Byzantine and Russian Painting

Title page illustration:

Icon
The Nativity
Tempera painting on wood
Venice, Hellenic Institute of
Byzantine and Post-Byzantine Studies

Cover illustration:

Empress Theodora and her retinue (detail from right) Ravenna, San Vitale

Byzantine and Russian Painting

Kostas Papaioannou

Translated by Janet Sondheimer   Funk & Wagnalls, New York

Series edited by Claude Schaeffner
Artistic advisor: Jean-Clarence Lambert
Illustrations chosen by André Held
Assistant: Martine Caputo

Library of Congress Catalog Card Number:
73-75700

Published by Funk & Wagnalls,
A Division of Reader's Digest Books, Inc.
by arrangement with Editions Rencontre
Printed in Italy

The colour illustrations in the first part were
provided by:
André Held, Lausanne: Cover, pages 3, 6, 10, 13
left, 15, 16, 17, 18, 22, 23, 25, 27, 28, 36, 37, 40,
43, 47, 48, 51, 54, 56, 58, 63, 65, 66, 67, 69, 70, 71,
72, 75, 76, 79, 80 and 83;
Deutsche Fotothek, Dresden: pages 84, 86, 87,
88, 90, 93 and 94;
Giraudon, Paris: pages 53 and 91;
Hirmer Verlag, Munich: pages 13 right, 24, 38,
50 and 62;
Hinz, Basle: pages 33 and 44;
Commercial Bank of Greece: pages 34 and 41;
Skira, Geneva: page 21.
The black and white illustrations in the dictionary
were provided by:
André Held: pages 148, 151, 157, 158, 164, 166,
168 right, 169, 170, 171, 172, 176, 178, 180, 183,
184, 187, 189, 191, 192, 194 and 197;
Giraudon, Paris: pages 147, 152 left, 153, 159,
165, 167, 168 left, 173, 179 and 199;
Alinari-Giraudon, Paris: pages 181, 190 and 195;
Anderson-Giraudon, Paris: pages 152 right, 182
and 193.

Table of Contents

The Baptism of Christ and St. Mark
Tetraevangelion
Manuscript, 13th cent.
Greece, Megaspileon monastery

Introduction

Today, after so many discoveries, reconstructions, and learned monographs, the kind of misapprehension concerning Byzantine civilisation which Western Europe entertained for so long seems more than ever unjustifiable, indeed quite unpardonable. It has left its mark on our dictionaries, which include 'otiose' as one sense under the heading 'Byzantine'. 'Byzantine discussion' means 'futile discussion', which shows the disdain of our realism for the supremely graceful metaphors of Byzantine theological speculation, 'the dance of the angels on the point of a needle', to quote the most famous of all. Of course, if a John Donne had composed it, it would have been the finest line he ever wrote . . .

At all events, it is to a poet, William Butler Yeats, that we are indebted for a striking rehabilitation of the 'holy city' of Byzantium in the European consciousness on the eve of the present century: I refer to his great poem 'Sailing to Byzantium', in which among 'the monuments of unageing intellect' Yeats sets out to rekindle the last sparks of the divine light, that spiritual gold which the Byzantine artists made to shine 'out of nature' in 'the artifice of eternity'. And that is where the Irish poet longs again to be.

To come still closer to our own time, when we consider some of the most important of the works of art to have been created before our own eyes, we see clearly enough how the 'transfigurative forces' which swept the Byzantine artists can join hands across the centuries with other expressions also dominated by the 'spiritual'. 'The spiritual in art': this is precisely one of the dominant themes of a creator of abstract art, the Russian, Wassily Kandinsky. And I cannot forget the questions, somewhat disturbed perhaps, which another modern master, Nicolas de Staël, also of Russian origin, was asking of Byzantine art shortly before his tragic death: he had been directed to it by Georges Duthuit, who was already meditating his great work 'Le Feu des Signes'.

The references could be multiplied by going further back into the past, references which are to a greater or lesser extent concealed. Kostas Papaioannou indicates some of them in passing, as for example when he speaks of the 'savage colouring' of Byzantine masters who 'drew and created space with colour'—such, too, was the ambition of a Matisse; or when he compares the mystical realism of Van Gogh with that of the mosaicists of San Vitale* and St. Sophia*: in relying on colour 'to create a nature larger, more exciting', to reveal 'the things hidden in colour', it is as though the unfortunate Vincent were all at once reviving a tradition.

To these examples must certainly be added the re-emergence of El Greco, which has recently led us back to Crete, where the late Byzantine style was still vigorous at the time Theotokopoulos was born there: and this is why he can justly be regarded as the last great Byzantine creator. Nor let us forget the impassioned pilgrimage of Ruskin to a Venice which conjured up from beyond the Ottoman reality, itself full of fascination (Loti said 'it is Istanbul, never Constantinople'*) the spirit of a civilisation fallen into purgatory: then we are ready to concede without reserve how much Western Europe owed to Byzantium in being able to prepare at such length for its own advent.

The truth is that in taking up the torch from Byzantium, having first contributed to its disappearance (the sack of Constantinople during the Fourth Crusade is one of the

7

---

* An asterisk refers to the dictionary where the word is the subject of an article or explanation.

blackest dates in medieval history), Western Europe succeeded to one of the longest political and cultural continuums in our history: for if Constantinople was indeed founded in 330, between that date and the successful assault on the city by Mahomet II in 1453 we see a destiny which prolonged its course, in a single uninterrupted sweep, over eleven centuries. What other Western nation, even today, can boast of such vitality, even of such longevity? What other city, Rome included, has spread its influence with such consistency and over so wide an area? The answer is certainly none.

Painting is but one strand in this exceptional continuity: in writing of it, Kostas Papaioannou has not treated it in isolation from the general synthesis, a wholly arbitrary procedure given the organic link between Byzantine art and the Byzantine state and religion. In these all too brief pages, he has succeeded in tracing a vision of the whole, a vision which readily assumes the values of an epic, a sacred epic. With the Jerusalem of the prophets and of Christ in ruins, Constantinople became a new Jerusalem built around the new Temple. The chroniclers tell how Justinian, at the consecration of St. Sophia, exclaimed 'Glory to God who has judged me worthy to accomplish this work. O Solomon, I have outdone thee!' And there is no denying that the basilica of Anthemius of Tralles* and Isidore of Miletus* remains one of the few edifices which can stand as the pride of the whole human race. Dedicated to the Holy Wisdom, so conceived that the celestial light illumined the footsteps of the basileus as he passed from the high portal of the narthex towards the central nave, this is none other than the scene of that glorious transfiguration to which the Byzantine soul so intensely aspired.

Constantinople was also the 'New Rome'—at a time when the Italian capital was succumbing to the barbarians. As such, Constantinople preserved the antique heritage and fused it with the revolutionary forces erupting from the Middle East, of which Christianity would prove the most decisive. The famous walls, so frequently assailed by enemy forces but defended with the utmost and unwearying heroism, made possible the elaboration of an unprecedented vision of the universe and of a new conception of man, which have never ceased to form the common patrimony of the Christian world.

A city doubly chosen to be pre-eminent, Constantinople escapes the sorry story of human conflicts—even though she was engulfed in her turn. And her art has little preoccupation with immediate reality except to sanctify it—to transform the world according to the revelations of the faith. This art is a ceaseless imitation of Jesus Christ and of the divine, its intention to manifest to the eyes of men values of the higher order and absolute verities. For the Byzantines, painting or decorating a building was always a form of worship. A late witness, the monk Dionysius of Fourna, says as much in his famous treatise: 'It is not only St. Luke who is blessed but all those who represent, and labour to show, the miracles, the sacred portraits of the Lord, of the Mother of God and of the other saints; for this work is pleasing to God and well regarded by him.' Thus it is easy to understand why monastic communities such as those who sought a life of austerity and meditation in the lunar valley of Göreme* in Cappadocia were able to turn a series of white rocks made fantastic by the mad whim of erosion into a fabulous ensemble of oratories and troglodyte churches, decorated with frescoes in profusion; this, too, was to show forth the glory of God.

The passion for luxury and pomp, however dazzling it may be, should not mislead us, nor should the most sumptuous decoration drown this 'gaze' which Byzantium has given to man, to all men. For Byzantium is a gaze: the gaze of the Spirit. Eschewing the terrestrial horizon, each time it points us in the same sublime direction, as one discovers from the cupolas or from the parchment of manuscripts, at Daphni* or Nerezi*, at Torcello* or St. Sophia. The whole impact of Byzantium is concentrated in those eyes: a supreme achievement of the human figure made in the image of God.

Jean-Clarence Lambert

Tetraevangelion
St. Matthew
Manuscript, second half of 10th cent.
From Dousikon monastery
(Western Thessaly)
Athens, National Library

The Birth of Byzantine Art

'East is East and West is West and never the twain shall meet.' This overworked formula can rarely have been less applicable than in the epoch which saw the emergence of Byzantium as the metropolis of the Christian world. The conquests of Alexander had been followed by the establishment of the first international cultural community, the Hellenistic 'koine'*, which extended from the Ganges to the Adriatic, from the Crimea to Egypt. In Greece, the Near East and the whole of Asia, south of the tomb route dating from the Stone Age which leads from the Caspian to the Great Wall, a vast mass of highly heterogeneous peoples, whose individual characteristics rested on age-old traditions, were drawn together round the cities strung out by Alexander and his successors. This huge 'koiné' was in no way impaired by the ending of Greek domination. Quite the contrary, for while the Parthians acted as intermediaries between Hellenism and the East, the Romans carried Hellenism to the shores of the Atlantic. If they Latinised the West, they merely gave a fresh impetus to the Hellenism they found East of the Ionian Sea. One remote consequence of the expedition of Alexander was that the texts of the New Testament and the majority of the writings of the Fathers would be written in Greek . . .

An oecumenical art, by reason of the Greek ascendancy more or less uniform, held sway from Gallia Narbonensis to India. A traveller in the time of Marcus Aurelius might encounter at Trier, Nîmes, Timgad, Palmyra and in the countless Antiochs*, Seleucias* and Apameas* scattered by the Diadokoi from the banks of the Orontes to the Aral Sea, the colonnades, public squares and temples he was familiar with at home. The Ionian temples of India, built in the first century, that is after the final extinction of the Bactrian Greeks*, might well be mistaken for the temples of N. Africa or Provence. A Graeco-Indian Boddhisatva and a Tripolitanian Apollo are well nigh indistinguishable. The resemblance between the relief from Gandhara* representing the Trojan Horse and the same scene as it appears on a ceremonial shield from Dura-Europos* on the Euphrates and in a manuscript of Virgil in the Vatican* has not passed unremarked. The Parthian word for painter is 'zahroub', derived from the Greek 'zographos' . . .

Nevertheless, it is wrong to imagine that this Hellenistic brand of cosmopolitanism entailed the absorption of the peoples of the East by the Greek spirit. As Droysen* liked to remind us, there were many brands of 'Hellenismos', Syrian, Iranian, Babylonian, Jewish, Egyptian: each people was led—one could go so far as to say compelled—to rethink its particular vocation in Greek and to act on the consequences.

Where nationalism failed, religion succeeded. At the very moment when the earthly Jerusalem was being reduced to ashes, the image of the heavenly Jerusalem was starting to shed over the oecumene the mystic light of its walls of jasper and gates of pearl. This is how the 'New Jerusalem', the 'city where there will be no more night', is described in the Revelation of St. John:

'The first foundation was of jasper, the second lapis lazuli, the third chalcedony, the fourth emerald, the fifth sardonyx, the sixth cornelian, the seventh chrysolite, the eighth beryl, the ninth topaz, the tenth chrysoprase, the eleventh turquoise, and the twelfth amethyst. The twelve gates were twelve pearls, each gate being made from a single pearl. The streets of the city were of pure gold, like translucent glass.'

Henceforth the world sees itself living under the sign of these fires. The cosmos resplendent with order. rationality and beauty, which was for the Greeks the unique and eternal reality, becomes a tenebrous prison, a nightmare from which one must awake, a fleeting spectacle which exists only so long as man alienates himself from God and surrenders to himself. 'The image of the world passes away', says St. Paul: the world is but an episode in the story of salvation, which must have its ending in a kingdom 'not of this world'. It is this utter transcendence, this resolute 'demonstration of things invisible' which from now on constitutes the domain of faith. 'We live not by sight but by faith': anyone who wishes to understand the evolution which proceeds from the anti-naturalistic painting of Dura-Europos to the stylisation of Byzantium must take this text to heart.

The great antithesis which expresses the new vision of the universe is no longer, as with the Greeks, that between cosmos and chaos, order and disorder, but between Light and Darkness. Light is the major theme of the immense literature of the period, pagan, Jewish, Christian or Zoroastrian. Plotinus* attributes beauty to the 'presence of an incorporeal light dominating matter, which is dark. . . .'

Related to this new experience of light is the new image of the soul. The antique image—Plato's two-horsed chariot guided by reason—cries out for plastic representation. By contrast, when Plotinus speaks of animated beings with 'illumined bodies', he conjures up a pictorial impression and one thinks of the touches of light which transpierce and mobilise the apparent fixity of Byzantine figures. The sculptural image of the Platonic 'auriga' is from now on replaced by an enigmatic division into three substances, spirit, soul and flesh, which entails a strict trichotomy between men as spirit ('pneuma'), men as soul ('psyche') and men as flesh: a man 'possesses' a body; he can himself attain to be a soul, but he can only 'receive' the spiritual breath which, descending from on high like a luminous wave, will make of him a new man, in communion with the 'new Adam'. The word 'soul' thus takes on a pejorative connotation unknown in antiquity: the man of the psyche, who lives according to the 'soul', reduced to the level of his own moral experience, is just as far removed from divine grace as the man of the flesh, wallowing in lust. St. Paul went so far as to distinguish between the 'body of the soul' and the 'body of the spirit': this distinction, to-day well-nigh unintelligible, must be kept firmly in mind if one wishes to understand the transfigurative art of Byzantium.

It was this world teeming with images, symbols and new concepts which was to descend like a spring torrent on the congealed forms of antiquity. 'The Syrian Orontes flows into the Tiber,' wrote Juvenal at the beginning of the second century. In 217, when Caracalla abolished the distinction between Roman and foreign deities, Rome had already long since become merely a province of the Orient in religious matters. And when Constantine*, a century later, was converted to Christianity, it was a Judaeo-Hellenistic religion which took possession of the Roman world.

The foundation of Constantinople in 330 set the seal on the economic, cultural and religious primacy of the East. Admittedly, the word 'East' may lead to confusion. From

the time of Alexander, the East and Hellenism had concluded an alliance. It was in a setting to a greater or lesser degree Hellenised that Christian theology came to birth and the earliest form of sacred art elaborated: when St. Clement of Alexandria* dared to raise Greek philosophy to the rank of a 'second Old Testament' he was merely translating into the language of theology what Christian art was already trying to express through its Good Shepherds, adolescent Christs and philosopher Apostles, which for a long time to come would associate the divine figure with human beauty. Concurrently with this Hellenistic iconography, however, a long tradition was in process of formation in the hinterland of Egypt and Syria, to which we are indebted for the majority of the sacred scenes in their settled form.

Art undergoes a Transformation

More important than the duality of the iconographic vocabulary was the profound transformation in the language of art which took place between the second and fourth centuries. Architecture, the ornamental code, the very image of man, undergo a decisive change: one by one, all the specific characteristics of the ancient aesthetic disappear, but at the same time we witness the unfolding of elements which will produce the Byzantine synthesis. In contrast with the flat-moulded architecture of the ancients, calm, rational and of this world, one sees a spherical architecture being elaborated, whose domes and cupolas will from now on mark the landscape with their sacred symbolism. True, these new forms do not portend the total elimination of antique architectural types: the basilica has a glorious career before it in the Christian world. But it is in the cupola that the new

13

community will recognise most clearly the all-embracing power of the sacred, the presence of 'new heavens' on the 'new earth'. Equally significant are the new functions of decoration. The simplicity and regularity of antique decoration is henceforth replaced by an exuberance of ornament, varied and complicated in the extreme, in which at times one recognises the pulsations of arabesque. This style, which treats ornament no longer as a means but as an end in itself, is already evident in the pagan temples of Syria. The orientals who built the palace of Diocletian at Split* transplanted the style to the shores of the Adriatic: two centuries later we shall see its flowering in the churches of Ravenna*. Lastly, a new artistic intention makes its appearance and finds its appropriate technique. Where men once strove after relief, they now try to achieve a pictorial effect by the opposition of light and shade. The substitution of the drill for the chisel reveals the transition from the tactile aesthetic of antiquity to the visual principle which prevails in the new world: instead of carving the stone with a chisel, one gouges it with a ferrule, hollowing out deep pockets of shadow which eliminate all appearance of materiality and give the design the aethereal aspect of lace embroidered with light. It was this image of matter wholly re-absorbed into light that the Byzantine masters would express in the sculptured decoration of St. Sophia.

Concurrently, a decisive transformation was at work in the image of man himself.

Subjectivity was unknown to ancient art. The sense of mystery, of inwardness and of anguish—together with their counterparts, the world of hope and transfiguration—were almost forbidden territory to the Greeks. So it is that even the most beautiful Greek figures seem immersed in an impersonal cosmos: their eyes at once open and shut, like those of an animal, as indifferent to hope and despair as the beating of a pulse or the course of the stars, resolutely exclude all possibility of personal expression. The truth is that the psychological dimension appears only with the Romans: the achievement of these centuries, harbingers of what is to come, is precisely that they lead the man 'with a soul' of the Graeco-Roman portraits to the threshold of the interior spirituality of the Byzantine icons and mosaics. The physiognomies of the third and fourth centuries, whether from Fayum or Palmyra, whether from Greece or Rome, lead us into the presence of an art no longer centred on glorification of the body but on the intensity of an expression. Here the ancient eye, 'close kinsman to the sun', as Plato said, loses its solar indifference and becomes the reflection of the luminous and sombre forces which henceforward divide the universe between them.

If the Fayum portraits are ancestors of certain of the icons, the Dura-Europos frescoes lead us to the threshold of the Byzantine aesthetic: the plastic shapes are contained by the severity of the line, the expanse is suppressed by the flat figuration of the people: these bodies without hint of roundness, having neither volume nor weight and supported by nothing, are no longer part of the wall but float in spiritual space, where prayer and adoration have completely abolished the distance between the object and subject of contemplation. If something is still lacking in these 'precursors of Byzantine art' is it not a setting related to their subtlety of content? The flat tints of vivid blue-green and Indian red link the painting of the synagogue at Dura with the past, with antique

14

The Good Shepherd
Mosaic, 5th cent.
Ravenna, so-called Mausoleum of Galla
Placidia, Lunette
above the entrance door

polychromy: it lacks the pure colours which will be the hall-mark of the Byzantine era. Subservient to the drawing, the antique colours were just as ill-adapted to the new aesthetic of light as were the antique mosaics made from pieces of opaque marble. Now, just as the new technique of sculpture with the drill had made stone amenable to light, so did the awakening of the soul transform the technique of mosaic: the marbles and hard stones of the Flavian epoch become intermingled with vitrified pastes and gilded scraps of glass and finally, in the Christian era, give place to cubes of enamel whose bluish and golden shimmerings fill the space with a light not of this world. When mosaic has been thus fully and finally enlisted in the service of light, the figures of Dura, who advance on the spectator while engulfing him in the profundity of their gaze, and also those charming Hellenistic figures, will at length, in their transfigured state, penetrate to the interior of that 'transparent sphere' Plotinus dreamed of, in which Byzantium would locate its imperial retinues and holy images.

15

The Byzantine Synthesis

Since the Byzantine Empire began as a continuation of the Roman Empire, Byzantine painting at the outset was inevitably a part of that Hellenistic and orientalising art which held sway not only in the Roman Empire but also in the vast Persian Empire. An artistic 'koiné' had come into being in the wake of the great religions which divided between them the Empire of Alexander and that of the Caesars, overriding political boundaries and ethnic differences. Despite violent political and religious disagreements, the fourth century world was remarkably uniform in its structure. In this world in which Orthodoxy took the place of nationality, men of all parties felt the need to establish their sacred texts in authoritative form: hence the almost simultaneous development of a sacred philology which would result in the Christian Bible, the Jewish Bible and the Avesta. In the East as in the West, all domains were invaded by a like religiosity. While the palatine ceremonies were finally being transformed into a liturgical celebration of the imperial power, strictly hierarchical clergies were also in process of formation, their rites often modelled on those proper to adoration of the emperor: the Church's use of candles and of incense, down to the end of the fourth century regarded as pagan custom, was borrowed from the ceremonial of the palace . . . Everywhere one finds the same mixture of Hellenism and Orientalism. Everywhere there is the same taste for polychrome decoration, the same

passion for costly fabrics, sparkling gems, enamel work, and lastly, for mosaic.

These profoundly 'Byzantine' modes of life were thus not in fact born in Constantinople. But it was Byzantium which perpetuated them for a thousand years, gave them time to mature and turned them into a style. The Roman state, Greek culture, Hellenistic cosmopolitism, the monumental order in palace and church, which during the fourth and fifth centuries enjoyed a relatively happy co-existence only to be sundered by the barbarian invasions and the rise of heresies and of provincial cultures, found at Byzantium not only a refuge but also a new home.

Hellenism and Orthodoxy

Greek in population, and possessing a university in the ancient tradition, Constantinople was the centre of a civilisation deeply influenced by Hellenism. In its libraries (Julian's* is said to have contained 120,000 volumes) were preserved all the treasures of Greek learning, while its streets, forums, gardens, palaces and the famous baths of Zeuzippos* were veritable museums, in which the masterpieces of Greek art were assembled. For a thousand years the ancient tongue continued to be the literary language. A fervent attachment to antiquity led the educated classes to reject demotic Greek, the true national language, in

favour of the language spoken at Athens and Alexandria in the Hellenistic epoch. 'By race and language we are the compatriots and heirs of the ancient Hellenes' says Theodore Metochites* writing at the end of the thirteenth century. In conformity with this principle, the patriarch Nicholas Muzalon ordered a saint's life written in vulgar Greek to be burned . . . Hence also the cult of Homer and Plato, the love of mythology and the steadfast loyalty to antique models. Homer continued to be learned by heart, and there exist poems on the Virgin and the Annunciation in which every line is borrowed from either the Iliad or the Odyssey.

The persistence and power of Hellenistic traditions can be observed at every period throughout the Byzantine millennium. Under Constantine, under Theodosius and on many later occasions during the Middle Ages, we find a crop of imitations of antique models. Slightingly described as 'renaissance', these copies created the elements of a genuinely antiquising school, to which many masterpieces of painting bear witness. Admittedly, these imitations express an outmoded aesthetic and are situated outside Byzantium properly understood: the truly profound influence of Hellenism is to be found rather in the restraint, moderation, sense of scale and of spiritual beauty for which Byzantine art provides monumental evidence in the days of its flowering.

The twenty different peoples inhabiting the Empire were united by the Greek language and the Orthodox faith, and if Byzantium was a second blossoming of Hellenism, the new graft was Christianity, whose rejuvenating effect was of capital importance. But it is precisely in the elaboration of Byzantine orthodoxy that Hellenism was able to make its true contribution. What strikes us in Byzantine patristic literature is just this old Greek confidence in nature, which shines out in St. Basil*, Gregory of Nyssa* and Maximus the Confessor. For them the world is not a gloomy prison: 'theophany', an 'appearance of God', says Dionysius the Areopagite*, father of Christian mysticism. It is highly significant that the debate between Maximus and Origen* turned on this feeling for the dignity of the natural world. 'Nothing is more to be feared', said Maximus, than the view that 'this unique masterpiece which is the visible world, in which God makes himself known by a silent revelation, has its origin only in sin.' In a universe where everything that exists is 'theophany', each being is a good thing, and evil but an unreal shadow. That is why Byzantine art refused to give house room to the demoniacal contortions and 'monstrous fauna' which apocalyptical visions conjured up on the portals of northern cathedrals, and it was no accident that the painters of the decadence who illustrated the Apocalypse had no better resource than to copy the engravings of Dürer and Cranach and the illustrated Bible of Piscator*.

Above all it was the great debate on the nature of Christ which allowed this transfigured humanism to demonstrate in most striking fashion the indissoluble union between Hellenism and Orthodoxy. To signify the union between the human and the divine in the person of Christ, early Christianity had hit upon the ecstatic formula of a fusion between God and man. The union between the two natures had been represented as a mingling of two liquids, a drop of vinegar dissolving in the sea. When the East started to use this language to suggest a volatilisation of the human nature of God, the Council of Chalcedon

Moses receiving the law on Mount Sinai
(fragment)
Mosaic from the presbytery
Ravenna, San Vitale

substituted for the idea of fusion that of synthesis and elevated the formula 'asynkhytos' ('without mixture') to the rank of a dogmatic principle. 'Christ is perfect God and perfect man' (Cyril of Alexandria*), and the union of the two natures occurs 'without mixture or confusion'. This formula should be kept in mind as a guide to the internal logic of Byzantine art. It was this sanctified humanism which enabled it to rescue the human figure from the shipwreck it suffered in the Monophysite* and Islamic East and in the barbarised West. While in the rest of the Christian world the human figure was reduced to an ornamental sign, as with the Copts* or the Irish, or was devoured by the barbarian bestiary, Byzantium was rediscovering its beauty. Intimations of this beauty are already evident in the countenances of the *Martyrs* of Salonika (mosaics of St. George)*, but it was in the great works of the classical period (from the tenth to the twelfth century) that Byzantium was able to express the mysterious 'union without mixture' of pure humanity and pure divinity: it was then, and only then, that the formula of Chalcedon revealed the full richness of its meaning.

Byzantium would be unwearying in its celebration of the mediations accomplished by Christ. Christ, says St. Maximus, 'unites man and woman, earth and heaven, sentient beings and spiritual beings, and finally, in a manner ineffable, created and uncreated nature'. He has shown 'that celestial and terrestrial beings make up a single solemn circle': it was this image of an existence conceived as a liturgical act, as ritual adoration and 'solemn dance' that Byzantium attempted to realise on earth through its ceremonial and ecclesiastical ritual.

The Imperial Order and the Church

'The Empire on earth is the reflection of the heavenly kingdom'; such was Eusebius' description of the Empire of Constantine. 'The executive power,' said Constantine Porphyrogenitus* in the tenth century, 'exercised with rhythm and order, is the image of the harmony and impulse imposed by the Creator.' The emperor will always be the 'thirteenth apostle', in whom the synthesis of the spiritual and the temporal, the union of Heaven and earth is at work. His person is sacred: at certain festivals the Gospels or the Cross are placed on the imperial throne, identifying it with the throne of Christ. Equally, the imperial cult had all the elements of a religion. Its chief sanctuary was the sacred Palace*. The effigies of the emperor were adored like icons. The ceremonial robes worn by the emperor and high dignitaries had the character of liturgical vestments. As we learn from the 'Book of Ceremonies' compiled by the emperor Constantine Porphyrogenitus, minute regulations prescribed the form and colours of the vestments appropriate to the different festivals and there were even supervisors whose office it was to see that they were put on in conformity with the ritual. Finally, the ritual of the court profoundly influenced the style of the ecclesiastical liturgy.

20

MOSE

Justinian and his retinue
Mosaic from the presbytery
Mid 6th cent.
Ravenna, San Vitale
▼

St. Demetrius and the Founders
On the left an ecclesiastic,
on the right a secular personage
7th cent.
Salonika, church of St. Demetrius,
pillar to right of choir
▼
▼

The Church, says the patriarch Germanus, is 'the terrestrial heaven in which the God of the higher heaven has his dwelling and moves'; the Mass is 'the reflection of the uninterrupted Mass which the angels celebrate in heaven'. It was this presence of the invisible which the Byzantine church tried to express through the splendour of its rites and the sumptuousness of its apparel. In this connection, there is nothing at once more 'Byzantine' and more 'Russian' than the legendary account of the 'choice of faith' made by Vladimir, the great prince of Kiev. To find out which was the best religion, Vladimir had sent emissaries to the Muslims, the Jews, the Latins and the Greeks. When they came to Constantinople, they were conducted on a feast day into St. Sophia and there, beneath the glittering mosaics, among the clouds of incense, amid the blazing of the candles, the astonished Boyars thought they beheld winged young men floating in the air and chanting the 'Trisagion' Hymn (in which the word 'holy' is thrice repeated in Greek or Latin), 'Holy, holy, holy is the Eternal'. Having been informed that in the Orthodox Church 'the angels themselves descend from heaven to celebrate the office with the priests', they declared to Vladimir: 'We know not whether we were in heaven or on earth, for on earth such beauty is not found. So we do not know what we ought to say, but one thing we know well: there God dwells among men . . .'

Codex Rossanensis,
6th cent.
Rossano, Archiepiscopal Museum

Madonna and Child
Icon, 6th cent.
Rome, Santa Francesca Romana

Virgin and Child, enthroned
Apse mosaic, 10th century
Salonika, St. Sophia

The mosaics, the enamels, the precious stones, the fabrics gorgeously decorated and stitched with gold are so many reflections of this pomp. For example, the fashion for precious stuffs helps to reveal the profound psychical changes of which late antiquity was the arena. The luxurious figured fabrics of the Orient, so despised by the Greeks who reserved them for hetairai, now gave an aura to ceremonial robes, liturgical vestments, church and palace ornament, and even determined the artistic image of man. The fauna from the Iranian bestiary, stories from the Gospels, picturesque scenes dear to the Alexandrians, were scattered over material with such profusion that Asterios, bishop of Amasia, rose in indignation against these garments which gave those who wore them the appearance of 'walking frescoes'.

'Walking frescoes': such must indeed have been the impression produced by these long vestments in stiff brocade, inspired by the robes of Chinese mandarins, which in the fifth century replaced the Roman toga. At the same time, the body loses the high and symbolic status it had possessed in ancient art: the new art makes it disappear completely behind its covering vestment, like a metal cope, which accentuates by its stiffness the impression of hieratic immobility created by the frontal pose. In the imperial groups of San Vitale* at Ravenna, as in the ex-voto of St. Demetrius* at Salonika, the bodies have been replaced by what might be described as curtains with vertical folds, above which rise countenances whose dilated eyes fill the space with a mysterious presence . . .

The Byzantine Language of Art

The passion for rich materials is another indication of the profound change in the language of art. In the system of patchwork ornamentation esteemed in East and West alike, precious marbles form an essential element in the polychrome decoration. On the floor of St. Sophia at Constantinople, marbles of all hues, alabasters, jaspers, porphyries and serpentines, create the impression of a garden strewn with purple flowers. All the lower part of the walls is lined with marble incrustations in prodigious variety: narrow lace borders or wide sculpted bands frame marble panels in rainbow hues or symmetrically veined. San Vitale at Ravenna, the church at Poreč*, St. Mark's at Venice and the Chora church at Constantinople are other monumental examples of this Byzantine taste for precious materials and resplendent polychromy.

Enamel work is another manifestation of this chromatic magic. At Byzantium the art of cloisonné reaches the peak of perfection, and the splashes of gold and coloured lavas invade not only the most sumptuous items of church furniture—icons, crosses, reliquaries, altars, gospel bindings, chalices and patens—but also the ceremonial uniforms and furniture of the Court, even down to the harness of horses on parade. The most ancient Byzantine pieces date from the seventh century, when the technique is still clumsy: the heyday of Byzantine enamel work is in the eleventh and twelfth centuries.

The passion for splendour, the intense striving after colour evinced by the use of coloured silk, precious stones and enamels, found their most powerful symbol in mosaic.

After its long subservience to paintings, mosaic now wins its autonomy and discovers its true destiny, which is to manifest the sovereign power of light. 'Here light is born or while captive yet reigns free' (Aut lux hic nata est aut capta hic libera regnat'), proclaims an inscription in the vestibule to the chapel of the archbishop's palace at Ravenna. The Byzantine mosaicists poured all their ingenuity into glorifying this reign. The first step was to coat the walls with two or three layers of mortar, whose irregularities produced as many facets on which the light played. The artists alternated cubes of a vitreous paste permeable to light, and thus in a sense lit up from within, with squares of opaque stone on which the light kindled lively and aggressive coruscations. The cubes were planted at various angles so as to catch the inflections of the light. Finally, by grouping the cubes as a fan, in regular rows, or otherwise, the artists suggested an abstract background in which the aerial play of the contours of the cubes created as many furrows of shadow and streaks of light. The cubes—no less than thirty-six million are reckoned to have gone into St. George at Salonika*—were coloured various shades with the help of metallic oxides mixed with a glass paste: manganese for violet, cobalt for blue etc. It is only in gilded or silvered cubes that the metal is not incorporated, but applied as a very thin leaf over the smalt and covered with a strip of plain glass. Lastly, in the sixth century, mother of pearl and even precious stones are mixed with the coloured smalts to enhance the effect.

The demands of this 'painting for eternity' were not immediately understood. The mosaics of Santa Costanza* are still merely pavement mosaics projected on to the vaults. Again, the mosaicists of Santa Maria Maggiore are still under the sway of traditional painting, whose shadings and graduations they try to imitate. Even the mosaics of the triumphal arch, in other respects very advanced, constitute a collection of enlarged miniatures rather than a monumental ensemble. But at Salonika and Ravenna the threshold has been crossed: the colours are at last given fearless treatment, with candid tones and strong tints, the relationships between the colours are fully assumed and one sees here affirmed, with incomparable mastery, that art of 'creating space with colour' which will later be the aspiration of Delacroix, Van Gogh and Matisse. Once Byzantium has learned to adapt this lurid palette to the exigencies of monumentality, the way will be open for the revelation of those 'hidden things which exist in colour': as Van Gogh said of them, they 'collaborate of themselves' to create 'a nature which is larger and more exciting'.

Byzantine Painting before the Century of Justinian

We do not know at what date Constantinople became a centre of art in its own right. The example of Ravenna, however, justifies us in supposing that this must have happened quite early on. Chosen in 402 as the seat of the Western emperor, within a very few years Ravenna had lost its centuries-old character of an obscure provincial city to become a magnificent city of art. A similar miracle could not fail to be the destiny of the former colony of Megara on whose site Constantine founded the new capital of his Empire. As is self-evident, political and ecclesiastical centralisation, the profusion of new buildings, the luxury of the court and imperial patronage must soon have produced an important and influential movement in art. The imperial will, for example, had been a decisive factor in the creation of Christian art. We know that the primitive churches were accommodated inside private houses and in outward appearance differed in no way from any other dwelling. The most illustrious sanctuaries of Christendom were imperial foundations and to a greater or lesser degree evinced the tastes of the capital. Thus at the beginning of the fifth century we find the empress Eudokia intervening directly in the arrangements for the church she was having built at Gaza in Syria: as well as providing the money, she despatched from Constantinople the plans, the architect and precious substances, marble columns and capitals, to adorn the new church. The 'Theodosian' capitals encountered in all the provinces of the Empire from Tunisia to Kerch in the Crimea were executed in marble from the famous quarries of Proconnesus*. The unity of style presented by all these capitals entitles us to suppose that from the fifth, and certainly from the sixth, century there existed a Constantinople school of decorators whose influence extended over the whole Empire.

Unfortunately, practically nothing survives of the paintings which decorated the palaces, thermae, public squares and churches of Constantinople. The Great Palace, with its hanging gardens and its harbour on the Sea of Marmara, has disappeared. Vanished too are the University and the sumptuous church of the Holy Apostles* which Constantine set aside for imperial burials; vanished are the eight public thermae, the two theatres, the four Courts of Justice, the fourteen palaces, the fifty-two porticoes. The 4388 lordly mansions which were Constantine's gift to the 'New Rome' are a further total loss. To form an idea of painting in Constantinople between 330 and the era of Justinian*, two centuries later, we have to rely on a single example of monumental painting, mosaic pavements from a portico of the Great Palace, and a solitary manuscript, the Dioscorides* from Vienna, which is in any case partly a copy of an Alexandrian work.

We are not much better informed concerning the earliest monumental art of the Christian East. We know nothing of the monuments of Alexandria. The 'thousand and one churches of Anatolia', the 'dead cities' of Syria, the sanctuaries of the Holy Land have retained nothing of their primitive decoration. On the other hand, there is an abundance of testimony from pavements in mosaic. But here we are still in the mainstream of the Alexandrian tradition. Hellenistic decoration prevails not only at Miletus, Nicopolis*, Delphi, Stobi*, at Antioch or Apamea, on the Orontes, Greek cities all, but also in

Palestine, Syria, Jordania and Tripolitania. At Gerasa*, a Graeco-Jewish town where Greek was the dominant language, the common-place Hellenistic motif of the foliated scroll combined with hunting scenes was reproduced in 610 in the church of bishop Genesios, twenty-two years before the Arab invasion. If Hellenistic models were abandoned, it was in favour of Sassanid models, or to leave the field free for popular primitivism: whichever was adopted, it always remained on the fringe of the Byzantine style in the strict sense. The only exceptions are the magnificent mosaics from the Beisan monastery, but they are too late to instruct us in the beginnings of the Byzantine style in the eastern provinces of the Empire.

The same anachronistic impression is given by the mosaic pavements which decorated part of the Great Palace at Constantinople. These mosaics, attributed to the sixth century, were laid over the four sides of a large square courtyard, each side measuring 64 m. in length and 9.50 m. in depth. A uniform white ground sets off a host of people, animals, idyllic landscapes and genre scenes of every description, remarkable for their subtlety and delicacy. But again, we are still in the presence of antiquity: the hunts, the 'landscapes with architecture', the 'woman with a pitcher', the 'philosopher' figure could as easily have been found at Delos or Herculaneum four or five centuries earlier. Nothing about these works, exquisite as they are, gives a hint of the new style evolving at that very moment in the capital. It is to Salonika, Ravenna, Poreč and the churches of Cyprus, Angeloktistos* and Kanakaria* that we must look for the secret of the earliest period of Byzantine monumental art.

The Mosaics of Salonika

The series of Salonikan monuments begins with the mosaics in the rotunda of St. George*. Holy martyrs, in the attitude of orantes (praying figures), stand erect against a gold background on the face of magnificent tabernacle structures which recall buildings in the second Pompeian style. Here we can indeed contemplate the new face of Hellenism, in the beauty of these wonderfully elegant saints whose gorgeous mantles seem to billow at a breath from another world. Formally, these young soldier saints and the architectural décor which frames them seem to come straight from the Hellenistic world. But one only has to compare them with the authentically Hellenistic-Roman figures of Santa Costanza at Rome to realise the serene authority with which the artists of the rotunda have grasped and held the Christian promises of peace and transfiguration. There is nothing antique and nothing antiquising in these tall ecstatic figures who seem to guard the gates of the heavenly Jerusalem. For centuries past antique art had produced nothing whose beauty was so steeped in spirituality: to find the equivalent of these masterpieces one must go back to the sculptures of the Parthenon.

The mosaics of the huge Acheiropoietos basilica* survive only in the decoration of the arches along the nave. Here we are indisputably confronted by a masterpiece of the decorative thinking of the early Byzantine era: the scrolls of vine-shoots, the multicoloured birds, the turquoise-coloured flowers and the profusion of papyrus and lotus which fill the space with indescribable intimations of paradise, call to mind the magic gardens of the East.

The mosaic in the apse of Hosios David* is the oldest apsidal mosaic to have survived intact within the territory of the Greek Empire and furnishes the earliest known representation of a theophany manifested to prophets from the Old Testament. This is the earliest Byzantine version of the 'landscape with rocks' found in Italo-Hellenistic painting and the first attempt at monumental composition: the Christ in glory, the symbols of the evangelists who soar up at his sides and seem to hurl themselves at the astonished prophets, generate a compact system perfectly adapted to the architectural structure.

The most important sanctuary in Salonika was the Basilica of St. Demetrius. Unfortunately its mosaics were almost totally destroyed in the great fire which ravaged the town in 1917. The fragments which survive from the decoration of the fifth and sixth centuries confirm once again the affinities between the art of Salonika and that of Ravenna: there is the same impressionist feeling of landscape with polychrome clouds, the same iconographic type of the 'Madonna surrounded by angels', the same expressiveness in the faces, the draperies and architectural décor fulfil the same monumental function . . .

Ravenna's fortune was made in 404, when Honorius, in flight from Alaric and his Goths, abandoned Milan and took refuge in this town protected by the swamps of the former Po delta.

Fifth century painting is represented at Ravenna by two magnificent ensembles: the mausoleum known as that of Galla Placidia* and the Baptistery of the Orthodox*. We have seen in the mosaics of St. George* how the Hellenistic figures were transfigured; we shall see in these two monuments the interval in which the transubstantiation of ancient art was effected.

In his essay on 'The Grotto of the Nymphs' the Neo-Platonist writer Porphyry identified the grotto as the supreme symbol of the cosmos. It is precisely this effect of a marine cavern bathed in nocturnal light that is felt in the mausoleum of Galla Placidia, with the slow breathing of its indigo colouring and phosphorescent iridescences. At the beginning of the century the plain glass of the small windows were replaced by alabaster slabs which diffuse a filtered light, so that the mosaics receive the degree of illumination demanded by their nature. At the top of the dome a great cross shines out from a field of more than eight hundred gold stars. Traced on this indigo ground, rich in frequent modulations within the grey-white tones and scattered with restrained accents of red, green and yellow, are little gold circles, stars, milky corolla waves, supple vine tendrils strewn among the lilies and the roses. In the half-light, thirst-stricken stags advance across a lattice of volute acanthus leaves to quench their thirst at the source of life, doves drink from little vases along the border. The eye guesses at the presence of beings, transparent to the point of evanescence, which melt away into the billowing depths of this unreal space and remain invisible, until fitful coruscations come by stealth to pick out the reflections of their mother of pearl and coral. The eight apostles, seen in pairs face to face beneath gigantic shell-shapes adorned with pearls, loom like spectres or apparitions; so do the figures of

David and Solomon
Detail from *The Descent into Limbo*
(*Anastasis*) 11th cent.
Chios, mosaic in the Nea Moni

the two matching compositions above the door-way and at the far end of the mausoleum (the Good Shepherd and St. Lawrence). We know the Good Shepherd as a conventional theme in ancient painting. In the magical space of the mausoleum it is liberated from all its Pompeian associations: we are travelling towards an essentially other world.

In the Baptistery of the Orthodox we have the first great example of the new monumentality: its polished marbles, stuccos and ornamental and figurative mosaics combine in an organic whole which marries perfectly with the architectonic structure. The blue ground of the mosaics, with its reflections now of lapis lazuli, now of cobalt, fiercely projects the gold, red and sulphurous yellow. In the setting thus created, coloured smalts of the most diverse hues combine like iron filings caught in a magnetic field to sketch out figures and objects by themselves.

The mosaics of the time of Theodoric and his daughter Amalasuntha in the Baptistery of the Arians*, the Archbishop's chapel and at Sant' Apollinare Nuovo* afford us a glimpse of the transition from the art of fifth century to the new aesthetic which comes to fruition in the era of Justinian and will appear at Ravenna after the reconquest of the city by Byzantine troops in 540.

The basilica of Sant' Apollinare Nuovo—originally designed for Arian worship—is the masterpiece of the period of Theodoric. Three zones of mosaic rise one above another on the walls of the central nave, above the arcades. The topmost zone is composed of a series of decorative panels alternating with twenty-six compositions, illustrating on the left-hand wall the Miracles and on the right the Passion of Christ: this is the most ancient cycle from the Gospels to have come down to us. The second zone develops in the intervals between the windows and presents thirty-two figures of prophets, apostles and saints viewed full-face. The third, which runs directly above the arcades, epitomises all the political, religious and aesthetic upheavals which Ravenna experienced towards the middle of the sixth century. Originally the two immense friezes depicted King Theodoric and the dignitaries of his court setting out from the city of Ravenna and the port of Classis and making their way towards Christ and the Virgin. The capture of the city by Justinian's troops, the quashing of the Arian heresy and the conversion of the basilica to orthodox worship led to the obliteration of the memory of the heretic king and a 'purge' of all the figures recalling the Gothic occupation. The procession of the defeated king was replaced by the two trains of saints and martyrs and the figures of the three Magi which precede them. It seems therefore that the two decorations were separated by a space of some forty years. During this period Ravenna changed both its master and its official confession and its art has undergone a profound transformation: with these long trains of saints and martyrs the new hieratic and rhythmical style of sixth century Byzantium makes its appearance.

What strikes one about the decoration from the time of Theodoric is the generalisation of the gold ground and the severe exclusion of any ornamental element: the spatial organisation rests solely with the human figures. But the presence of these elements, so characteristic of the most advanced tendencies in the art of the sixth century, in no way signified the disappearance of the ornamental and naturalistic style of the preceding

ONIΠTHP

century. Quite the contrary: in the sixth century it was still possible for the most divergent
paths, old traditions and new trends, to meet and cross. The mosaics of San Vitale,
masterpiece of the painting of the age of Justinian, offers us a monumental image of these
heterogeneous movements in harmonious co-existence. In the presbytery we find the re-
emergence of all the ornamental luxury of the fifth century. Framed by colossal shell-
work, vine branches spilling out from two large vases develop in a series of volutes
which cover the entire surface of the extrados of the arch. The vault is ornamented in
fabulous richness. On alternating grounds of gold and green, amid a luxuriant foliage
of acanthus leaves in which sports a myriad of birds; four angels, resting on azure
globes, support with outstretched arms in a starry sky a garland which frames the
image of the Lamb of God. Surrounding this paradise garden are landscapes ('Moses
on Sinai', 'Abraham entertaining the angels', 'Sacrifice of Abel') which elevate
the naturalism of this epoch to a degree of vernal splendour beyond men's previous
dreams.

If the mosaics of the presbytery recapitulate the ornamental and naturalistic experiments of the fifth century, the mosaics on a gold ground found in the apse lead us to the
heart of that supernatural space in which Byzantine hieraticism will henceforth move:
Justinian, Theodora and their retinues advance in slow motion to bring their offerings to
the Church of Christ. The luxury of the materials employed matches the splendour of the
ceremonial accompanying the 'oblatio Augusti et Augustae' (customary offering of
liturgical vessels made by the Byzantine emperors to the largest churches of the Empire).

36

The Washing of the Feet
Mosaic, early 11th cent.
Phocis (Greece), monastery of Hosios
Leukas, wall of narthex

Here is a profusion of gold cubes and mother of pearl, actual precious stones are scattered in handfuls over the heavy draperies of the palace vestments and the splendid apparel worn by the empress and the ladies of her suite. We are on the frontier between two worlds: from the art of representing the 'psyche' we pass into that of 'pneumatic' presences. The intensely expressive heads of the emperor and his dignitaries conduct us to the threshold of the world of the icons, in which it is no longer a case of seeing but of adoring. Invisible now beneath the sumptuous ceremonial costumes, deprived of all material substances, these bodies seem transformed into a rhythmical notation. The same principle can be seen at work in the slightly later mosaics of the 'Train of Saints and Martyrs' at Sant' Apollinare Nuovo.

But it must be said once again that these new tendencies, harbingers of the great compositions of the classical period, in no way implied the withering away of the previous aesthetic. The basilica of Sant' Apollinare in Classe, with its columns of Proconnesus marble and its Byzantine capitals whose leaves flutter in the wind, perpetuate the naturalism, and indeed the naïve symbolism, of primitive Christianity. The gold ground gives way to grounds of blue and green; a cross standing in the sky in front of three sheep symbolises the Transfiguration on Mount Tabor*. The mosaic ensemble in the apse gives the impression of tapestry rather than painting; the only reminder of Byzantine monu-mentality are the two archangels, robed as emperors, the imperial standard in their hands, who guard the entrance to the apse.

37

The Descent from the Cross
Left, the Virgin and Nicodemus,
Right, St. John and a kneeling figure
Fresco, early 11th cent.
Phocis (Greece), monastery of Hosios
Leukas, crypt.

Poreč, Cyprus and Mount Sinai

In the beautiful basilica built about 550 by bishop Euphrasius at Poreč, one is struck first by the presence of Byzantine capitals on the pillars to the arcades in the narthex* and by the columns of Proconnesus marble which separate the naves. The mosaic of the triumphal arch, with its apostles advancing towards Christ with slow and measured tread, recalls the 'Train of Martyrs' at Sant' Apollinare Nuovo. In the touching scenes of the 'Visitation' and the 'Annunciation' the affinities with the art of Ravenna are less evident. Generally speaking, the mosaicists of Poreč aim at a kind of compromise between the naturalistic decoration and the supernatural gold ground. Thus, in the 'Visitation' and 'Annunciation', the ground is formed by multi-coloured bands: blue, grey, pink, black, but the bottom band is always green as though to suggest an expanse of fantastic meadow. The same green band, strewn with fanciful flowers, occupies the lower portion of the magnificent mosaic in the apse. Here, the gold ground is not, as at St. Demetrius of Salonika or at San Vitale, merely interrupted by narrow strips of multicoloured cloud: it is literally pulverised by a cloudy whirlwind in which harmonies of white, pink and blue are merged. Exquisite because of the harmony of its colouring, this hybrid work, unique of its kind, can be regarded as symbolic of the hesitations attending this century of transition.

Unfortunately, the surviving frescoes at Nis*, in the basilica at Stobi and in the Red Church near Philippopolis in Bulgaria are too fragmentary or too effaced to give any idea of monumental painting in the Balkan provinces of the Empire. The only monuments from the epoch of Justinian extant in the East are the apsidal mosaic of the Panaghia Angeloktistos* on Cyprus representing the Virgin between two angels and the mosaic of the 'Transfiguration' in St. Catherine's monastery at Sinai. On a silver ground, Christ rises in a blue mandorla* between Moses and Elijah; at his feet are the three apostles, prostrate or raising their arms. Thirty medallions of prophets, apostles and evangelists, and portraits of the two founders of the monastery, compose a glory surrounding the scene of the Transfiguration. Higher up, two angels rhythmically displayed support a cross within a circle. Finally, at either side of a window, there are two mosaics showing 'Moses and the Burning Bush' and 'Moses receiving the Law'. These rigorous and austere compositions are far removed from the lavish decoration of San Vitale and the pleasant scenes of Poreč. The hieratic pole of the Byzantine world is in evidence here, that pole whose attraction would eventually prove the stronger. However, it is as well to bear in mind the admirable personifications of the months in the pavement mosaics from the convent at Beisan: in the beaming figure of February we recognise an important pointer along the route which leads from the 'Martyrs' of Salonika to the angelic forms of Nicaea* and St. Sophia.

The same tendencies recur in all the productions of this age: in the great illuminated manuscripts, in the gorgeous figured fabrics preserved in the Egyptian necropoleis, in the sculpted ivories and in the priceless goldsmiths' work.

Reliquary for fragment of the True Cross
Cover of the central portion
c. 960
Limburg-on-the-Lahn, Cathedral Treasury

The Virgin. Detail of *The Crucifixion*
c. 1050
Chios, mosaic of Nea Moni

St. John. Detail of *The Transfiguration*
c. 1050
Chios, mosaic of Nea Moni

Frieze of angels
Detail: three angels on the right
11th cent.
Ochrid (Yugoslavia), St. Sophia

The Manuscripts

What is striking about the manuscripts is the extreme variety of their style. Thus the antique tradition is perpetuated not merely in profane manuscripts—the Virgil, 'The Iliad', and the Dioscorides illustrated before 524 at Constantinople for the princess Juliana Anicia*— but also in sacred texts in Greek or Latin.

Among the original creations of the fifth and sixth centuries mention must first be made of the 'Alexandrian Chronicle'*, a work more Coptic than Byzantine, and of the magnificent series of 'codices'* with a purple ground. If the miniatures of the Vienna Genesis* take their inspiration largely from Hellenistic painting, the new solemn and emotive style makes a splendid debut with the Rossano and Sinope Gospels. Here the illusionist naturalism of antiquity has been almost completely suppressed. As with the gold ground mosaics from the time of Theodoric, the purplish ground of these miniatures plays a double role: whilst repelling every element of naturalistic representation, it affirms itself as the supreme colouristic value. A deliberate counterpoint of candid, sonorous tones (red and black) and cold colours (white, bluish white) from now on controls the space, in which nothing is interposed between the figure and the ground, and gives the miniature an uncannily monumental dimension.

One can follow the emergence of this new monumentality through the five miniatures of the Sinope Gospels, the thirteen illustrations to the Rossano Gospels and the five large compositions of the Rabula Gospels. In the tragic Christ of 'Sinopensis' we again meet the spirit of the Dura-Europos paintings: this manuscript, written in Greek, is perhaps the sole testimony to the grandeur of fifth century Syrian art. But it is in 'Rossanensis' that the new hieratic and monumental spirit most forcefully declares itself.

The style of 'Rabulensis' is less advanced than that of 'Rossanensis'. While the painter of 'Rossanensis' has stripped his pictures of all illusionist accessory detail and virtually discarded the decorative element, 'Rabulensis' delights in the representation of colourful, animated skies and ornamental elements: the architectural decoration, flowers, animals and birds, with which he embellishes the illustrations, are still treated in a style whose grace and sophistication leads back to the fifth century.

This impression of stylistic 'anarchy' is a fitting conclusion to our brief evocation of the Byzantine painting of the sixth century. It seems that Byzantine art had not yet attained the homogeneity characteristic of classical epochs. In any case, we shall never know just when the art of the Empire became truly Byzantine. The reason is that virtually no paintings from Constantinople have survived from that 'First Golden Age', the time of Justinian. We know this emperor filled the Empire with magnificent buildings. Procopius' treatise 'On Buildings' shows the emperor's architects at work in all the cities of the East, the buildings of the capital serving everywhere as models. The discovery in 1959 of pavement mosaics from the episcopal church of Qasr el Lebia* has yielded moving confirmation of the threefold activity of this emperor. 'Construction', 'Renovation' and 'Decoration' are represented under the features of three feminine figures: Ktisis holds in her hand the charter containing the imperial grant; Ananeosis sits enthroned beneath the imperial baldachin and Kosmesis brings incense and roses. Unfortunately, neither these beautiful allegories nor the long lists of the hundreds of buildings erected, renovated or adorned through the good offices of Justinian, can make up for the loss of the mosaics which adorned the Holy Apostles, St. John of Studius*, the hall of the dome in the Great Palace, where the victories of Justinian were displayed, or the famous church of St. John at Ephesus*.

Today there remains as testimony to that 'Golden Age' one of the greatest architectural masterpieces of all time and the most powerful symbol of orthodox spirituality: namely that work 'at once admirable and terrifying' (Procopius, 'On Buildings') accomplished between 532 and 537 by Anthemius of Tralles and Isidore of Miletus when they raised more than fifty metres above the ground the dome of St. Sophia. It was in this luminous sphere that the dissonances of the sixth century would find their unity and mingle in a supreme harmony.

The Crisis over the Icons

Never since the time of Constantine had the Mediterranean world been so close to unity as in the time of Justinian, and never had the lack of unity been so cruelly felt. The presence of conflicting forces can be sensed throughout the Byzantine world. In an excess of Christian zeal, Justinian deprived pagans of their right to teach at the University of Constantinople and in 529 closed the Academy at Athens, the refuge of pagan Neo-Platonism. The Persian king immediately invited the Athenian philosophers to his court, so great was the continuing influence of Hellenism. On the other hand, it was at the court of Justinian himself that Alexandrian poetry enjoyed its last flowering. The sixth century is the century both of Romanus*, the greatest religious poet of Byzantium, and of Dioscorus, the last Alexandrian. Paul the Silentiary, who has left us a poetic description of St. Sophia, was also the author of erotic poems verging on the obscene. Similarly, a century earlier we find Nonnos composing hexameters on the voyages of Dionysos to the Indies and also writing a poetic paraphrase of St. John's Gospel.

Christian art had not escaped these contradictory attractions. Its soaring attainments in the fifth and sixth centuries had not obliterated its original hostility towards any representation of sacred personages and subjects. 'Thou shalt not make any graven image nor any likeness at all': in the name of this Commandment, the Council of Elvira* in 306 forbade the decoration of churches with paintings 'so that the object of our adoration shall not be exposed on the walls'. Accordingly, when at the end of the fifth century Serenus, bishop of Marseilles, ordered all the images in the city to be destroyed, Pope Gregory the Great praised him for having prevented adoration of the images by the masses.

The symbolism of Early Christian painting was a compromise solution between this iconoclastic attitude and history painting which seeks to illustrate a religious narrative.

42

However, despite the progress made by narrative iconography, symbolism was still being practised down to the end of the seventh century, when it came under attack in an ordinance of the Council of 692, which vetoed the 'former shadows' the Church had accepted as 'symbols of the truth' and insisted on the representation of Christ as a human figure:

'We ordain that Christ shall be represented not as the traditional Lamb but in his human form. This image will make us understand the greatness and humility of God the Word and remind us of his life as a man, his passion, his saving death and the deliverance of the world which issued from it.'

To uncertainty over programmes was added heterogeneity of styles. The ornamental style of the fifth century had its final flowering in the Byzantine mosaics of Syria and Palestine, from 640 under Arab occupation. Complex architectural forms, candelabra and a paradise of plants adorn the mosaics of the basilica at Bethlehem*. The same prolixity or ornament characterises the decoration of the great Ummayad sanctuaries: the Mosque of Omar* at Jerusalem and the Great Mosque* of Damascus. Unfortunately, most of the mosaics in the Great Mosque have disappeared, the result of numerous fires. Nevertheless, magnificent compositions still extant in the court-yard give us an idea of the splendour of profane painting in seventh and eighth century Byzantium. Artists came from Constantinople to work for the Caliph Al-Walid, artists who knew how to give their landscapes and Pompeian architectural motifs an indescribable magical charm. Airy edifices, at times fantastical, appear on a gold ground in the midst of gardens shaded by great trees and watered by streams tumbling in cascades. Nothing animated is to be seen. These are places from which life seems withdrawn, as though by enchantment, and one expects at any moment to glimpse those speaking statues of bronze and trees loaded with precious stones which figure in oriental tales. The chromatic range of the mosaics, nourished by a prodigious variety of phosphorescent blues, grass greens, burning yellows and pearly whites, enhances this feeling of withdrawal and the imminence of magic. And yet this masterpiece of ornamental painting is contemporaneous with the decoration to the palaces of Kusejr' Amra* and Khirbet el-Mafjar*, filled with hunting scenes, portraits, and figures of naked women, prolonging Alexandrian naturalism well into the eighth century . . .

In Byzantine territory there survive only the fine mosaics of the Kanakaria Virgin on Cyprus, the provincial mosaics at Dsromi* in Georgia and the ex votos of St. Demetrius, Salonika. The greatest evidence of Byzantine painting of the seventh and eighth centuries is to be found at Rome, untouched by iconoclastic ravages: the beautiful apsidal mosaic at St. Agnes*, the mosaics of St. Venantius in the Lateran* and in the former oratory of the Greek Pope John VII in the Vatican. Among frescoes, mention may be made of those in the catacomb of Comodilla and in St. Maria Antiqua, which range from the seventh to the eleventh centuries. Built in the sixth century, this church was decorated almost entirely by Greeks, as is attested by the predominance of Greek inscriptions and the large place occupied by Byzantine and Syrian iconography. These frescoes, which are unhappily becoming more and more faded, are the best testimony to the position of Byzantine painting in the eighth century.

An extreme diversity characterises these Roman paintings. While at St. Agnes and St. Venantius the hieratic style is dominant, the presbytery of St. Maria Antiqua presents an astonishing sequence of beautiful Hellenistic figures, whose plasticity and richly graduated colouring carries us back three centuries. We are here confronted by the school which has also left us a fine manuscript of Job* ('Patmos 171'). Yet in this same church, at this same period, side by side with these oddly Neo-Antique figures which presage the paintings of Castelseprio*, there is a sequence of votive pictures for which, try as we may, we can find no equivalent in the monumental art of the preceding centuries. Their art is fundamentally different; it is no longer merely an art with symbolical or didactic intentions but a profound collective experience, a new manner of envisaging the relationship of the work of art to the sacred on one hand and to the spectator on the other: in short, we have defined the icon.

Like the Fayum portraits, the earliest icons were painted on sized wood or by the encaustic method. And Egypt was the home of some of the earliest icons now known: *Christ and St. Menas, Bishop Abraham*. But it was not in Egypt that the icon acquired its distinctive physiognomy, nor was Egypt the source of Byzantine iconolatry. The adoration of the icons which is the characteristic feature of the Orthodox Church, and perhaps reveals its Hellenic roots, was known neither to the Copts nor to the Monophysites in general. In archaic Greece men knew of primitive wooden statues which had been sent down from the sky, for example the Athena Nike of the Acropolis. The Hellenism of Byzantium would encompass the adoration of icons attributed to St. Luke, to the magical activity of the Saviour or to the presence of supernatural and miraculous forces, as in the case of the *Holy Face* of Edessa*.

It was in the catastrophic atmosphere of the seventh century—the true Byzantine 'Middle Ages'—that the cult of the icons mounted to a frenzy. And it was then, and only then, that icon art found its style. Most of the icons of this period were destroyed by the iconoclasts. With those which survive, in the monastery on Sinai, at Kiev and at Moscow, together with the colossal icon of the Virgin at Santa Francesca (Rome), which is an encaustic painting, we have reached the threshold of Byzantine classicism. From the seventh century, in fact, the icon style breaks out from the domain of painting on wood and invades the frescoes and mosaics. The first effect of this irruption of the 'iconic' conception of painting into the churches was a breach with the monumental order. The great compositions and their grounds disappear. Parsimony is carried to extremes, votive pictures, having the appearance of enlarged icons, are found ranged side by side, with no connection between them. The frescoes in the catacomb of Comodilla and in St. Maria Antiqua give one the impression that 'they reproduce images which on portable objects, such as bracelets and seals, would fulfil the function of an amulet' (A. Grabar). But it is in the ex votos of St. Demetrius of Salonika that the new style is seen at its most successful: the saint, clad in the sumptuous costume of an imperial officer, appears flanked by his devotees, men and women, aged and young. A mysterious action from a distance links the world of these mosaics with the sphere of the spectator, who feels he breathes the same air and moves in the same space as these solemn figures who fix him with the gaze

of their dilated pupils. This fusion between the subject and the contemplated object will be the basis of the new monumental order built up by Byzantine classicism.

This profound change in Byzantine art is to be seen against its background, the terrible crisis of the seventh century. Byzantium was being forced to fight simultaneously on two fronts, in the west against the Slavs, the Avars and the Bulgars, in the east against first the Persians and then the Arabs. By the end of the seventh century the Empire had lost most of Justinian's conquests in the West; in the East it had lost Syria, Mesopotamia, Palestine, Egypt and Cyrenaica. Territorially speaking, the Empire was reduced to less than half its former size and on two occasions, in 626 and 686, the enemy laid siege to Constantinople itself. At the beginning of the eighth century the citizens were ordered to lay in provisions to last them three months.

In the seventh century Byzantine literature suddenly dried up. Writing and building came to a halt: the only emperor with a reputation as a builder is Justinian II. Superstition reached terrifying proportions: unspeakable scenes involving black magic took place at Pergamon during the siege of the city by the Arabs in 717. It seems as though the struggle for survival and the cult of the icons absorbed all the vital energies of the Byzantine world. The two preoccupations were closely linked. On more than one occasion when Salonika was being besieged by the Slavs the city owed its preservation to the miraculous intervention of St. Demetrius. The icons were weapons of war. During the great siege of 626 the patriarch Sergius, at the head of the Senate and people, made a procession round the walls bearing the images of Christ and the Virgin 'exhibiting them to the powers of darkness': the barbarians, says Pisides, the poet-chronicler, turned away their heads to avoid the sight of the 'invincible Theotokos' . . .

It was this apocalyptical atmosphere which gave birth to the inexhaustible store of legends about icons which spoke, wept, bled, worked miracles, crossed the sea, flew in the air, appeared to men in dreams and revealed the places where theophanies would be found. It was against this inextricable mixture of gross superstition and ecstatic spirituality that the iconoclast emperors launched their offensive.

These great emperors, who set the state on its feet again and saved Byzantium from the Arab peril, were just as much prisoners of the icon magic as those whom they regarded as 'slaves to the icons'. For Leo III the icons were 'idols' because they were 'mute and lifeless': and in the name of this almost Islamic principle he embarked on what amounted to a civil war, by ordering the image of Christ over the bronze doorway to his palace to be destroyed. His successor Constantine V prohibited all images of divine things, 'whose dead colours cannot represent their splendours', and ordered all images in churches to be destroyed. The images were everywhere replaced by symbols or even by secular paintings. The most frequent substitute for figures of Christ and of the Virgin was a cross: a typical example can be seen in the church of St. Irene at Constantinople*. The geometrical decoration of certain Cappadocian churches is perhaps a reflection of the iconoclast style, but the iconoclast emperors seem chiefly to have restored to a place of honour the symbolism and naturalism of primitive Christianity. Thus at the Blachernae church*, Constantine V ordered representation of 'trees, birds and animals of every kind, framed in ivy-leaves, in which cranes and peacocks were mingled'. The birds of the St. Kyriaki church on Naxos explain how the iconophiles came to accuse the iconoclasts of having turned the church into 'an aviary and an orchard' . . .

48

For Byzantine Orthodoxy, the iconoclast crisis was the ordeal by fire, the salutary shock which forced it to rethink and purify its doctrine. To defend themselves against the accusation of idolatry, the great Orthodox thinkers—St. Germanus, patriarch of Constantinople, St. John Damascene, the greatest theologian of his day, and St. Theodore the Studite, who reformed the famous Studite monastery at Constantinople—elaborated a theory of the icon which ushers in the monumental art of the Byzantine classical period.

They saw iconoclasm as the last resurgence of Monophysite transcendentalism, which denies the incarnation and with it Christ's mediation between heaven and earth, between things visible and invisible. 'Having become perfect man, Christ allows himself to be represented by an image like the rest of us in order that he may not be anything other than we are,' the patriarch Photios was to say at a later date. But the word image must be taken in its strict meaning: the icon is not the arbitrary creation of the painter's imagination. If it is made 'correctly', that is, if it reproduces models whose authenticity is guaranteed by tradition, the icon becomes a 'reflection' of its divine prototype and participates in its sanctity. There is the same relation between the icon and the sacred as between the Son and the Father, since it is said that 'the Son is the reflection of his splendour and the stamp of his person' ('hypostasis', Hebrews i, 3). Christ is the 'image of the invisible God' (Colossians, i, 15), 'in whom the complete fullness of Godhead dwells embodied' (Colossians, ii, 9): these passages from the Epistles, in which Christ appears as the 'icon' of God on earth, are always recited at the Orthodox mass for the consecration of icons.

The icon is the 'mirror' in which the invisible world is reflected: it is 'existentially' identical with its model while being 'essentially' different. To venerate the icon is to identify with it and receive grace from it through the 'sympathetic' process described by the apostle: 'We who having no veil over our face contemplate as in a mirror the splendour of the Lord, are transformed into the same image.' (II Corinthians, iii, 18.) Just as the liturgy is not a dramatic representation but the presence 'hic et nunc' (here and now) of the Passion, so does the icon make the saintly hypostases present in person. Pushing the specifically Byzantine belief in the incarnation of divine forces to its final conclusion, St. Theodore the Studite congratulates John the Spatharius for having chosen the icon of St. Demetrius as god-father for his son, and hastens to add: 'It is the saint himself, spiritually present, who will serve as the child's god-father . . .'

It was on this doctrine, of which the Studite says it is 'intelligible only to piety and inaccessible to profane ears' that the classical system of painting would be erected.

Deesis
Mosaic, 13th cent.
Constantinople, St. Sophia
▼

The Madonna (late 12th century)
and *Apostles* (11th century)
Mosaics of the apse
Torcello, near Venice   ▶

Brief Cappadocian Interlude

Before embarking on the 'Second Golden Age' of Byzantium, this will be a convenient place to say a few words about the art of a Byzantine province which remained more or less foreign to the style being elaborated in the capital and in the great cities of the Empire.

In the volcanic region of Urgüp in Cappadocia*, numerous colonies of monks had taken up residence inside tufa rocks of fantastical shapes from which they fashioned churches and convents whose walls, vaults, pillars and cupolas were literally carved out of the rock, in imitation of masonry work. The Cappadocian frescoes introduce us to a regional popular art which preserved its independence and peculiar tradition from the end of iconoclasm until the beginning of the thirteenth century. The oldest paintings in these sculpted churches date from the beginning of the post-iconoclast era. Hence the pictorial decoration of the chapels of St. Basil, and others, knows nothing of icons. Conversely, the 365 churches and chapels of the eleventh to thirteenth centuries which stud the lunar landscape of Göreme and Soghanli* bear witness to a revival of the old narrative tradition of Early Christian and proto-Byzantine art.

This art derives from its Byzantine roots its simple grandeur, the authority of that large-scale mural handwriting which is as necessary to painters as to mosaicists, the practical skill in the linear undulations which link the figures with the curves of the vaults and the blind arcades. What is peculiar to itself is the popular accent, the instinct for telling a lively tale through image and gesture, and above all, the passion and asperity which perhaps found its way into Anatolian art and was from there widely disseminated. 'Monastic' art had always been the great purveyor of realistic and dramatic cycles. At all events, the tone if not the style of Cappadocian art has its echoes in all the provinces of the Empire: Cyprus, Aegina in Greece, southern Italy and even in certain manuscripts from Constantinople.

The Second Golden Age

In 843, the Seventh Oecumenical Council restored the cult of the icons. In 867, a new dynasty known as the Macedonian came to the throne with Basil I* and governed the Empire for close on two centuries. In these two centuries Byzantine power, wealth and civilisation were at their peak.

Constantinople, with a population of at least a million, was a fabulous city. Its reputation had penetrated to China, where it was taken for the Empire itself and is described in the Foulin Chinese texts as 'The City'; to the Russians it was 'Tsarigrad', the supreme imperial city. When the Crusaders stormed Constantinople in 1204 'they could not believe the world could contain so rich a city, when they saw those high walls and prodigal towers which completely encircled it, and those rich palaces and lofty churches, to a number no one who had not seen them for himself would believe, and the length and breadth of the city which was of all others the sovereign' (Villehardouin, *The Capture of Constantinople*, 1204).

A splendid intellectual flowering accompanied the economic and political renaissance of the Empire. This was the 'Macedonian Renaissance', a time in which the 'consul of the philosophers', Michael Psellos, the first modern Platonist, dared to write to the patriarch: 'I myself occupy a throne no less elevated than your own. . . .' But this epoch of littérateurs and mannerists was also and above all that which heard the 'song mingled with tears' of St. Symeon*, the first modern mystic, who alone shares with St. John the Apostle and Gregory of Nazianzen* the title 'Theologian', conferred by the Orthodox Church to signify an existential participation in the divine Word.

Reinvigorated by the Studite reform and the patriarchate of Photios, the Church successfully resumed the missionary work which had been interrupted during the iconoclast crisis. The ninth century saw the evangelisation of the Slavs and the Bulgars. The great event of the tenth century would be the entry of the Russians into the Byzantine 'koiné'. St. Vladimir, the great Prince of Kiev, was baptised in 987 or 989. He married Anna, a Porphyrogenita princess, and summoned from Kherson, the ancient Greek colony on the Black Sea, priests to organise the Russian clergy. Kherson or Korsoun was regarded as a holy city and in Russian the epithet 'korsounki' is applied to any object especially antique and venerable. It was from Kherson, if not Constantinople itself, that painters came to decorate the churches of Kievan Russia* and to initiate the Russians into Byzantine painting. Nearly all the Russian words relating to painting—'izographe' (painter), 'iconopis' (sacred painting), 'levkas' (white preparation for icons and frescoes), 'finift' (enamel work) are Greek words, only superficially Slavicised.

The conversion of the Slavs and the Russians enormously enlarged the field for the expansion of Byzantine painting. The tenth and eleventh centuries witness the establishment, centring on Constantinople, of a vast 'koiné' embracing the Balkans, Asia Minor, Georgia, Venice and southern Italy, and 'all the Russias' from Kiev to Novgorod and Suzdal. Furthermore, it is in large part thanks to this internationalism of Byzantine painting that we are able to reconstruct its history. Practically nothing survives of the countless churches and palaces which were the ornament of Constantinople in the Macedonian era.

The few ninth century mosaics which still survive rank among the masterpieces of Byzantine art, indeed of art in general. In the first place are the colossal 'Virgin and Child' and the 'Archangel' in the apse of St. Sophia. The mosaics of the church of the Dormition* at Nicaea surpassed in beauty those of St. Sophia. Unfortunately, this church, which also possessed magnificent mosaics from the eleventh century, was destroyed during the Graeco-Turkish war of 1920-1922. A third undoubted masterpiece is the immense composition of the 'Ascension' in the dome of St. Sophia of Salonika*: this is all that remains of the mosaics of the ninth century.

Traces of mosaics from the tenth century are rarer still. Most are to be found at St. Sophia in Constantinople. In all probability the emperor seen kneeling before Christ in the lunette of the narthex is Leo VI*. In the south porch, another mosaic represents Mary with the Child receiving offerings from the emperors Constantine and Justinian. The tribunes above the sanctuary carry a fine portrait of Alexander and a panel representing Constantine IX and Zoe* before Christ enthroned. Lastly, on the side walls of the nave there are fine mosaics of prophets and the patriarchs of Constantinople these, together with the seraph wings to be seen on the pendentives, make up the tale of tenth-eleventh century Constantinopolitan mosaics.

To gain an idea of the splendour of Byzantine painting in the tenth century, it is necessary to turn to the minor arts.

The marvellous fabrics of the tenth to twelfth centuries yield nothing in magnificence to the other works of pomp and piety executed in mosaic and enamel. The crowning glory

St. Goachim offering sheep before the
Birth of the Virgin
Wall Painting
Mis'tra, Peribleptors Church (Greece)

of this art form is undoubtedly the shroud of St. German of Auxerre: the ground is violet-purple; the eagles are pale gold, their eyes and rings green; each eagle is more than half a metre high.

This period was the golden age of Byzantine enamel work. Mingled with precious stones, lapped by the milk of alabaster and blood of onyx, aureoled with gold, the enamels with their harmonies of purple, lapis lazuli and sky blue are, with the mosaics, the most powerful symbol of the sumptuous Byzantine idea of beauty. In the ninth century, probably as the result of some technical discovery, the art of enamel cloisonné*—one of the most difficult of all techniques—achieved its maturity: the votive crown of St. Basil among the treasure of St. Mark's is one of the earliest examples of the astonishing mastery the Byzantines acquired in this field. It is at Venice that the largest number of pieces enriched with enamel are preserved, chalices, patens, Gospel bindings, icons, retables such as the celebrated Pala d'Oro*; practically all of them were carried off from Constantinople after the sack of the city by the Crusaders in 1204. Among the treasure of the Cathedral of Limburg* is the finest specimen of the style to come from the tenth century: a reliquary containing a fragment of the True Cross which belonged to Constantine VII and Romanus II. Here, as elsewhere, one is left astounded by the mystery of Byzantine monumentality: the sixteen tiny enamel plaques which adorn the cover of this reliquary compose an ensemble as imposing as any giant iconostasis.

It is above all in the miniatures that one can observe most clearly the genesis of the classical Byzantine style in the ninth and tenth centuries. With 'Parisinus 65'*, whose painted decoration is composed solely of linear ornament, we are still in the iconoclast orbit. On the other hand, the psalters with marginal illustrations known—wrongly, it seems—as 'monastic', have a lively pictorial quality, popular, sometimes bordering on expressionism. Among the eight psalters of this type, the most famous is the Chludov psalter at Moscow. This piece of anti-iconoclast propaganda, in which the heretical patriarch John the Grammarian comes in for especially malicious treatment, was inspired by the circle centred on the patriarch Photios.

Rich in landscapes, architectural features and secular subjects, the iconography of the 'Cosmas'* in the Vatican reflects the antiquising art of the sixth century; at the same time, a series of monumental figures indicates the transition towards the hieratic style of the classical epoch. But the most important testimony to the state of Byzantine painting immediately following the iconoclast crisis is the magnificent collection of the 'Homilies of St. Gregory Nazianzen'*, illustrated about 880 for Basil I, who with his family is represented on the frontispiece. The revival of interest in things ancient which took place in the tenth century is represented in painting by a sequence of fine manuscripts, first and foremost the magnificent 'Joshua Roll'*. This is a parchment some 10.50 m. long and 31 cm. high, on which the exploits of Joshua are displayed in unbroken series. One is struck by the anachronism of these paintings: while the art of the tenth century keeps to brilliant colours, the painting of the 'Roll' perpetuates the antique genre of the tinted sketch. Antique art is sovereign here, not only in the iconographic details, but also in the very structure of the composition, down to the cubist architectural structures which perspectively serve as background. In the same way the famous Paris Psalter* seems to ignore the most decisive acquisitions of Byzantine art. Other ninth century miniatures appear to copy fifth and sixth century models. Thus, in contrast to the vigorous drawing of the ninth century, the painters who depicted Moses on Sinai in the Bible of Leo the Patricius* in the Vatican and the Vision of Ezechiel in 'Paris 510' are almost wholly ignorant of linear contours. One of the painters of 'Paris 510' has expressed his atmospheric sense of landscape through a grouping of pink, blue and green splashes. Here we again encounter the blue and pink grounds of antique painting and even the elegant frame of the original, probably an Alexandrian painting of the fourth or fifth century.

This antiquising school is a constant feature of Byzantine painting. It was predominant in the pavement mosaics of the fourth and fifth centuries. We have seen it reappearing in the frescoes of St. Maria Antiqua in the seventh century. It is seen at its grandest in the miniatures of the ninth and tenth centuries, the frescoes of St. George on Naxos and above all in the frescoes of Castelseprio.

It is not until near the end of the tenth century that manifestations of the style of the classical epoch appear in the miniatures. The sequence opens with Gospels preserved at Paris, at Athens, at Sinai, at Stavronikita* and elsewhere. The gold ground becomes general, naturalism disappears, graphic values are accentuated, even the smallest paintings acquire the monumental breadth we find in the mosaics and the icons: the tall and pensive figures of these miniatures seem to move in the same immensity as the apostles and prophets on the walls of St. Sophia and on the pendentives and cupolas of eleventh century churches. This specifically Byzantine monumentality blossoms out in the 430 miniatures of the celebrated Menologion of Basil II*. Other menologia of the eleventh century take their inspiration from this masterpiece: the one in Baltimore, with its 24 full

55

page miniatures, was probably executed on behalf of Michael IV. Other great works of miniature from the eleventh century include the Psalter of Basil II in which the emperor is shown triumphing over the Bulgars, the Psalter Vienna 336, the Gospel No. 1 of Iviron* and above all the magnificent 'Paris 64'. Lastly we have Coislin 79*, with its superb frontispiece representing the emperor Nicephorus Botaniates* between the archangel Michael and St. John Chrysostom, which marks the transition to the more individual style of the Comnene period*.

It is in these works that the Byzantine miniature attains its classic perfection. In the Martyrology of Basil II, the composition obeys a supple rhythmical movement which is a sensitive accompaniment to the musicality of the colour: the same theme recurs in the mysteriously immobile silhouettes, in the undulation of the hills and the structure of the objects. The plasticity still visible in the tenth century Gospels recedes before the intense spirituality which now emanates from ascetic countenances with huge expressive eyes: the image of St. John the Theologian in Bodleian* 110, the double image of Christ and the prophet Jeremiah of manuscript V, 9 in the Laurentian Library, proclaim the reign of the icon under the same title as the great figures of Daphni. Likewise, the ornamentation is reduced to its simplest expression: it is with 'Paris 64' that one sees the emergence of the canons of concordance in richly decorated frames which will become general in the twelfth century.

In contrast with these works, which transpose the monumental art of the eleventh century to the space of the miniature, the 372 illustrations of 'Paris 74' confront us with another source of inspiration. The virtuosi to whom we are indebted for these minuscule miniatures carried stylisation to a degree at times reminiscent of certain Romanesque works. Moreover the touches of light which normally punctuate Byzantine draperies have here been replaced by a network of gold lines in evident imitation of the design of cloisonné enamel: together with the mosaics of Nea Moni*, the miniatures of the Gospel Book of Ostromir*, the most ancient of the Russian manuscripts with miniatures, and the miniatures of 'Paris 74' are the first indications of the profound influence enamel work was starting to exert over painting.

Monumental Painting

The monumental painting of the eleventh century is represented in Greece by three great mosaic ensembles. These are the mosaics of Hosios Leukas (1050) near Delphi, of Nea Moni at Chios (1100) and of the convent of Daphni (1100) close to Athens. To these mosaics one must add the fine frescoes in the crypt of Hosios Leukas, those of Panaghia Chalceon at Salonika and, above all, the admirable frescoes which Leo, a former administrator of St. Sophia at Constantinople, had executed about 1040 for the church of St. Sophia at Ochrid*.

At this same period, Byzantine masters decorated with frescoes the narthex of San

57

Procession of Archbishops
Lower register of *Communion of the Apostles*
(the archbishops are shown as successors
of the apostles)
Church of Sopočani monastery (Yugoslavia)

Dormition of the Virgin
In the centre, Christ receiving the soul of
the Virgin in the form of a new-born infant;
angels, apostles, bishops
1260-1265
Church of Sopočani monastery (Yugoslavia)

Angelo in Formis and other Italian churches in Calabria and Apulia. But the most important monument to the Byzantine 'koiné' of the eleventh century is at Kiev, 'the Byzantium of Asia', the city described as 'the rival to Constantinople and the finest ornament of the Greek world': the mosaics and frescoes of St. Sophia. These frescoes, unfortunately over-restored, are the sole survivors of Byzantine secular art: a variety of scenes, containing not less than 130 figures, represents the sports of the hippodrome and festivals at the court of Constantinople.

The texts mention three other large Kievan churches decorated with mosaics. The few remaining fragments in the church of St. Michael-with-the-Roof-of Gold* date from the beginning of the twelfth century. Together with the 'Communion of the Apostles' in the apse, this is the most subtle art of the Comnene period to make its appearance on Russian soil.

On the political plane, the epoch of the Comnene dynasty was a series of disasters: it saw Turkish and Norman invasions, the loss of Italy and the Anatolian plateau, the devaluation of the currency and the rise of the great feudal estate. The transformation of Anatolia into a new Turkestan ruined the whole military and economic structure of Byzantium: the Empire attacked in 1204 by the infamous diversion of the fourth Crusade was an Empire reduced to the Greek peninsula and a handful of cantons in Asia Minor.

Nevertheless, this terrible thirteenth century was one of the most brilliant epochs of Byzantine civilisation. Unhappily, its monuments in Constantinople have almost all perished. The sole vestiges of Comnene painting surviving at Constantinople are to be found in the gallery of St. Sophia. The panel representing the Virgin and Child between the emperor John II* and the empress Irene, accompanied by their son Alexios*, is one of the earliest examples of the new technique of modelling by touches of light, later to become general in the frescoes and icons; lastly, in the Deesis panel, one can admire one of the masterpieces of Byzantine mosaic.

While Byzantine paintings were multiplying in the Balkans and in the north of Russia, at Pskov* and Vladimir*, Byzantium's deadliest enemies in the West, Venice and Norman Sicily, were also becoming provinces of Byzantine art. They offer the largest ensembles of Byzantine or Byzantinising mosaics to have come down to us: the mosaics of St. Mark's at Venice cover an area of 5,000 square metres, those of Monreale*, near Palermo spread their compositions over 6,340 square metres.

According to Amari*, at the time of the Norman conquest Sicily was 'more than half Arab and in the remainder Byzantine'. Successors to the Greek basileis and the Arab emirs, and like them, great builders, the Norman kings used the Arab, Byzantine and Latin elements to compose a bizarre ensemble, unique in the Middle Ages. In architecture they were eclectic, crowning Gothic basilicas with Byzantine and even Muslim domes, combining Latin shapes with stalactite Arab ceilings, but for the pictorial decoration of their churches they drew exclusively on Byzantium. They borrowed Byzantine painting, sacred and profane, just as they copied the vestments, ceremonial and customs of the court of Constantinople. The hunting scenes, fanciful beasts, stylised flora and ornamental

luxury of the chamber of King Roger at the palace of Palermo and in the palace of Ziza*
are evocative of the Arabo-Byzantine decoration of iconoclast palaces. Again, the art of
Daphni finds itself continued, with greater or lesser felicity, in the mosaics of churches
built by the Norman kings and high dignitaries of their court at Cefalù*, Palermo and
Monreale.

What strikes us about all these monuments of the classical epoch is their extraordinary
unity. Gone is the stylistic anarchy and arbitrary iconography of the epoch of Justinian.
One and the same style now makes itself explicit in architecture, monumental painting, icon
and manuscript painting, in enamels and in textiles. In the time of Justinian all types of
building were essayed simultaneously: basilicas, domed basilicas, buildings on the circular
plan crowned with a dome, cruciform churches. From now on, whatever may be its
internal structure, externally the Byzantine church presents itself as a cubic building
surmounted by a central cupola or group of cupolas, the middle one higher than the rest:
a strictly iconic conception of the image unifies the style of painting, while a rigorous order,
governed by a thought-out theology, regulates the iconographic scheme. In fact, the church
is regarded as the very image of the world: the cupolas and vaults are the heavens; the
sanctuary, the intelligible world; the naves, the world of the senses, redeemed by the
Incarnation and sacred history. This hierarchical tripartite division of the cosmos is
jointly conveyed by the palette of the building and its iconographic arrangement.

The dome of St. Sophia at Salonika is an imposing example of the early classical style.
At its centre the Pantocrator*, seated on a rainbow, rules enthroned from a medallion
borne up by two angels. In the circular band a gold ground sets off the Virgin in a violet
robe, flanked by two angels and accompanied by twelve apostles whose emotive heads,
modelled with green shadows, whose twirling bodies and swirling draperies form a vivid
contrast to the mysteriously sensuous beauty of the angelic countenances. This vast
composition, rising twenty-five metres above the ground, creates an atmosphere of ecstatic
uprooting and spiritual violence, an impression reinforced by the vehement counterpoint
of the draperies, the verticality of the trees veined with gold which separate the figures and
the rhythmical undulation of the deliberately asymmetrical rocks which punctuate the
lower border of the dome. By these very qualities, this work locates itself as on the threshold
of the classical system. The agitation and violence which characterise the Salonikan
mosaic will be re-absorbed into the massive inwardness of the effigies of the Macedonian
era. It becomes exceptional for the Ascension to be represented on the central dome: one
finds this only in certain peripheral or provincial buildings. From the tenth century the
Ascension is relegated to the secondary vaults, as for example at St. Sophia of Ochrid
where it is framed by a marvellous frieze representing angels in flight.

Henceforth the Pantocrator occupies the central dome. 'One might say,' writes the
patriarch Photios, 'that he is inspecting the earth, meditating its order and governance.'
Surrounded by archangels, and more often than not by prophets holding unfurled parch-
ments in their hand from which they read the sacred texts, the Pantocrator is not the
Christ of the Gospels but the 'Master of the Universe', 'the All-Seeing One'. It is this gaze
become God which is represented in the impressive cupola at Daphni.

At the conch of the apse—the point where the celestial cupola meets the square earth—is placed the Virgin, symbolising the Church and the union of earth and heaven. 'Cloud illumined': such is the invocation of the Virgin in the great Acathist Hymn, and so she appears at St. Sophia when the rays of the sun fall on the gold ground to kindle a blaze of glowing embers and amber. The same impression of a theophany is produced by the huge Virgin of the Basilica at Torcello. 'Joy of the angels', the Virgin is escorted by angels in full ceremonial dress, like the Dynamis angel at Nicaea and the colossal archangel of St. Sophia. Confronted with these figures, one can visualise the miraculous apparition commemorated in the Russian festival of Pokrov ('Intercession to the veiled Virgin'): recalling how one day, in the Blachernae church at Constantinople, where the veil of the Virgin was preserved, Andrew the Innocent and his disciple Epiphanus saw the Mother of God rise up above the 'gate beautiful' of the iconostasis, doff her mantle of mercy and spread it out over the people. A Muscovite icon from the beginning of the sixteenth century celebrates this 'intercession' in marvellous harmonies of clear blue, vermilion and white.

In the apse, above the Virgin, we have the eucharistic cycle which contains two magnificent symbols almost unknown to the art of the West: *The Communion of the Apostles* and *The Divine Liturgy*.

Lastly, the church itself is dedicated to illustration of the twelve great festivals of the Church: Annunciation (with spinning wheel or well), Nativity, Presentation, Baptism, Transfiguration, Raising of Lazarus, Palm Sunday, Crucifixion, Resurrection*, Ascension, Pentecost, Dormition*.

This scheme is completed by portraits of saints and martyrs; in some instances the Last Judgment is represented on the west wall, as at Torcello, Sopočani* and in numerous Russian churches. This completes the systematic ensemble in which, as one theologian expresses it, 'all the mysteries of the Incarnation of Christ are represented, from the Annunciation to the Lord's Ascension and his second coming'.

From one end of the Byzantine 'koiné' to the other, one encounters the same themes, treated in the same fashion and arranged in the same order. The apostles of Hosios Leukas and of St. Sophia at Kiev* could almost change places. The mannerism of Kurbinovo* and Kastoria* shows itself simultaneously on Cyprus. The frescoes of Staraya Ladoga and of Lagoudhera* on Cyprus are so alike they could be taken for each other. The 'petasos', the hat affected by Athenian dandies, which the antiquising passion of the Byzantines has placed on the head of some shepherd from the Nativity, crops up both in thirteenth century paintings on wood at Pisa and in the frescoes of Volotovo* in Russia. Formerly, teams of monumental masons carrying their pattern books with them travelled through the provinces of the Roman Empire. Now the use of pattern books reproducing models sanctified by the Church and by tradition is again the general custom. But it goes without saying that these procedures do not account for the unity of style. The arresting homogeneity of Byzantine painting is to be attributed above all to the strict surveillance of the Church and to the rigour of the iconic conception of the image.

In 787 the Seventh Oecumenical Council had laid down the strict subordination of

61

art to theological and liturgical ideas, and popular adoration of the icons tended in the
same direction. By its essence, the icon is not a 'work of art' but an 'apparition', an
objectified prayer, a petition answered and become a figure. By its essence, the icon places
itself outside representation whose concern is to give an 'illusion' of the reality. The veneration of which it is the object abolishes the distance between the appearance and the reality:
the adorer is not the spectator of a distant God but a participant impregnated with the
presence of the sacred.

The element in which the image of the icon or mosaic bathes is a substance beyond all
natural colouring: the gold ground. The midnight blue of Galla Placidia still belongs to the
world of the senses; but the glowing gold—the only colour never encountered in nature—
strips space, matter and bodies of everything which might suggest extent, weight, the
hazards of an existence riveted to the earth. Everything the Neo-Platonists and the great
Orthodox scholars said about the 'subtle light' of the intelligible world and the illumination
of obscure matter by the divine ray, will find monumental expression in the manner by
which the icons and mosaics realise the transfiguration of colours through their gold
grounds.

The gold strewn with russet which unifies the space of the church has a double
function. Through its agency, the light becomes co-extensive with the pictorial space: the

◀ *Dormition of the Virgin*
Christ, in the centre, receiving the soul of
the Virgin in the form of a new-born infant;
angels, apostles and bishops; apostles and
the Virgin, accompanied by an angel,
shown above.
1295
St. Clement, Ochrid (Yugoslavia)

Christ on the Mount of Olives
Fresco, 1295
St. Clement, Ochrid (Yugoslavia)
▼

light is no longer natural but 'pneumatic' light, which surrounds the figures like a nimbus of sanctity and projects them with complete lucidity into the midst of the worshippers. As Otto Demus* remarks, the gold ground abolishes the fictitious space behind the personages and makes them loom up in the real space in which the spectator moves. The captive light in the gold grounds confers a mysterious mobility on figures apparently immobile. The accents of the light shift continually with the movement of the spectator and the course of the sun; at night, the light from the candles creates changing reflections on the gold surface where the giant figures detach themselves as silhouettes. Contemporary descriptions constantly harp on the 'whirling movement' created by these incessant scintillations. Venantius Fortunatus, bishop of Poitiers, says: 'The figures move, they come and go at the whim of errant rays of the sun, and the entire surface ripples like the waters of the sea.' Procopius says: 'There is perpetual sudden change in the spectacle.' Referring to the Pharos Church, the patriarch Photios remarks: 'The circular movements in every direction induce in the spectator a kind of vertigo . . . Everything seems to him in ecstasy while the temple trembles in all directions . . .'

As a mirror reflecting the intelligible world, the iconic image is required to avoid everything reminiscent of the earth as such: the third dimension, perspective, distracting ornament, landscapes evocative of distance.

Ornamental decoration is banished not only from the mosaics and frescoes but also from the miniatures: the only surviving reminder of the ornamental luxury of the preceding centuries is the decoration of the concordance tables in the manuscripts.

Landscape is likewise reduced to a strict minimum; often enough there is absolutely nothing to break the unity of the gold ground. At Nea Moni, the landscape of the *Descent into Limbo* is reduced to a calligraphy formed from a few arrow-shaped strokes; that of the *Transfiguration* is indicated by a serpentine plant with unreal flowers. The only landscape permitted to be the object of 'representation' is that of the *Nativity:* at Hosios Leukas the cave is boldly reduced to a coloured schema which suppresses all appearance of naturalism.

Since the space of the church is the 'true world' spherically shut in on itself, the painting resolutely ignores perspectives tending to open false windows on nature and to re-establish contact with the profane world. It hollows out no space behind the figures, but by alternating blue and gold grounds creates a sort of tonal space which, without imposing the illusion of the third dimension, leaves the mural unity intact and multiplies expressivity as may be desired.

If the wealth of ornament disappeared, so too did the historico-didactic cycles of pre-iconoclastic art. The church is neither a stage for spectacle nor a school for educating the people. Byzantine classicism has no room for variety, still less for profusion. The epic side of Romanesque art, the 'encyclopaedic' side of Gothic remained wholly foreign to it. If with its abundance of edifying stories the Gothic cathedral has something in common with the Buddhist temple, the Byzantine church of the eleventh century recalls rather the sober decoration of the Greek temple. The Pharos Church—a key monument of the classical period—contains no scenic compositions while at Hosios Leukas the large number of individual figures, 147 in all, shows how vigorously the icon style took possession of the monumental decoration.

The decoration of the classical churches curtails the number of compositions: nine at Hosios Leukas, fifteen at Nea Moni. The drama is enacted with a repertory of gestures reduced to the strict minimum, but whose concentrated power is authoritative: in the *Crucifixion* at Hosios Leukas (the first monumental representation of Christ dead on the cross) and above all at Chios and Daphni, the Virgin who brings her left hand up to her neck, stricken with a simple and speechless grief, St. John and the women in their tragical robes, compose ensembles in which one meets again the sober grandeur of antique funerary stelae.

In the mosaics of the Nea Moni at Chios this art of presence and transfiguration attains its perfection. Nea Moni is one of the favoured places in which burns that 'fire of signs' spoken of by Georges Duthuit*. In no other Byzantine work is the art of 'drawing with colour' affirmed with such mastery. The colourism of Ravenna was not achieved without some relaxation of the drawing. At Hosios Leukas, on the other hand, the colouring is faint and the composition is based on a symmetry broken only by the agitated rhythm of the draperies. At Nea Moni the effort has gone not so much into choosing between line and colour but into multiplying the systems of equivalences. The traditional graphicism is

The Marriage at Cana
Christ, accompanied by his mother,
ordering the servants to fill the jars with
water
Vault of the outer narthex
Early 14th cent.
Constantinople, Chora monastery

The Flight into Egypt
On the left, an angel appears to Joseph
asleep, ordering him to flee to escape the
massacre of the Innocents.
Exterior wall of the narthex
beginning of 14th century
Constantinople, Chora monastery

re-absorbed into the burning expanse secreted by the interchange of colours in an out-
burst of purples, greens, blues and yellows: here once again are all the pure colours
transfigured to create a mixture, unique to Byzantium, of tragic tension and spiritual
serenity. By this same stroke, the drawing, almost evanescent in the Baptistery of the
Orthodox at Ravenna, finds its quality re-enhanced: forceful circles in black localise the
personages and define the action, but here—and in this Byzantium is unique—black is
freely employed as a colour in its own right: the stroke, the contour and the colour are but
one power and the composition is formed as much by the vigour of the drawing as by the
energetic movement of the planes of colour as they collide, advance and retreat in the
luminous space.

The mosaics of Daphni mark the beginning of the 'age of Praxiteles' in Byzantine
painting: the moment of happy equilibrium between monumental power and refinement
of form. In the sixteen prophets of the dome and the thirty-two isolated figures of the
church, the hieratic asperity of Hosios Leukas is raised to a broad spirituality which in
the faces of Nea Moni still lay hidden beneath the black and green shadows. The style of the
eleventh century, evident in the earliest mosaics of St. Mark's and in the Basilica of
Torcello, here reaches maturity. In the Christological scenes one perceives the manner in
which Comnene Byzantium expressed the 'union without mixture' of the divinity and the
humanity of Christ. In the *Nativity* the divine impassivity of the Virgin balances the

The Census at Bethlehem
The Virgin and Joseph before Quirinus,
the pro-consul. Wall of the outer narthex.
Early 14th cent.
Constantinople, Chora monastery

touching figures of the expectant Joseph, the proclamation to the shepherds, the Infant's bath. In the *Crucifixion* it is the balance of the composition itself which translates the vision of Chalcedon. Christ dead, but with a living gaze, is beyond the drama incarnate in the gesture and countenance of his Mother, but the Evangelist looks straight ahead and not at the Christ at whom his hesitant hand points: 'He has rather the attitude of a contemplative meditating on the mystery of the Passion.' (Michaelis.) Lastly, with the cycle of the Virgin in the narthex, and in particular the *Prayer of Joachim* and the *Annunciation to Anne*, the new aesthetic of Grace makes its first appearance: a direct line of descent connects these mosaics with those of the Chora convent and the Palaeologue* style of the late Byzantine period.

The twelfth-century mosaics in St. Mark's are still this side of the art of Daphni. In the twelfth century, Byzantines, assisted by Venetians trained in their school, decorated the domes with the Ascension, Pentecost and Christ Emmanuel: the first like the one in St. Sophia at Salonika, the second derives from that of Hosios Leukas and the third offers us a provincial version of the Byzantine prototypes. The remainder belong to the thirteenth and fourteenth centuries. The most faithful reflections of Comnene art will be found at Torcello and above all in Sicily, at Cefalù, Palermo and Monreale.

There are two main reasons for the uneven quality of the Sicilian mosaics. The first and chief is that the Latin basilicas, with their elongated naves, lent themselves ill to

67

The Descent into Limbo (*Anastasis*)
Christ breaking down with his feet
the gates of Hell
14th century fresco
Constantinople, Chora monastery

Byzantine forms which were indissolubly linked with a spherical architecture. Next, to cover the immense surfaces of the naves, it was necessary hastily to devise extended narrative cycles which had no equivalent in the temperate decoration of the Byzantine churches of the twelfth century. It was also necessary to call on inexperienced local craftsmen to whom Byzantine rigour remained a dead letter. Already evident in the naves of the Palatine Chapel*, at Monreale, where moreover Latin inscriptions predominate, this necessity becomes really oppressive: innumerable anecdotes sprawl complacently over the walls. The gold grounds are strewn about with a complete want of discrimination and the figures, over-humanised, lack authority. The sacral character of the icons, the sober Byzantine economy, Comnene moderation, all are submerged in the superabundance of narrative cycles and humanising indulgence.

The two most important foundations of the Comneni at Constantinople were dedicated to Christ Pantocrator and to the Virgin of Grace: and it was under this two-fold banner of Power and Grace that Comnene art would evolve. The Christ of Cefalù and Monreale is not the Monarch of Daphni with a closed book in his strong grasp. It is the Christ who is king and judge, but to these aspects is added a third, indicated by the inscription on the open Gospel: 'I am the light of the world.' The terrible Pantocrator is replaced by the Christ 'friend to men' of the mosaic icon in the Bargello Museum at Florence, the 'merciful' Christ of the mosaic icon in the museum at Berlin. His image in the mosaics, frescoes and miniatures in no way evokes the idea of wrath nor even of severity: rather, that of the grave gentleness of the Christ who listens to the supplication of the Virgin and St. John the Baptist in the wonderful 'Deesis' panel of St. Sophia. Again, the concentrated inwardness of the Macedonian effigies begins to be externalised in faces illumined by the touches of light which gradually replace the green shadows of the preceding epoch. The transition can be observed by comparing the icon of St. Panteleimon in the museum at Kiev with that of Nerezi*, the icon of S. Maria Maggiore at Rome or the mosaic icon of the Virgin of the Greek patriarchate of Constantinople with the icon of Our Lady of Vladimir*. This icon of the 'Virgin of Tenderness', held to be miraculous, was brought from Constantinople to Kiev about 1140. In 1155, at the instruction of the Mother of God who appeared to him in a dream, Prince Andrew transferred the icon to Vladimir*, where it became the palladium of the nation. With a softness at once grieving and meditative, this icon is perhaps the most sublime expression of 'the union without mixture' of the pure humanity and the pure divinity as Byzantium understood it.

Thus a new style, in which the experience of Grace prevails over the sacramental objectivity and ecstatic spirituality of the Macedonian era, acquires definition, vibrant with a reinforced sense of the sacred but imprinted with a moving humanity.

In the icons, frescoes and mosaics of the twelfth century, the bodies, less imposing in stature and of more slender dimensions than formerly, bend at a greater number of axes. The gentle inclination of the heads, the radiant beauty of the faces, the gracefulness of the gestures and the very movement of the draperies create an air of tender benevolence, but all the rest is sober and reserved. In the fresco of the *Crucifixion* at the Mavriotissa* convent near Kastoria the Virgin is shown in a swoon before the dead Christ: this is the

68

'svanimento', or swooning theme, which will leave so profound a mark on the thirteenth century at Byzantium and in Italy.

Already evident in the mosaics of Daphni and Serres, this trend towards humanisation has found striking expression in the frescoes which Alexius Comnenus, a nephew of the emperor Manuel, had executed in 1164 at Nerezi, by artists who came probably from Constantinople. Discovered in 1924, these frescoes completely upset the traditional image of the history of art. Whereas formerly Byzantine painting of the fourteenth century was explained by hypothetical Italian influences, one now sees that the Italian painting of the thirteenth century has its roots deep in the Byzantine art of the twelfth. The Nerezi paintings are a landmark in the history of European painting; through their beautiful organisation of the voids and the intense expressivity of the faces they are monumental, yet at the same time they know the nuances and secrets of the life of the psyche. A profound life, which is at once personal and ideal, radiates from the array of saints and makes their faces glow with disturbing phosphoresence. But it is in the two huge compositions of the *Descent from the Cross* and the *Threnos* (funeral lament, Pietà) that the new sensibility asserts itself with greatest force. In the *Descent from the Cross*, the expressive asymmetry of the composition draws attention to the emotional stresses of the subject, but the solemnity of the gestures and the nobility of the attitudes raise the tragedy of the Cross to the supernatural peace of the Crucified. Joseph of Arimathea* on his ladder resembles a priest offering the sacrifice . . . In the *Threnos* the anguish of the Virgin, as she grips the dead body of her Son in a close embrace, is underlined by the pathetic curves described by the bodies of the prostrate disciples—but all is resolved in adoration, in the certainty of the Redemption.

69

In the miniatures, too, one finds variety intruding on the unity of the preceding epoch and dynamism prevailing over its static order. A life freer and more spontaneous, although always conforming to the hieratic gesture and subjected to monumental rigour, manifests itself in the manuscript painting of this period and is in keeping with its spirit.

Another sign of the times is the proliferation of ornamental decoration. In the ninth and tenth centuries, the concordance tables are protected by simple arcades; during the second half of the eleventh century the decoration is enriched with zoomorphic and architectural motifs. In the twelfth century the initials become compositions in their own right; magnificent frontispieces with fountains, porticoes and a whole population of birds, stags and tigers cover whole pages with splendid illuminations. The delectable representation of St. Mamas in 'Paris 550' is perhaps the masterpiece of this new art, in which the rigour of the icon is alleviated to leave more and more scope for the pursuit of the purely aesthetic.

70

The Entry into Jerusalem
Mosaic, 14th cent.
Salonika, Holy Apostles

The Thirteenth Century and the Limits of Byzantinism

The thirteenth century was a time of trials for the Orthodox world. After the sack of 1204, Constantinople, the greater part of Greece and the island of Cyprus were occupied by the Latins. When Michael Palaeologus* liberated the capital in 1261 he found a ruined city whose population had fallen from a million to a hundred thousand inhabitants. Russia in its turn was invaded by the Tartars. Kiev fell in 1240 and for nearly two centuries the whole of Russian territory lay under the Mongol yoke. The brilliant urban civilisation of Kievan Russia collapsed, the buildings fell into ruin and artistic activity was interrupted, save at Novgorod* and Pskov, protected from the disaster by their geographical situation. Wall painting suffers an almost total eclipse until the second half of the fourteenth century: the only monuments of thirteenth-century Russian painting which survive today are the wonderful

71

Transfiguration
Christ between Elijah and Moses. In the
lower portion, the apostles, Peter, James and John
Mosaic, 14th cent.
Salonika, Holy Apostles

icons preserved in the Tretiakov Gallery and the Cathedral of the Dormition* at Moscow.

At Byzantium, too, artistic production suffered cruelly from the plundering of the Crusaders and the general misery. Luxury arts such as enamelling and painting on silk fell into an irreversible decline. Output inevitably fell also in the workrooms of the miniaturists, but though diminished in quantity, the quality of their work remains of a very high standard and, thanks to the researches of Weitzmann*, we now know of a whole sequence of fine manuscripts, illustrated at Constantinople, Nicaea or Salonika, some on behalf of Latin patrons. The most important miniatures of the thirteenth century are to be found in the magnificent psalters of the Stavronikita convent on Mount Athos and in the Vatican Library*. Evident in them is the new feeling for humanity, characteristic of the thirteenth century, which would blossom about 1265 in the Sopočani frescoes*.

The period of the 'Babylonian Captivity'—the name given by Byzantine chroniclers to the Latin interlude—coincides with a magnificent flowering of mural painting.

The thirteenth century saw the formation of new centres of political power: the Empires of Nicaea and Trebizond* in Asia Minor, the Despotates of Epirus and Mistra in Greece*, the Empire of Tirnovo in Bulgaria; the feudal kingdom of Serbia would become the chief representative of the Byzantine 'koiné'. New patrons came to take the place of the basileis of Constantinople, and their portraits multiply on the walls of their foundations: the Serbian kings Stephen I at Žiča and Vladislas* at Mileševo, the Bulgar tsar Constantine and his wife Irene, together with the grandee Kalojan and his wife Dessislava, at Boiana*, the Serbian king Uros I and his son Dragotin, Queen Helen and her son Milutin, Queen Anna Dandolo at Sopočani.

The only thirteenth century mosaics to survive on Byzantine territory are those of the Virgin 'Parigoritissa' at Arta, capital of the despotate of Epirus, and at Porta Panaghia near Trikkala in Greece. The mosaics in St. Mark's at Venice, in particular the scenes in the nave and narthex, are a composite collection, frequently devoid of style, of proto-Byzantine elements, of belated reflections of the classical style and of nordic influences. In general they show a misunderstanding of the role of the gold ground and of the plastic value of the colouring which is so profound that they place themselves almost altogether outside the Bzyantine system. Emotion is stifled by the sterility of the drawing, linear in the extreme; the neutral background flattens the design. Thus in the *Temptation*, the *Washing of the Feet* and the *Last Supper*, Byzantine undulation is reduced to an intensive, somewhat empty, schematic form. From time to time the faces are illumined by vivid shafts of light and now and then the compositions acquire the calm authority of Byzantine forms.

The mosaics which adorn the dome of the Parigoritissa Church* at Arta have a quite different importance: through their rich and bold colouring, they participate in the great urge to experiment whose effects can be seen on the walls of thirteenth century Greek, Serbian and Bulgarian churches.

The sequence opens with the frescoes of the church of the Mother-of-God at Studenica*. In the imposing *Crucifixion*, one sees the new dramatic sense which emerges in the thirteenth century: the prevailing inspiration is clearly models originating in Constantinople, from which the Giunta Pisano crucifix and the majority of Italian paintings on wood of the Duecento* are derived.

Another dimension of this multiform century appears in the magnificent frescoes of the Mileševo convent. The Virgin of the *Annunciation* prefigures the gentle Madonnas of the Siennese school, while the colossal angel of the Resurrection has the presence of the Hellenistic figures of St. Maria Antiqua. One would like to know the mosaics which inspired the Mileševo paintings, even down to the imitation of the gold grounds. The mosaics of the Rotunda of Salonika have been suggested; the radiant beauty of Mileševo, however, presents a terrestrial aspect, resolutely non-transcendental, for which there is no equivalent in the Byzantine tradition. The portrait of Vladislav in the narthex is likewise a landmark in the history of painting. The colours of secular life reign here, with absolutely no concession to the sacred. One must wait for the fourteenth century in Italy before discovering portraits so individualised, so rooted in the earth as that of the old Serbian king.

The same secular realism appears in the frescoes of St. Sophia of Trebizond*, recently discovered. The personages of the *Feeding of the Five Thousand* and even the Christ of the *Miracles* stand on the extreme boundary of Byzantinism. Their blue-orange universe is no longer transfigured by Grace but presents a new humanity, based squarely on itself, justifying itself by nothing other than the beauty of its natural truth.

These strains will not be encountered again in Byzantium. In the paintings of the two-tiered church at Boïana near Sofia the Byzantine balance between the 'aestheticism' of Mileševo and the 'naturalism' of Trebizond is already re-established. Here the spirituality of Nerezi and of Vladimir takes on a tragic density which rings round in black the *Christ*

73

among the Doctors and the beautiful faces of the Pantocrator and the young soldier saints. In effect, the Boïana paintings are the only productions of the thirteenth century which allow us a glimpse of the transition from Comnene classicism to the mystical style of the fourteenth century.

During the second half of the thirteenth century Byzantine painting was working in a quite different direction. The Sopočani frescoes, the highest creation of Serbian painting, can be considered the last manifestation of Byzantine classicism. In the imposing compositions of the nave, the monumental use of rhythm characteristic of the classical epoch achieves maximum intensity. A pure melodic line is created by the antithetical curves of the prostrate apostles in the scene of the Virgin swooning and in the sublime representation of the Dormition, and this impression is further reinforced by the subtle contrast of greens, blues and purples which alternate on the blue or gold ground of the frescoes. Likewise, in the isolated figures, the classical icon rises to a degree of realism never before attained. Finally, the pictorial element, once timid and sporadic, here occupies a larger place. Architectonic grounds start to invade the frescoes, signifying the disruption of the transcendant space in which the classical icon had hitherto moved.

Unfortunately we do not know the name of the artist of genius who painted the most beautiful icon of the thirteenth century: the *St. James* of the convent of Patmos*. In no other Byzantine work had the feeling for the human been pressed as far as in this exceptional piece, which recalls the portraits of the high Renaissance. But we do know the name of Manuel Panselinos*, the painter who about 1300 decorated the Protaton church* at Karyes*. At the same period, a group of painters with Astrapas* and his sons Michael and Eutychios at their head decorated a series of Macedonian and Serbian churches.

A profound affinity exists between the early works of Eutychios and Michael at Ochrid and the frescoes of Panselinos at the Protaton. In no other monumental Byzantine painting was the humanisation of sacred figures carried to such lengths as in these lofty creations, the work of a school which seems to have been centred principally on Salonika.

Here, the liturgical art of classical Byzantium becomes epic and manifests a dynamism previously unsuspected. Byzantium had never before brushed so closely against the 'all-too-human' element in man, it had never carried psychological exploration to such lengths as in the 'portraits' of saints painted by Panselinos for the Protaton. The figures, so astonishingly reminiscent of Dürer's drawings for the Heller-altar, those agitated crowds which people the *Dormition*, or graceful girls who accompany the *Virgin in the Temple*, show us Byzantinism on its furthest-flung frontiers: what appears on the horizon of these paintings is the Giotto* of the Arena Chapel in Padua, and the 'desacralised' western world of naturalistic observation and psychological analysis. That is why Byzantium prudently drew back before the new opportunities opened up by the experiments of Eutychios, Michael and Panselinos. Admittedly, in the works of their maturity the Astrapas group continued their exploration of the Passion: at Staro Nagoričino*, the 'Mocking of Christ' puts one in mind of a late medieval Flemish *Ecce Homo*[1]; and in the scene where Christ is being led

---

[1] Name given to the representation of Christ wearing the crown of thorns and purple raiment, as he was when Pilate showed him to the Jews with the words 'Ecce Homo'.

Annunciation
Icon, 14th cent.
St. Clement, Ochrid (Yugoslavia)

75

to execution he is here shown actually mounting the ladder resting against the cross. But in Astrapas' wonderful frescoes for the church of the Mother-of-God at Prizren*, the too worldly realism of the 'Macedonian' school has already been modified to make way for the new aesthetic of 'Grace' emanating from a liberated Constantinople, once again the capital of Byzantine art.

The Palaeologue Style

For the last two centuries of its existence, the Empire was no more than a shadow of its former self. In the time of Byzantine greatness, Constantine Porphyrogenitus declared there were three things an emperor ought never to yield to a stranger: a crown, the secret of Greek fire[1] and the hand of a Porphyrogenita princess. Under the Paleologi, the imperial crown and the pomps of the court had become a farce. At the coronation of John VI in 1347, says Nicephorus Gregoras*, all the world knew that 'the gems of the crowns were made of glass, that the robes were woven not from real gold but from tinsel, that the plate was copper and that all the seemingly rich brocade was only painted leather'. Gone were the days when Nicephorus Phocas could declare 'I alone have control of the sea' . . . The Byzantine fleet was no more and Greek fire was no longer a secret. Once it was thought degrading for a Byzantine princess to marry even the greatest of Christian princes. Now they married Mongol Khans, as for example that princess Mary whose mosaic portrait is in the Chora convent at Constantinople, and might even enter the harem of a Turkish

---

[1]A war material invented in the seventh century by Callinicos and employed by the Byzantines. It had the property of burning on water.

sultan, like the unhappy Theodora, daughter of John Cantacuzenus . . . Dismembered by the Turks, attacked by the Serbs and Bulgars, bled white by the Venetians and Genoese, the Empire was the 'sick man of Europe': the state the Turks would liquidate on 29 May 1453 was a phantom, reduced to Constantinople and its suburbs.

Nevertheless—an example unique in the history of civilisations—this period of misery and impotence was one of the most fertile of Byzantine culture. The decadence affected only the luxury arts. Painting on silk, therefore, disappears completely. Textile art is represented only by some marvellous embroideries in gold and silver on ecclesiastical vestments or eucharistic veils. A few fine works still come from the work-rooms of the miniaturists at Byzantium, in Bulgaria, in Serbia and in Russia; but taken as a whole, the quality of the Byzantine miniature shows a serious decline during the last two centuries of the Empire.

In compensation, letters and the monumental arts shone with such brilliance that this period has been named the 'second Byzantine Renaissance'. The fourteenth century was equally the golden age of Byzantine science, with Theodore Metochites and Gregoras, the first reformer of the Julian calendar. Men begin to know something of Western thought: Demetrius Kydones* translates St. Thomas Aquinas and chides his contemporaries who 'continue to class the Latins in the category of barbarians' . . . Now in its heyday, Byzantine humanism would exert a decisive influence over the humanism of Italy: Plethon* and Bessarion* belong at once to late Byzantium and to the European Renaissance. This epoch of great humanists is also one of great spiritual figures: St. Gregory Palamas* and Nicholas Kavasilas*. Late Byzantine painting will range itself under the banner of the 'uncreated light of Mount Tabor'.

Despite the miseries of the time, Byzantine prestige remained intact both in the East and in the West. The fourteenth century witnesses the entry of the new Moldavian principalities into the Byzantine 'koiné': the frescoes in the church of St. Nicholas at Curtea des Arges, the capital of Wallachia, are numbered among the finest productions of the fourteenth century, and it was in the Rumanian churches of the sixteenth century that Byzantine painting would have its last flowering. In the West, the journeys of Manuel II* and John VII had stirring effects on letters and the arts. Not long before 1453, the future pope Pius II wrote that 'no Latin could claim to be learned if he had not studied for a time at Constantinople'. After the catastrophe of 1453, the emperor Frederick III paid supreme homage to Byzantium by declaring that 'with the loss of Constantinople mankind had lost the true resting place of letters and learning'.

This epoch, which heard the pagan appeal of Plethon, saw also the triumph of mysticism. The painting of the Palaeologi reflects in its own fashion this eternal Byzantine polarity. The full Hellenistic décor makes its reappearance in pictures crowded with architectural fantasies or romantic rocky landscapes, which act as a frame for religious scenes in mural paintings as well as in icons. At the same time, mystical fervour enriches iconography with new cycles relating to the Old Testament or illustrating canticles and prayers, for example, the twenty-four Stations of the Acathist Hymn, which appear for the first time at the Marko* monastery near Skoplje. These narrative tendencies complete the ruin of hieraticism, already foreshadowed by the art of the thirteenth century. In place of the monumentalism expressive of religious orders, we now find a personal piety and a style which extends increasingly to mural decoration the refinements associated with icon painting: one no longer has the sense of being sustained by the encircling presence of the sacred, but of addressing the isolated image 'as one alone with another'. It is in any case in the style that the new spirituality shows itself most clearly: the drawing, light of touch, improves the contours; the graduations multiply, warm and dark; the characters, sharpened into ideal figures, vibrate with an interior life which is translated by the rhythm of the draperies and the fleeting touches of light.

The paintings of the Chora convent at Constantinople present us with an arresting image of this double aspect of late Byzantium. Marial devotion had already inspired the frescoists of Sopočani to paint the touching scene of the *First seven steps of the Virgin.* In the Peribleptos at Ochrid*, one finds a *Mary caressed by her parents.* Panselinos at the Protaton, and the painters of the Church of the King (1314) at Studenica* and of St. Demetrius (1310) at Peč, recounted the story of Mary and her parents in frescoes shining with the poetry of a life at once natural and supernatural. This poetry of childhood and womanhood reaches its perfection in the mosaics in the narthexes of the Chora church. The scenes are apocryphal: the Annunciation to St. Anne, in a verdant garden of springing waters, the Nativity of the Virgin, her seven first steps, the caresses of her parents, the distribution of the purple, the reproaches of Joseph. All bring out the innocence of the infant form, all are radiant with the tenderness of youth. The same art, at the same time meditative and intense, imprinted with a beguiling bonhomie, but transposed now to a higher register, can be read in the narrative of the Miracles; and the same feeling of luminous peace and intimacy with the divine is experienced before the reflective or radiant figures of the saints and martyrs.

But the masterpiece of late Byzantium is undoubtedly the *Descent into Hell:* the God-man in raiment of supernatural whiteness, aureoled with a triple blue glory flashing with stars, snatches a bewildered Adam and Eve from the tomb. In the mosaics of Chios, the gestures and faces of the revived express supplication rather than certainty. In the Sopočani fresco, as in the marvellous mosaic of the Holy Apostles, Salonika*, gravity still follows its own law, but here God and men float above the vanquished abyss and their being is no longer anything but pure dance, liberating whirlwind, royalty and tenderness.

The mosaics of the Holy Apostles and the frescoes of St. Nicholas-Orphanou at Salonika*, recently cleaned, show us how this spiritualism gradually drove out the dramatic realism of the 'Macedonian' school. The epic ardour of the thirteenth century makes room, in the mosaics, for a sort of serene majesty: the great themes of the 'Dormition', 'Transfiguration', 'Entry into Jerusalem', receive a quieter interpretation and more polished modelling. In the same way, the frescoes of St. Nicholas-Orphanou have the lofty severity, the broad modelling, the monumental character of the high Byzantine era. Equidistant between the realism of the thirteenth century and the spiritualism of Constantinople, this second 'Macedonian school' produced a series of remarkable frescoes in Greece and Serbia and cast its influence as far as Rumania. But at Dečani, the display of

Virgin
Icon, late 14th cent. Left wing of a diptych
Meteora, monastery of the Transfiguration

twenty iconographic cycles, each comprising numerous scenes (46 for Genesis, 43 for the Passion, 26 for the Apocalypse), totally destroys the organic relationship between the decoration and the architecture: the 'cinematographic' narration of sacred history, which is reduced to a series of incidents, has completely emptied the building of its sacred character. Concurrently, at Lesnovo*, at Matejic*, and at the Marko convent, Byzantine art, indeed art of any kind, was being replaced by local Serbian work of popular character. It was at Mistra, close to ancient Sparta, that Palaeologue spirituality would find its ultimate expression.

In the earliest of the Mistra monuments we see at work the three tendencies characteristic of the painting of the early fourteenth century. A traditional provincial school has been responsible for the rows of saints and the passion of St. Demetrius in the Metropolitan Church. The imposing *Last Judgment* and most of the Christological scenes, including the *Betrayal by Judas* in the same church, are the work of a second school, related through its realism and its bold animated compositions to the style of the mosaics in the Holy Apostles of Salonika. Finally, the mystical idealism of the Chora frescoes is represented at Mistra in the angels of the chapel and in the superb *Procession of Martyrs* in the narthex of the Afendiko*.

There can be no doubt that the art of Mistra reaches its peak with the frescoes of the Peribleptos*: the Palaeologue style, with its delicate drawing, sumptuous colouring, animated and expressive composition, its storm-dark tints illumined by flashes from the interior life, has here produced the last masterpieces of Byzantine painting. The Mary cycle is developed in twenty-one compositions of exquisite grace. In the *Transfiguration* the ruddy-haired Christ, clad in a white tunic with orange reflections, stands out luminous

against the blue ground. In the *Ascension*, the fluid elegance of the angels and their aerial movement form a musical contrast with the hieratic immobility of the Virgin and the distress of the apostles. The Nativity takes on a fairy-like quality: a light which seems to issue from the bowels of the earth gives the rocky landscape the transparence of alabaster, and at the centre of this radiant expanse, the divinely impassive silhouette of the Mother of God stands out like a dark patch. This art of transfiguration comes to perfection in the *Divine Liturgy*. On a ground of intense blue, angels draped in flowing white dalmatics advance with a swift, light motion, bearing under veils the instruments of the liturgy or carrying candles and censers in their hands. A white ribbon binds their ruddy locks; fiery carnations with greenish shadows give emphasis to the gossamer tones of their robes; their faces, animated by an intense inwardness, are modelled in those minute layers, in which slender, parallel lines are pressed close together, that one finds in the icons: nowhere else is Byzantine mysticism expressed with such felicity as in this signal masterpiece.

The development of this aesthetic of Grace was promoted by the ruin of the former concept of sacrality, the disruption of the old harmony between the rite and the monumental décor. An assembly of pictures, as it were, each with its own merit, came to supplant the severely balanced compositions with which classical art had served the liturgical order. Without interfering with the projection and purity of the architectural lines, the frescoes gradually create for the church a décor designed for the presentation of icons, indeed of enlarged miniatures. Late Serbian painting, of the Moravan school, would still offer a number of monumental works, to a greater or lesser extent impaired by sentimentalism, by excess of analytical observation and by the artifices resorted to by chroniclers. But it is obvious that the breath of the spirit is no longer stirring. In the church of the Pantanassa*, the last of the Mistra monuments, the figures, barely monumental, have become figurines, while a characterless eclecticism replaces the style which in the Peribleptos is still unitary: from now on the major art of the Palaeologi will be represented only by icon painting.

The development of a giant-sized iconostasis is a further manifestation of the mystical fervour which swept the Byzantine world in the fourteenth century. In the earlier churches the clergy and congregation were separated only by a simple enclosure; in the classical Byzantine period, the people could still see what went on in the sanctuary, and in particular the priest at the altar, who faced the assembly. From now on an actual wall of separation is interposed between the apse and the nave, completely hiding the sanctuary and making the liturgical ceremonies invisible to the people: to Symeon of Salonika this barrier marked the boundary between the sensible and intelligible worlds.

Made of wood, pierced by three gates which correspond to the three altars (the central entrance is known as the 'royal gate'), the walls which sheltered the mystery of the holy of holies from the eyes of the faithful offered a vast field for icon painting. As substitutes for the now invisible paintings of the sanctuary, monumental icons rise up one above another in three or five parallels on the wall of the enclosure. In the central range, above the gates of the iconostasis, we have the 'Deesis' theme, enriched with archangels, apostles and martyrs who add their supplications to those of the intercessors. Above them are the smaller icons of the Trinity, of the Virgin, of the patriarchs and prophets of the

81

Crucifixion
In the border: *Betrayal by Judas, Mocking, Scourging, Bearing the Cross, Nailing to the Cross, Descent from the Cross, Laying in the Tomb*
Icon, 14th-15th cents.
Venice, Gallery of the Academy

Old Testament and of the twelve great festivals of the Orthodox Church. Lastly, the lower portion of the iconostasis is occupied by large-scale icons of saints and martyrs, while the folding door of the royal entry is figured with the Annunciation, flanked by the four evangelists.

This monumental iconostasis, increasingly to become the focus of Byzantine, and above all of Russian, painting, gave rise in the fourteenth and fifteenth centuries to some spectacular masterpieces. The period which brought God closer to man did not neglect to give a new face to the Pantocrator. In the thirteenth century there was the human Christ of Sopočani, the beneficent Christ of Boïana. In the fourteenth century there will be the softly serious Christ of the Chora mosaics, the 'beautiful Christ' of the dome of the Pammakaristos* at Constantinople and of the 'Beautiful Church'* of Athens. This art of Grace is encountered again in a long series of icons in mosaic or painted in tempera. The comely, serious Virgins of the museums of Athens* and Skoplje* always retain the tragic nobility of the twelfth century icons, but the Virgin with painted eyelids in the museum at Skoplje and the Virgin of Pimen already exhibit the more human style which the 'Graeco-Italian' icons of the fifteenth to seventeenth centuries would disseminate throughout Italy, the Balkans and Russia. The Chora style is in evidence in the mosaic panel of the twelve festivals in the Opera del Duomo at Florence, as also in the exquisite icons of the Annunci-ation in the Skoplje Museum, in the Victoria and Albert Museum*, London, and in the Tretiakov Gallery. In the same way, the spirit of Mistra has left its mark on the poignant *Crucifixions* of the Athens and Skoplje museums and on the colossal icon (166 × 145 cm.) in the Elkomenos* church at Monemvasia.

These panels stand midway between miniature and mural painting. They have the elegance and mannered colouring of the former; they retain the quiet mimicry, the con-centrated energy, the encircling presence of the latter. In the superb *Sacrifice of Abraham* at the Benaki Museum, the sacred is presented with an affecting familiarity and yet loses nothing of its inaccessibility. Lastly, we have a whole sequence of tender and beautiful saints in which the intense lyricism of late Byzantium finds expression.

There can be no question of enumerating the great icons in the Palaeologue style which survive by tens and hundreds in the churches or museums of Greece, Serbia, Bulgaria, and Russia. They show us a world of supreme refinement, in which the recharged sense of the sacred does not exclude earthly beauty, in which classical reticence combines harmoniously with the charms of the new spirit. The golds which sparkle and blend with one another from their contact with the various tones of the earth of Umbria, ochre and the earth of Sienna bring out their velvety harmonies and accentuate the shimmering effect of the colours as they combine in the light and shade. The drawing, at once definite and aethereal, translates the reserved emotion of the gestures, the full-blown spirituality of the faces, the mysterious mobility of the draperies hatched with strokes of gold: it was in the icons of the fourteenth and fifteenth centuries that the severe purity of Byzantium, banished from the churches, found a last refuge.

These final productions of the Byzantine genius are bathed in a soft evening light. For Russia, a new dawn was breaking.

Annunciation
Icon, 12th cent.
Moscow, Tretiakov Gallery

Annunciation
Icon, 12th cent.
Moscow, Tretiakov Gallery

The Golden Age of Russian Painting

While Byzantium was drowning under the mounting Turkish tide, Russia was freeing herself from the Mongol yoke. As we have seen, the great mercantile republic of Novgorod and its satellite town Pskov had escaped destruction. In the fourteenth century they recovered their former prosperity: the mere fact that between 1228 and 1462 no less than 150 churches were built at Novgorod gives some idea of its wealth . . . In the fourteenth century these cities of the North were the main artistic centres. It was here that the great schools of icon painting were formed and here that the principal monuments of mural painting are preserved: the church of the Snetogorsky convent close to Pskov, the churches of the Transfiguration* and of St. Theodore Stratelites at Novgorod, the church of the Dormition at Volotovo and the church of the Nativity at Kovalyovo close to Novgorod.

The dominant feature of Russian history in the fourteenth century is the slow rise of the principality of Moscow. The amalgamation of Russian territories and the foundation of the unitary State was begun by Ivan Kalita*. In 1380, at the battle of Kulikovo on the Don, his grandson Dimitri won a great victory over the Tartars. He was surnamed Donskoy, victor of the Don, and the Virgin whose image adorned his standard was given the name Donskaia. Held to be miraculous, the icon of the *Virgin of the Don* would be venerated for centuries to come in the Cathedral of the Annunciation* in the Kremlin.

The movement of the 'poustinniki' or solitaries, the spiritual revival associated with the name of St. Sergius of Radonezh, is another essential aspect of the fourteenth century Russian Renaissance. In 1340 Sergius built a hermitage and a small wooden church in the depths of a forest north of Moscow. Such were the beginnings of the Troitse-Sergiev Lavra*, the richest and most celebrated of all Russian monasteries. His example stimulated contemplative vocations in prodigious numbers. Over 150 monastic foundations are recorded for the period between 1340 and 1440, and nearly half of these were due to the saint's immediate disciples. The foundation of the most famous Russian houses goes back to this period: the Kirillov convent* at Belozersk, founded by St. Cyril of the White Lake; the Ferapontov monastery*; the Walamo convent on Lake Ladoga; the Murmansk convent on the Onega; the Solovetski* convent on the White Sea.

It was in these solitudes, in the midst of forests stretching as far as the eye could see, that the Russian ideal of sanctity was formed. St. Sergius, St. Cyril and St. Nil Sorski are first in a line of ascetic custodians of the deep-seated life forces, uniting the tragic sense of sin with the bliss of the earthly paradise regained.

Lastly, the renaissance of Russia reveals itself in painting which reaches its heyday from about 1350 to 1450. Miniatures, icons and frescoes of the fourteenth century testify to the abandonment of Byzantine canons and the emergence of a specifically Russian type of painting, at Novgorod, Pskov and Tver*. In the manuscripts, there is a sudden irruption of human and animal life in their infinite variety and with a profusion of motifs, at times reminiscent of the traced scrolls and interlaces sculpted in wood in old Scandinavian and Armenian churches, and soon inspired by the art of the steppes. A Gospel of 1346 preserved at the Lenin Library in Moscow is perhaps the most compelling witness to

◄ *SS. Boris and Gleb*
Moscow school
Icon, late 13th cent.
Leningrad, Russian National Museum

St. Paraskeve and the three Hierarchs
School of Pskov
Icon, 14th cent.
Moscow, Tretiakov Gallery
▼

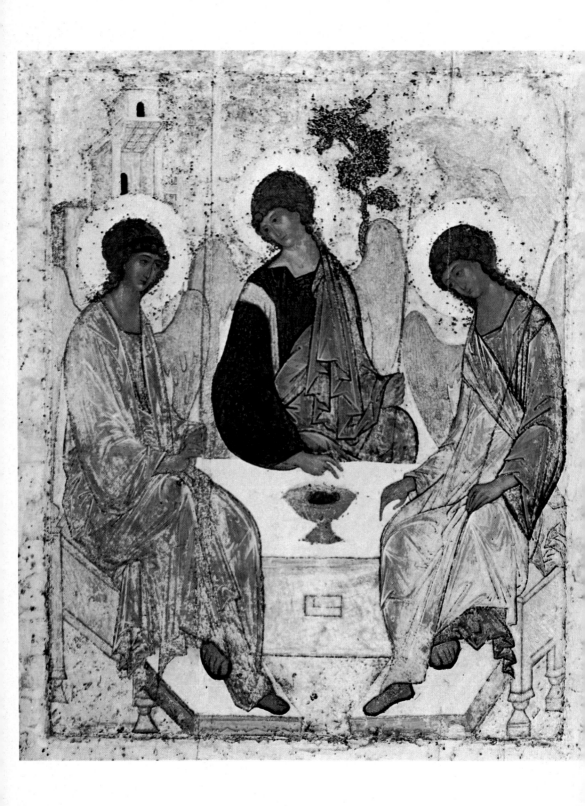

this strange resurrection. Another indication of emancipation from Byzantine standards is the transformation in the monumental frontispieces which represent a many-domed church in section. In the Svyatoslav Gospel, dated 1073, the Byzantine model is still honoured. During the thirteenth century the motif changes and becomes unrealistic. In the fourteenth century it is metamorphosed into an abstract oriental ornament: in Novgorod Psalter 8662 in the Lenin Library the architectural decoration has vanished in a flurry of abstract lines, in places suggestive of plaited cords.

The icons express the emancipation of the Northern painters in a variety of ways. True, Byzantium did not cease to be a source of inspiration, and we know of a whole sequence of fine icons from the fourteenth and fifteenth centuries painted either by Greeks or by more or less Graecised Russians. The icons of the *Virgin of the Don* and of the *Annunciation* in the Tretiakov Gallery and the icon of St. Demetrius in the Russian Museum at Leningrad are purely Byzantine works, although they are attributed respectively to the schools of Novgorod, Moscow and Pskov*. Other icons are directly linked with classical Byzantine art, yet the linear-ornamental interpretation of the hair and of the eyebrows, the brutal opposition of lights and shadows, represent ideas totally strange to the Byzantine tradition. The progress of this stylisation can be followed if one compares the fresco of Staraya Ladoga, representing St. Basil, with the icons of St. Nicholas in the Tretiakov Gallery and in the Russian Museum at Leningrad. Elegant Byzantine undulation is here replaced by an art which expresses itself through an unrestrained graphicism, brilliant colouring and in a markedly popular accent. The continuous relief of Byzantine modelling has given way to a linear stroke which juxtaposes surfaces of intense colour, devoid of depth. Colourings, which almost entirely lack graduation and are vividly contrasted, replace the deep, darkling halftones of Palaeologue art. The pale blues and olive greens of the *Dormition* in the Tretiakov Gallery demonstrate the delicate colouring of the school of Tver. On the other hand, the school of Pskov, related to that of Novgorod, is characterised by its mystical intensity, shown in a sombre concentration and in the acidity of the colouring, in which an intense green and orange-red predominate: the *Glorification of the Virgin*, an icon of the school of Pskov, brings us face to face with one of the possible sources of the art of Theophanes the Greek*.

It was at Novgorod, above all, that Russian painting developed its original tendencies to their furthest limit. The city styled itself 'Novgorod the Great Lord'; its motto ran 'Who can dare anything against God and Novgorod?' Three remarkable icons representing a battle between the men of Novgorod and the men of Suzdal' show how municipal pride arrogated the sacred character of the icon to itself. Novgorod was also the first Russian city to produce a bourgeoisie of the western type, and it is a bourgeois piety which appears in the icon of the Novgorod Museum, dated 1467, showing a patrician family at prayer. The worshippers and the holy figures are shown with the same dimensions, something quite unthinkable at Byzantium. We meet this world of the 'all too human' again in the aerial compositions, vigorous cast of countenance and vibrant and contrasted colouring of the fine icons of the Novgorod school preserved in the Tretiakov Gallery and in the Russian Museum at Leningrad. In all these paintings, where the dominant colour is a

89

The Redeemer
Icon, Andrey Rublev
Moscow, Tretiakov Gallery

Crucifixion ▶
Novgorod School
16th century icon
Paris, Louvre

candid vermilion and where gold is replaced by a clear yellow, nothing remains of any consequence from the spirituality of Byzantium. Although he scrupulously respects the Byzantine models, there is nothing of the contemplative in the master who painted the great four-part icon representing Lazarus, the Presentation, the Sacrifice of the Son and St. John dictating his Gospel to Prochoros. The only reminder that this was also the period of St. Sergius and Andrey Rublev* is the marvellous *Archangel Michael*, formerly part of the Rabouchinski collection and now in the Tretiakov.

But the masterpiece of this Northern painting is indisputably the festival register of the iconostasis of Kargopol. In the *Entombment*, the *Descent from the Cross*, the *Last Supper* and the *Beheading of John the Baptist*, Russian painting has achieved full independence. Modelling and plasticity are reduced to zero in the limpid blaze of reds, yellows, greens and whites; the colours, flat and intense, are rigorously defined by long straight

90

lines or firmly inscribed curves which compose a rhythmical, almost geometrical schema, with a rare power of suggestion. In the *Entombment*, this art is at its most dynamically concise: the cosmic lament which rises from it is echoed, as it were, by the ground of yellow rocks, which a daring stylisation has converted into a cascade of zigzag lines.

The fresco-painters of the North were not as revolutionary as the anonymous master of the Kargopol iconostasis. Paradoxically, it was a Byzantine of pure descent, Theophanes the Greek, who diverted monumental painting into new channels. Fresco-painters, miniaturist, icon painter and 'philosopher', Theophanes had worked successively in Constantinople, Feodosia in southern Russia, Nijni-Novgorod and Moscow. History relates that he had decorated forty large churches before he arrived in the Russian capital. His frescoes in the church of the Transfiguration at Novgorod (the only ones to survive) reveal him as the most original artist of any who lived in the Byzantine world. While ignoring none of the efforts of the Chora painters, Theophanes from the outset places himself quite outside the Byzantine norm and conventions, in a strictly personal world for which there is no precedent in Byzantium, Italy or Russia. Theophanes' element is not sacred drama as understood at Ochrid and the Protaton, it is not the lyricism of Mistra nor the idealism of late Serbian painting, neither is it the quest for earthly values, still less the solid popular faith of the icons from Northern Russia. A 'modern' disquiet, reminiscent of Pascal, has caused the disappearance of that classical order which elevated the certainty of the presence above the changes and chances of existence. Even the Pantocrator assumes a mask of remoteness. A bitter inward-turning, more familiar with spiritual conflict than the certainty of redemption, dissolves the previously organic shapes and conjures up from the 'dark night of the soul' feverishly stylised figures, given a significant place by streaks of light which seem to float in an indefinite space, neither terrestrial nor celestial: youthful figures of Abel and Acacius, patriarchs and Stylite saints.

This art, whose stress is on human pathos rather than eternal certainties, appears again in the Volotovo frescoes, with their disturbing mobility of countenance. Nevertheless, its radically subjective nature condemned it to remain without issue. When Theophanes came to execute the magnificent icons for the Cathedral of the Annunciation in the Kremlin he was obliged to temper the originality of his style. That this was so was due not only to the conservatism of the icon, but doubtless also to the fact that the pure Byzantine tradition was held in much greater honour at Moscow than at Novgorod.

At Moscow, the metropolitan throne* was frequently occupied by priests of Greek origin, and there were close links binding the court of the Grand Duke to that of Byzantium. Despite its loss of ground at Novgorod, at Moscow the influence of Byzantine painting reappears in full strength. In 1344 the metropolitan Theognostes invited Greek painters to decorate the walls of his cathedral. In 1386 Athanasius imported from Constantinople seven large icons representing the *Deesis*, two *Archangels* and *St. Peter and St. Paul*, which provided the point of departure for the Russian iconostasis. When Theophanes came to Moscow, he may have found already in being a school of painters more faithful than himself to the bland spirituality of late Byzantium. These were the painters who were responsible for the spendid miniatures of the Khitrovo and Morozov Gospels. The same broad fidelity to the Palaeologue spirit is met with again in the icons painted by Theophanes' Russian collaborators for the iconostasis of the Cathedral of the Annunciation in the Kremlin, as also in the earliest works of St. Andrey Rublev, the greatest of the old Russian painters.

Andrey Rublev, who had been a monk at the Troitse Lavra of Zagorsk and thus followed in the immediate footsteps of St. Sergius of Radonezh, is described by the chroniclers as a man of great humility, 'full of joy and brightness'. His art was the same: limpid and deep, supremely luminous, invested with the privilege of a perpetual childhood. The opposite of Theophanes, he does not express the night and conflict of the solitary soul, but joy and brightness. A chronicler remarks that his icons were 'as though painted with smoke' and indeed his unique talent lies in his drawing, at once firm and gossamer-like, in the mysterious artistry by which he unites the rigour of the composition with its

tender and musical colouring. As Alpatov* observes: 'In no other country of Europe were the principles of Greek composition felt so profoundly as they were by Rublev, who made them incarnate in his work.' With Rublev and his pupils, the fluid art, at once incisive and allusive, of the antique draughtsmen makes a paradoxical appearance on the plains of Muscovy, but illumined by the spirituality of the Gospel at its purest.

In his earliest works, certain discreet touches of light are still reminiscent of the methods adopted by the Palaeologue style, but the serene benevolence of the faces, the limpidity of the tints, already express a profound calm which Byzantium could no longer attain. At this date the school of Rublev was not yet fully autonomous; for example, the fine icon of the Nativity in the Tretiakov Gallery looks like a copy of a Mistra fresco. In 1408 Rublev and his 'fellow-faster' Daniil Chyorny* are found decorating the Cathedral of the Dormition at Vladimir. A fresco fragment still in situ represents the Last Judgment. The Hell has completely disappeared, but above the throne of the Hetimasia we can see Paradise, with the Good Thief bearing his cross and the patriarch Abraham sitting beside Isaac and Jacob, a nestful of tiny souls in his bosom. This work, together with the colossal icon of *Christ in Majesty* (314 × 220 cm., Tretiakov Gallery) are nowadays attributed to Chyorny, but another icon from the same iconostasis and representing the apostle Paul (311 × 105 cm., Russian Museum, Leningrad) shows us Rublev's style as it unfolded. However, his masterpiece, the celebrated icon of the *Trinity**, was painted in honour of St. Sergius of Radonezh. Adopting the traditional theme of the angelic visitation of Abraham, Rublev expresses with unrivalled felicity the boundless implication of the divine sacrifice, at once an act of love and a promise of life. It was in the days and vibrant harmony of this work that orthodox spirituality found its loftiest expression.

At this same epoch another artist of genius produced the *Archangel Michael and his Deeds of War*, ablaze with turquoise, red and green. The artist's fiery style, the menacing aspect of the archangel and the colouring, reveal an original personality, totally foreign to the peaceable spirituality of Rublev. All the same, the best Russian icons of the fifteenth century range themselves under Rublev's banner. It is from Rublev, and the whole Byzantino-Russian continuum, that they derive their purity, grace and profound musicality.

Dionisy* is the first Russian lay painter. In his frescoes and icons, a kind of idealist unrealism supplants the spiritual realism of the preceding epoch. The figures are shown as intangible, almost evanescent; the silhouettes are of inordinately elongated proportions; the buildings, in hydrangea or coral pink, stand out from grounds of turquoise cerulean blue; the creamy or silvery whites are used to give value to other pale and tender tones abruptly spattered with strokes of bright red or black. The same mottled colours and aethereal figures are found in paintings of his school. Hereafter, even though the icon preserves its nobility and formal qualities, it becomes a 'work of art' and thus loses its meaning.

The End of the World

After 1453 Constantinople is no longer the 'God-defended city' but 'Istanbul'. The Church, however, remains, and patriarch Gennadios, enthroned in accordance with ancient Byzantine ritual, is accepted by the Sultan as head of the Christian nation. In 1472, Ivan III, prince of Moscow marries in great pomp Sophia Palaeologua, the niece of the last basileus. The two-headed Byzantine eagle finds its way into the armorial bearings of Russia, whose prince now styles himself 'Czar of all the Russias'; Moscow is about to proclaim herself the third Rome. Philotheus, 'staretz'[1] of Pskov writes to Vassily, son and successor of Ivan III: 'Two Romes have already fallen, but the third still stands and there will not be a fourth.' In 1551, a century after the fall of Constantinople, the Council of Hundred Chapters, concerned with preserving Russian painters from errors of doctrine in their iconography, will indicate the old icons and the icons of the Greeks as canonical.

The final flowering of Byzantine art, in Greece and Rumania, belongs to the sixteenth century. In the seventeenth century the churches of the Upper Volga will be covered with huge fresco cycles. But everywhere quantity exceeds quality. In the monasteries of Mount Athos and the Meteora*, decorated by the 'Cretan school'*, all the virtuosity of a Theophanes of Crete* or a Catellanos* cannot disguise the spiritual sterility. At times popular emotion succeeds in breaking through the academism, and this intrusion of popular elements is still more marked in the frescoes of the Moldavian and Wallachian churches*. The great mural tradition gradually fades, ousted by local workmanship, while the growing westernisation disturbs icon painting at its very roots. Cretans such as Michael Damaskinos*, Andrea Ricco* and Emmanuel Tzanes* uphold the nobility of the old icons and Russia still produces several painters of talent: Prokop Tchirin* (head of the 'Stroganov school'*), Nicephorus Savin*, Jacob Kasanets* and Gabriel Kondratiev. But their paintings are illuminations rather than icons; and the western 'free style' is substituted for the Byzantino-Russian. Towards the middle of the seventeenth century, Simon Ushakov*, the last great name in Russian painting, tried to rid the icon of the tiresome details with which it had become encumbered. He thought he could save it by copying in sickly-sweet style Our Lady of Vladimir and the 'Trinity' of Rublev, introducing elements borrowed from Raphael and Veronese. In vain. The West was henceforth to reign without rival. It was already more than a century since the last Byzantine, Domenicos Theotokopoulos—El Greco—had found a new fatherland at Toledo.

[1]Abbot of a convent; name also given to religious endowed with gifts of prophecy.

Evidence and Documents

Byzantium and the Renaissance

The numerous discoveries made in recent years, extending over the whole field of Byzantine art, have shown what exceptional resources its tradition discloses. Around the twelfth century, and within this art itself, there developed a powerful trend towards freedom and life, a movement, in short, contemporaneous with the one so noticeable in French architecture and sculpture and Italian architecture and decoration, premonitions of which are already found in frescoes of the eighth, ninth, tenth and eleventh centuries in certain churches at Rome. If the movement never came to fruition in the Greek East, it is doubtless reasonable enough to blame the Crusades, and still more the repeated Turkish assaults on Byzantium, leading to its gradual encirclement and eventual fall. But the frescoes at Nerezi and Sopočani in Serbia and at Vladimir in Russia show that Greek individualism lived on, in the embrace of the collective rhythm imposed on the Hellenised barbarians by the Orthodox Church to keep them in check, and that this individualism, with its usual celerity, was starting to spread its wings at a time when the appearance of the same phenomenon in central Italy, the point from which it would conquer the entire West, was still a century away. These frescoes, unmistakably the contemporaries of the great French cathedrals, demonstrate that the role of the Greeks in the Christian world was what it had been in the antique and that, as before, Italy and then France, were their intermediaries, although this time the Greeks faded into the background much earlier, at a time when the supreme manifestation, although announced, was yet to come. The sublime paintings at Sopočani, in particular, can be regarded as possessing a plastic quality equal to the Hellenic productions of the period immediately preceding Phidias. But in their spiritual quality they surpass them, deepened by ten centuries of Christianity. These frescoes are equal, and perhaps superior, to the highest inspirations of Duccio and Giotto which are descended from them by an indirect route and recall them to an astonishing degree, despite their greater weight, breadth and majesty. As in the past, Italian art would emerge from the meeting between this impressive annunciation and local preliminary essays stimulated by Byzantium: for the past five centuries—if one looks no further than the decorations of St. Maria Antiqua—this genius with fresco had been pointing Italy on her right road. Here, as at Santa Saba, there is an ease of mastery in the medium that mosaic can never attain, and an orientation towards that fruitful 'Romanesque' civilisation which, when married to the Byzantine acquisitions, would result in the unfolding of a truly Italian art.

Elie Faure

'Histoire de l'Art: l'Art médiéval'
Jean-Jacques Pauvert, Paris 1964.

Aesthetic Considerations

The position and movement of Byzantine representations stands in relation to the gold ground which for many constitutes a 'void'. This is why Demus remarks that the figures are never in profile but three-quarters, so that they appear to advance into the real space of the church where they are equally in motion. That is to say, the pictorial space is not behind the picture but in front of it; and so Demus holds that this is the reason why during the classical Byzantine period the representations are lodged in niches in a way that creates a space. This theory of 'magical realism' imprisons the figures within the natural space of the church and abolishes the aesthetic distance between them and the spectator; it denies to the imagination the possibility of conceiving the pictorial space at the back of the picture, because this is not represented in an illusionist fashion. In 1946, with reference to the *Annunciation* of Daphni, I myself observed that because it is situated in a niche, the Angel appears to be on the point of crossing the space of the niche to reach the Virgin. But this merely signifies that in this case the painting exploits the concave form of the niche, not that this impression should be erected into a general principle. Nor is it any longer possible to conceive of the gold ground as a 'void': this ground represents the depth of celestial space or of a transcendent space. The mere fact that the little cubes of gold follow diverse inclinations and reflect the light gives depth to the surface; and because the figures in this setting appear to move, they create the third dimension. It goes without saying that for two-dimensional representations, like those of the Byzantines, the mono-chrome ground is the only one appropriate; it is only thus that they harmonise, as they do so perfectly, with the curved surfaces of the vaults.

In Byzantine painting, the light too is a 'studio light'. It comes not from a single source, as in a naturalistic art, but from several, in conformity with the desire of the artist and with his intention of suggesting the sublimity of his vision. This is why the shadows often become white, as in the negatives of photographic plates. Nor does this happen, as is thought, only in places where there is insufficient light in the church; it also occurs where there is an internal necessity for it.

Because at certain points the perspective appears inverted, it has also been said that Byzantine art uses 'inverse perspective' in general, that is to say that the vanishing points occur in front of the picture and not behind it. But in the first place, the perspective of the Byzantines is not always inverted; therefore it does not follow a system. It can happen that the same picture has vanishing points both in front and behind (mosaics in St. George's, Salonika), that certain objects are shown from the bird's eye view, others from ground level. There are thus several vanishing points in the same picture because order in perspective is sacrificed to a visual order whose secret rests with the artist, who arranges the planes to suggest what he wants. And when, as in the *Last Supper* of Kaisariani at Athens (sixteenth century), the inverted perspective appears as integral, the obvious intention is not to diminish the Christ who is shown at the bottom, but, on the contrary, to raise him to the place he merits, from the moment he finds himself at the summit of the hierarchy. The truth is that this inversion is a negation of the negation which the normal perspective would have introduced into the hierarchical order of magnitude, and thus demonstrates the true magnitude. To avoid assigning an inferior rank to Christ, Leonardo da Vinci in his *Last Supper* places all the apostles on the same side of the table, and to re-establish the equilibrium of the picture, underlines the horizontal. Tintoretto, on the contrary, in his

Last Supper, dwarfs the Christ to conform with the system of perspective and for emphasis surrounds him with an aureole, but in vain. The Byzantine work surely remains far more telling!

Panayotis A. Michelis
'Consideration esthétiques sur l'Art byzantine' 1964.

A Light that can be Called Poetry

What I would describe as the Byzantine vision—and for me, 'Byzantine' implies a certain artistic attitude rather than an art with geographical limits, granted that manifestations of this art at its best moments can be found throughout the Mediterranean basin between the sixth and twelfth centuries—is characterised first and foremost by its conception and treatment of the atmosphere, of the environment, of the ambient space. The close-guarded treasure of the Parthenon is answered by a place of communion eminently accessible, San Vitale of Ravenna. One can say that in contrast with the Greek temple it has no façade: the exterior is a model of discretion. The marvel begins with the interior, immediately one crosses the threshold, as though the builders were willing to lavish their care solely on space which contains and includes. If the architecture, mosaic, sculpture and liturgy work together in such harmony, the reason is that the function of all these elements is to invest and modulate real space. From now on images no longer recede down paths open only to the spirit. They are no longer imaginary windows opening on to an ideal world. The surfaces are those supplied by the walls and vaults, the distances are those which separate the surfaces. The Greeks, we are reminded, called this upper sphere, the source of all life, the Cosmos; and taking this Cosmos to be pre-existent, they thought all man could do was to learn by heart the role he must play in it. For the Byzantines the Cosmos was not something which existed once and for all, it had to be constantly created and re-created by man himself. Thus art was an integral part of life.

The elaboration of this new vision, so profoundly different from those of Greece and Egypt, amounts to one of the most important revolutions in the history of Western civilisation. It is easy to formulate.

Two types of vision, or of art, succeeded one another: that of the Greeks, founded on a quantitive conception; and that of the Byzantines, which can be called qualitative. These two types are fundamentally opposed. Nevertheless, there is a certain level or sub-stratum at which their antagonism ceases: that of perception. The Byzantines admittedly transform reality, but they do not deny it. The transfiguration to which they aspire does not rule out figuration. And figuration—an ensemble of realistic observations of nature, presentation of identity as well as of recognisable themes and symbols—is common ground to the Greeks and the Byzantines. In a word, the transformation which took place between the sixth century B.C. and the sixth century A.D. is even greater on the moral than on the physical plane. The physical changes took place only to the extent that they followed the moral metamorphosis.

Georges Duthuit
From an unpublished lecture.

The Principle of Byzantine Mosaic

To describe these mosaics, encased in cupolas, apsides, squinches, pendentives, vaults and niches as flat, or two-dimensional, would be inappropriate. True, there is no space behind the 'picture plane' of these mosaics. But there is space, the physical space enclosed by the niche, in front; and this space is included in the picture . . . It opens into the real space in front, where the beholder lives and moves. His space and the space in which the holy persons exist and act are identical, just as the icon itself is magically identical with the holy person or the sacred event. The Byzantine church itself is the 'picture-space' of the icons. It is the ideal iconostasis; it is itself, as a whole, an icon giving reality to the conception of the divine world order . . . It is one of the aspects of the Byzantine conception of forms in space that forms were taken at their face value: a line which appeared broken or curved owing to secondary optical effects was taken by the beholder to be really angular or curved. Lines, on the other hand, which were to be taken as straight, because they were meant to depict straight objects, could not be placed in situations which would destroy their appearance of straightness. . . .

. . . The images of Byzantine church decoration are related to each other and welded into a unified whole, not by theological and iconographical concepts alone, but also by formal means which create an all-embracing and homogeneous optical unity. The optical principles used for this purpose aim, broadly, at eliminating the diminution and deformation of perspective. The most obvious of them is the 'staggering' in size of the images and figures according to their height or distance from the beholders' viewpoint . . . with the primary aim of preserving the essential size of the image from optical distortion. . . .

. . . Contemporary descriptions of pictorial decorations are couched in terms which suggest the presence in reality of the scenes and persons depicted. Their authors did not write: 'Here you see depicted how Christ was crucified' and so on. They said: 'Here Christ is crucified, here is Golgotha, there Bethlehem.' The spell of magical reality dictated the words. This magical reality of the decoration which, formally speaking, expressed itself in the spatial character of the whole and in the life imparted to it by the movement of the beholder in space, cannot be rendered satisfactorily by photographs. Byzantine church decorations reveal their supreme qualities only in their own *ambiente*, in the space in and for which they were created.

To this spatial *ambiente* belongs the actual light. Just as the Byzantine decorator did not represent space but made use of it by including it in his icons, just as he took into account the intervening space between the icon and the beholder, so he never represented

101

or depicted light as coming from a distinct source, but used real light in the icons and allowed for its effects in the space between the picture and the beholder's eye in order to counteract its disturbing influences. The first resource is illustrated by the inclusion of shining and radiating material in the picture, especially gold, which is so arranged as not only to produce a rich colouristic effect but also to light the spatial icon. The deep niches under the cupolas of Hosios Leukas and Daphni are effectively lit by highlights appearing in the apices . . . This economy contrasts strongly with the indiscriminate use of golden highlights in the colonial sphere of Byzantine art (Venice, Sicily). In Byzantium proper the golden cubes stress only the formal and iconographic foci. The centres of iconographic interest and those of formal composition, which in classical Byzantine art are identical, are stressed by the strongest light. It surrounds the main figures as with a halo of sanctity. The reflections shift with the movement of the beholder and with the course of the sun, but thanks to the nature of the spatial receptacles of the icons they always play round the main figures. At night, the light of the candles and lamps creates fitful reflections on the golden surface from which the figures stand out in significant silhouette.

Otto Demus

'*Byzantine Mosaic Decoration*'
London, Kegan Paul, 1947.

The Icon

The icon is the perfect expression, the most immediate there could be, of both the religious and the aesthetic feeling proper to eastern Christianity, and above all of the profound fusion of these two sentiments, a fusion which prevailed in the East much longer than in the West and is kept alive there underground even today. What the icon represents—sacred personages or events—was present initially only to the spirit; it makes visible only the invisible. It is not in the least 'abstract', in no way refrains from figuration, still less from resembling, but what it uses in its striving for resemblance is not of this world and could not be connected with it by reproduction of objects from which this world is made or by submission to the laws which govern it. Since Christian belief in the Incarnation forbids the icon to discount the human form, it retains it: a retention all the more permissible since in the teaching of the Church this form is not necessarily material. Body and flesh are two distinct things, and it is possible to figure the body without suggesting the flesh—or the charnel-house. From now on what the painter imagines and reveals to us is to be none other than that 'spiritual body' which St. Paul speaks of in the fifteenth chapter of the First Epistle to the Corinthians, opposing it to the 'animal body': although it would be a closer rendering of the exact sense of his words than is given by the Latin translation if we said he opposes the body of the spirit to that of the psyche. And the essential departure made by this art consists precisely in this, so much so that its definition could indeed come close to that of faith itself, as given in the Epistle to the Hebrews, xi, 1:

sperandarum substantia rerum, argumentum non apparentium (faith gives substance to our hopes, and makes us certain of realities we do not see).

Vladimir Weidlé

'Les icones byzantines et russes'
Ed. Electa, Milan 1962.

The Russian Icon

The Russian icon painter pays no heed whatsoever to the third dimension; he makes no use of chiaroscuro; he organises his composition in height and not at all in depth; he subordinates his creation to the flat surface of the panel on which he paints. In most cases the saints he represents are draped from head to foot in a robe which conceals their bodily shapes; in their completely rounded faces, the individual features are subordinated to the type; if the personages are placed in a landscape, it is one reduced to the most elementary forms and so stylised that it loses any organic character. The Russian icons reflect an acute feeling for the distance which separates earth from heaven . . . They identify themselves by an air of calm concentration, by their friendly and open countenances, by the purity and clarity of their contours, by their luminous colours—all qualities which evoke a singular feeling of inward buoyancy, as though all the spiritual forces were reconciled and one felt that ineffable sensation of harmony engendered by the sonorousness of the most exquisite music.

For the purposes of Russian icon painters the drawing was just as important, just as expressive, as the colour: they were past masters of drawing. They knew how to give line an allure which was soft, elastic, undulant, angular, monumental, as precise as a calligraphy. With them, tracing the line was always associated with the idea of rhythm. They assigned a particular importance to the contour; in the Russian icons it is characterised by an exacting sobriety which calls to mind the contours, so clear-cut, of the personages represented on Greek vases. Simplification of the contour is due in part to the position of the iconostasis, which had to display the icons situated on it from a distance. The iconostasis accustomed the painter to feeling the beauty of the 'continuous' trace, which gave the contour the sense of order, the monumental character, demanded of it.

Victor Lasarev

'Icônes anciennes de Russie'
UNESCO, 1958.
[English version in UNESCO publication]

The Quinisext

The first council to discuss a question of iconography: 'In certain venerable images a lamb is drawn, pointed to by the Forerunner, sign of grace, allusion to the real lamb,

Christ our God. Now in place of types and ancient shadows, symbols and inklings of the truth, we prefer the grace and truth which is the fulfilment of the law. We decree that the lamb which carries the sins of the world, Christ our God, shall figure on the images seen by all and be painted in the colours of his human nature in place of the ancient lamb. This image makes us understand the greatness of the humility of the God-Word and recalls to us his life as a man, his passion, his saving death and the deliverance of the world which issued from it.'

Canon 82 of the Quinisext Council (in trullo), 692.

Iconoclasm

At the Gate of Bronze, beneath the cross:—
The voiceless image, deprived of breath,
in earthly matter, which represents the Christ
is forbidden by the lord (God)
and repugnant to the scriptures.
Leo and his young son Constantine
engrave the eternal sign of the cross,
glory of the faithful, on the gates of the palace.

Epigram beneath the image of the cross which Leo III had placed in 726 instead of the figure of Christ above the Bronze Gate (Chalké) of the Great Palace.

The guilty art of painting is a blasphemy. Christianity has overthrown paganism root and branch, not only the pagan sacrifices but also the pagan images . . .

From a sacrilegious lust for gain, the ignorant artist represents what ought not to be represented and seeks, with his soiled hands, to give a shape to what ought only to be believed in the heart.

Decree of the Iconoclast Council of 754.

The Restoration of the Icons

The more a person contemplates the icons, the more he will be reminded of what they represent, the more he will be inclined to venerate them by kissing them, prostrating himself, without, however, evincing towards them the true adoration which belongs to God alone, yet they are to be offered incense and lights, as are the holy Cross and the holy Gospels . . . Whoever venerates an image, venerates the person it represents.

Declaration of the Seventh Oecumenical Council at Nicaea (787).

Epigram

Methodius the Patriarch to the image at the Chalké Gate:—
On seeing your immaculate image, O Christ,
And your cross traced in relief,
I prostrate myself and venerate your true flesh.
Being the Word of the father, your nature is outside time,
But you were once seen in time, mortal by your mother.
So in describing you and representing you through signs
I do not describe your immaterial nature
which is itself superior to the image and to suffering.
But in describing your flesh which suffered, O Word,
I declare your divinely ineffable nature.
But the disciples who follow the teachings of Mani
with their stupid and pretentious chatter
categorise as unreal appearance
your incarnation through which you have united the human race,
and intolerant of seeing you represented,
in a burst of anger and leonine insolence
hauled down your venerable image
which from time immemorial was traced here.
But Empress Theodora, guardian of the faith,
with her descendants robed in porphyry,
refuting their illicit error
and imitating pious kings,
showing themselves most pious of all,
piously restored it
above this gate of the palace,
for its glory, praise and reputation,
for the good of the whole church
for the happiness of the human race,
to the damnation of our wicked enemies and of the barbarians.

> Epigram of the Patriarch Methodius on
> the image of Christ reinstated by the
> empress Theodora (843–847).

The Light of St. Sophia

The sun's light and its shining rays fill the temple. One would say the space is not lit by the sun from without, but that the source of light is to be found within, such is the abundance of light . . . So light is the construction, the dome seems not to rest on a solid structure, but to cover the space with a sphere of gold suspended in the sky . . . The scintillations of the light forbid the spectator's gaze to linger on the details; each one attracts the eye and leads it on to the next. The circular motion of one's gaze reproduces itself to infinity, since the spectator is never so much as allowed to choose what he prefers from the whole ensemble . . . The spirit rises towards God and floats in the air, certain that He is not far away, but loves to stay close to those whom He has chosen.

> Procopius
> (Sixth century)
> 'The Building of Justinian'.

Pharos Church

The vault of the temple, composed of five cupolas, shines with gold and figures like the starry firmament . . . Surrounded by beautiful things which, like the stars, shine from all sides, the spectator is left stupefied. Everything seems to him to be in ecstasy while the temple is stirring in all directions, not permitting the spectator to fathom what he sees, drawing him to all parts, interrupting him, forbidding him to possess himself of the object of his ravishment. The circular motions in all directions and the incessant displacement demanded of his gaze by the multiple variety of the spectacle produce in the spectator a kind of vertigo . . .

> Photios the Patriarch
> 'Description of the Pharos Church' (864).

The Mosaic of the Virgin and Child in St. Sophia

The lips of the Mother of God are closed and seem to seal a mystery, but the artist, both inspired from on high and faithful to nature, has drawn them with such verisimilitude that one can nevertheless imagine she is about to speak. Instrument of a divine inspiration, the art of the painter has transformed the representation into reality. Moved by the affection of her womb, she looks with love on the face of her Son, but because of the impassive and supernatural being of her Son, she too sets herself in the attitude of an imperturbable and untrammelled soul and her look comes to resemble the being which she contemplates.

> Sermon preached by Photios at St. Sophia
> at the inauguration of the mosaic of the
> Virgin and Child (867).

The Oratory of the Saviour

The splendour and brilliance of this chapel cannot be believed by anyone who has not seen it, so great is the quantity of gold, silver, precious stones and pearls to be found massed within its walls. The pavement is entirely of solid silver, wrought with the hammer and enriched with niello inlays. The walls, to right and to left, are also covered with great leaves of silver damascened with gold and highlighted with the gleam of precious stones and pearls. As for the enclosure which shuts off the sanctuary, what riches are not gathered there! Its columns are of silver, so is the stylobate on which they rest; the architrave supported on their capitals is of pure gold and in every part loaded with what all India can offer by way of treasure. The image of Our Lord executed in enamel is to be seen there at many points. As for the splendid decorations of the sanctuary and the sacred vessels it contains, because of its special fitness as a place for custody of treasures, words refuse to describe them. Such, if I may put it in this way, are the beauties of the Orient which have poured forth from the bosom of the living faith of the illustrious emperor Basil into the works built by his hands in the imperial dwelling.

Constantine VII Porphyrogenitus (905–959).

'Description of the Oratory of the Saviour built by Basil I in the Great Palace' French translation by Charles Diehl.

Chronology

Dates	Political and other events	Byzantine art
IVth cent.	From Diocletian the Roman Empire moves towards a system of rigid state control: theocratic type of monarchy, all-powerful bureaucracy, controlled urban economy, spread of serfdom in countryside. Barbarian invasions in Europe, incessant warfare against Sassanid Empire in East, where the Neo-Persian Sassanid dynasty is in control.	The new spirit manifested only in the third centu‹ frescoes of Dura-Europos, but there are pointers the coming of icon art in the evolution of portraitu‹ (Fayum and Palmyra portraits, statues of high di‹ nitaries in the Istanbul Museum, funerary portrai‹ Salonika Museum), just as the decoration to paga‹ temples in Syria and the palace of Diocletian at Sp‹ etc., prefigures the ornamental 'baroque' of the fif‹ century.
300		
313	'Conversion' of Constantine the Great.	
323		
325	First Oecumenical Council at Nicaea: Arian heresy condemned.	
330	Foundation of Constantinople, new capital of the Roman Empire.	
337	Constantius.	
340		
361	Julian the Apostate. Last outburst of paganism.	
371	Important state trials in the East (suppression of magical practices).	
378	The Goths annihilate the Byzantine army at the battle of Adrianopolis.	
379	Theodosius I, the Great, founds the Theodosian dynasty. Christianity becomes the state religion. The Roman army commanded by German barbarians.	Antioch pavement mosaics.
381	The Second Oecumenical Council gives the Patriarch of Constantinople second rank after the Patriarch of Rome.	
392	Sustained attack on paganism. Suppression of the Olympic Games and Eleusinian mysteries. Beginning of Egyptian, Byzantine and Syrian monasticism.	
397		

Contemporary art	Intellectual life	Dates
	From the time of Plotinus (204-270) Neo-Platonism dominates the spiritual life of declining antiquity. The most active centre of Christian thought is Alexandria: St. Clement (d. 215), Origen (d. 253). In the West, Tertullian (d. 240) ends by founding his own church. Birth of Athanasius the Great (295-373).	**IVth cent.**
	Death of Porphyry, Neo-Platonist.	300
Predominance of traditional Graeco-Roman forms. Frescoes in Roman catacombs: Priscilla, Domitilla, St. Sebastian, 'papal crypt' of St. Callixtus.	Birth of Libanius of Antioch, last of the great pagan orators (314-391). Birth of Sallust, Neo-Platonist.	313
	Arius, theologian and author of a liturgical drama. In the fifth and sixth centuries Arianism will spread to the Ostrogoths and Lombards.	323
		325
Mosaics of Santa Costanza, Rome. Pavement mosaics at Aquileia and Piazza Armerina, Sicily.	Death of Iamblichus, Neo-Platonist. The great Fathers of the Church, Basil the Great (330-379), Gregory of Nazianzus (330-390) and Gregory of Nyssa (335-394) effect the first synthesis between Christianity and Platonism.	330
		337
	Death of Eusebius of Caesarea, first historian of the Church and theorist of the Christian state. Heyday of Christian rhetoric: Athanasius of Alexandria (d. 373), St. John Chrysostom (d. 407); monastic piety: Evagrius of Pontus (d. 399).	340
	Pagan philosophers: Julian the Apostate (d. 363) and Themistius (d. 387), commentator on Aristotle. Theon of Alexandria, astronomer and mathematician.	361
		371
		378
		379
		381
		392
	Death of St. Ambrose. St. Augustine (d. 430): *Confessions*. Heliodorus: *Ethiopian Tales*, romance. Chief centres of intellectual life: Alexandria, Antioch, Athens, Beirut and Gaza in Palestine.	397

Dates	Political and other events	Byzantine art
Vth cent.	Partition of the Empire between Honorius and Arcadius. Roman West ravaged by the Visigoths.	
402	Victory of the anti-German party at Byzantium. The Western emperor takes refuge at Ravenna.	
408	Theodosius II (d. 450).	Mosaic decoration of the church of St. George, Salonika.
410	Sack of Rome by Alaric.	
415		
425		
431	Third Oecumenical Council at Ephesus. Nestorianism condemned.	
438	Theodosian Code codifies the legislative work of the Christian emperors.	
450	West invaded by the Huns.	Mosaics of Hosios David and the Church of the Acheiropoietos Virgin at Salonika. Mosaics of the Mausoleum of Galla Placidia and the Baptistery of the Orthodox, Ravenna. Pavement mosaics of the Great Palace, Constantinople. Pavement mosaics of the churches of El Tabgha, Beth-Guvrin, etc., Israel. Frescoes of the tomb at Nish in Yugoslavia.
451	Fourth Oecumenical Council at Chalcedon: Monophysite heresy condemned. Monophysite unrest in Syria and Egypt. Foundation of Venice.	
457	Thracian dynasty founded by Leo I. Western emperors under the tutelage of their barbarian generals.	
475	Accession of Zeno. War with the Goths. Capture of Rome by Odoacer.	Icons painted in encaustic, Sinai monastery.
488	Italy occupied by the Ostrogoths: Theodoric the Great (493–526).	
489	First schism between Byzantium and Rome (484–518).	
491		
492	Ravenna captured by Theodoric.	
VIth cent.	Anastasius I favours Monophysitism to placate the Christians of Egypt and Syria. Economic revival of the Eastern Empire, decadence of the West.	

Contemporary art	Intellectual life	Dates
Mosaic of the apse of St. Pudenza, Rome; mosaics of St. Sabina, Rome.	Death of Ammianus Marcellinus, last of the great Latin historians. Nemesius of Emesa: *On the Nature of Man.* St. Jerome completes Latin version of the Bible, the Vulgate.	**Vth cent.**
		402
	Synesius, Neo-Platonist, becomes bishop of Cyrene.	408
		410
	Christians massacre the philosopher Hypatia, daughter of Theon the mathematician.	415
	University of Constantinople founded.	425
	Death of Plutarch, founder of the Neo-Platonist Academy of Athens. Olympiodorus, alchemist.	431
		438
Pavement mosaics of Hellenistic inspiration at the Sassanid palace of Bishapur (Iran). Mosaics of the chapel of St. Aquilinus, at San Lorenzo, Milan.	Works of Proclus (410-485), last great Neo-Platonist philosopher. The theological school of Antioch sparks off the Nestorian heresy (from 428). Alexandrian poetical writings of Nonnus (*Dionysiacs*) and Musaeus (*Hero and Leander*). *Cyprian of Antioch*, romance by the empress Eudoxia. Church historians: Socrates, Sozomen, Theodoret. Political history: Priscus. Dionysius the Areopagite, founder Christian mysticism (dates uncertain).	450
		451
		457
Mosaics of the Baptistery, Albenga.		475
		488
Egypt, frescoes of the mausoleum of Bagawat. (Coptic art).	Nestorian school of Edessa closed, Nestorians take refuge in Persia.	489
	Theological school of Gaza (in Palestine): Enaeus (d. 534), Zacharias (d. 533), Procopius (d. 529). Choricius of Gaza, rhetorician. John Philopo and Leontius of Byzantium, theologians. St. Sabas (Jerusalem) lays down rules for monastic life.	491
		492
		VIth cent.

Dates	Political and other Events	Byzantine art
518	Justininian Dynasty, Justin I.	
527	Accession of Justininian.	
529	Code of Justininian promulgated; this, completed by the 'Digest' and the 'Institutes' has been the basis of all jurisprudence down to modern times. After 30 years of warfare against the Vandals in Africa, the Ostrogoths in Italy and the Visigoths in Spain, the Mediterranean is once more a Roman lake.	Ornamental mosaics, St. Sophia. Mosaics of San Vitale and Sant' Apollinare-in-Classe, Ravenna. Frieze of saints and martyrs, Sant' Apollinare Nuovo Ravenna. Mosaics, basilica of Poreč, Yugoslavia. Mosaics, Sinai Monastery and Virgin Angeloktisto Cyprus. Frescoes, Red Church, Bulgaria.
540	Reconquest of Ravenna. Capture of Antioch by Chosroes.	
546	546–554, Rome occupied by Totila.	
551	Destruction of Beirut.	Pavement mosaics, Apamea on the Orontes, Syria
553	Fifth Oecumenical Council at Constantinople: Monophysitism condemned. Evangelism in Nubia.	Maria monastery Beth-Shean and church-outside-the walls Caesarea, Israel, churches of Madaba, Jeras and Mt. Nebo in Jordan. Illuminated manuscripts: Vienna Genesis, Rossan
565	Justin II.	Gospels, Sinope Gospels, Syrian Gospels of the mon
579	Tiberius II.	Rabbula.
582	Maurice.	
585	Frankish raids in Italy. Lombard invasions. Visigothic reconquest of Byzantine Spain. Avar attacks in the Balkans.	
591	Treaty with Persia.	
VIIth cent.	Heraclian dynasty. Heraclius I (d. 641).	Palestine, pavement mosaics at Madaba and Siyagh Mosaics, Virgin Kanakaria, Cyprus.
610		
614	Persian invasion of Syria and Egypt.	
617	Avar and Slav attacks in Balkans. Military system of the Empire reformed. System of petty peasant proprietorship extended.	
626	Constantinople besieged by the Avars. Victorious campaigns by Heraclius, Persian might annihilated.	Mosaics, St. Agnes, Rome.
634	Syria, Palestine, Mesopotamia and Egypt fall into Arab hands.	Moraics, Oratory of St. Venantius, Lateran. Frescoes, Santa Maria Antiqua and St. Sabas, Rom Mosaics, church of the Nativity, Bethlehem.
661	Ummayad dynasty at Damascus.	
668	Constantine IV victorious over Arabs.	
673	Constantinople besieged by Arabs.	
678		
680	Sixth Oecumenical Council at Constatinople. Invention of Greek fire.	
693	Byzantine Africa falls to Arabs.	Pavement mosaics, Quvesite, Ma'in, Mafijer (Jordan

Contemporary art	Intellectual life	Dates
Mosaics of SS. Cosmas and Damian, Rome.	Stobaeus: *Anthology* (exact date unknown).	518
		527
Frescoes, catacombs of Comodilla, Priscilla and Callixtus. Mosaics, St. Theodore and San Lorenzo-outside-the-walls, Rome. Pavement mosaics, synagogue of Beth-Alpha (Israel).	Closure of Neo-Platonist school of Athens, last refuge of paganism. Its teachers invited to the court of King Chosroes in Persia. Hymns of Romanus, the greatest Byzantine poet. Evagrius, church historian. Procopius: *Book on Wars, Treatise on Buildings, Secret History.*	529
Basilicas of Qalb Louzeh, Ruweha and Turmanin, Syria.	John Malalas: *Universal Chronicle.*	540
		546
	Revival of Alexandrian poetry: Paul the Silentiary (*Description of St. Sophia* poems) and Agathias, poet and historian.	551
		553
	Monastic piety: *The Spiritual Prayer* of John Moschos; St. Dorothea; *The Spiritual Leader* of John Climacus.	
	Rise of Syriac literature; Greek culture disappears from Egypt, where Greek is replaced by Coptic.	565
	Nestorian school of theology at Nisibis.	579
	John of Skythopolis, theologian, commentator on Dionysius the Areopagite.	582
	Menander, historian.	585
St. Augustine's' Gospels. Coptic frescoes, Baouît and Saqqara. Visigothic art in Spain.	Romance of *Barlaam and Joasaph*, Christian transcription of the story of the Buddha (uncertain).	591
		VIIth cent.
	Sergius, patriarch of Constantinople.	610
	Theophylact Simocatta, historian.	
	Antiochos the Strategos: *Capture of Jerusalem.*	614
Ashburnham Pentateuch.	The Koran. Acathist Hymn (attributed to patriarch Sergius). Works of St. Maximus the Confessor: *Mystagogy, Ascetic works, Minor theological and polemical*	617
Merovingian art in France.	*works.*	626
First flowering of Armenian and Georgian architecture.	Isidore of Seville (d. 636). George Pisides: *Poems.*	634
	The Nestorian mission reaches India and China. Nestorians and Monophysites translating Greek texts into Arabic.	661
		668
	Birth of the Venerable Bede.	673
	678-681: a Greek Pope, Agatho.	678
	A Byzantine, Theodore of Tarsus, archbishop of Canterbury, founds schools based on ancient culture in English monasteries.	680
Dome of the Rock at Jerusalem.	Spread of Paulician sect in Asia Minor.	693

Dates	Political and other events	Byzantine art
698	Arab occupation of Carthage. 20 years of anarchy (695–717).	
VIIIth cent.		Mosaics of Oratory of John VII, Vatican.
709	Loss of Ceuta, last Byzantine base in Africa.	Frescoes, Santa Maria Antiqua, Rome.
717	Isaurian dynasty. Leo III victorious over Arabs.	Mosaics, Grand Mosque of Damascus.
725	Beginning of Iconoclast period.	Icons of the Virgin of St. Francesca and St. Maria in Trastevere, Rome.
732	Battle of Poitiers: Arab expansion halted. Publication of the *Ecloga* (Selection of Laws). Freehold peasant proprietorship becomes general at Byzantium.	Pavement mosaics, Ummayad palace of Kirbet Al Mafjia, Jordan.
740	Arabs defeated at Acroinon, and evacuate the western part of Asia Minor.	
741	Constantine V. Attack on icons intensifies. Persecution of monks and confiscation of their property.	Frescoes, Santa Maria Antiqua, Rome.
751	Fall of Ravenna. Byzantium loses its Italian positions. Abbasid dynasty (750–1258). Foundation of Bagdad. Ummayads at Cordova.	Iconoclast frescoes, St. Kyriaki, Naxos. Antiquising frescoes, Castelseprio (Lombardy); date uncertain.
755	War with Bulgars.	
768	Accession of Charlemagne.	
774	Charlemagne destroys the Lombard kingdom.	
780	Constantine VI.	Mosaics, St. Sophia, Salonika.
781		
786	Accession of Harun al-Raschid, caliph of Bagdad.	
787	787–813: return to orthodox veneration of icons under regency of Irene. Seventh Oecumenical Council at Nicaea, the last recognised by the Orthodox Church.	Mosaics, SS. Nereus and Achilleus, Rome.
797	Reign of Empress Irene.	
IXth cent.	Coronation of Charlemagne.	Mosaics, St. Prassede and chapel of St. Zeno, Santa Maria-in-Domenica, St. Cecilia, Rome.
813	Beginning of second Iconoclast period; Constantinople besieged by the Bulgars.	Ptolemaeus Miniatures, Vatican Library.
820	820–867: Amorian dynasty.	
843	Cult of images restored. In the West: Norman invasions.	St. Sophia, Constantinople: mosaic in narthex, decoration of the choir and part of the nave.
846	Rome sacked by the Arabs.	
853	Michael III. Paulician persecution.	Cosmas miniatures, Vatican, gr. 699. Miniatures, *Sacra Parallela*, Paris 923, Pantocrator Psalter 61, Chludov Psalter (Moscow).

Contemporary art	Intellectual life	Dates
Sculpture decoration, Ummayad palace, Mchatta.	Melodic poems of Andrew of Crete (650-720).	698
Important Ummayad mosques, Jerusalem, Damascus, Medina, Aleppo and Cairo.	John VII (705-707), a Greek Pope.	**VIIIth cent.**
		709
Mural paintings of the Ummayad castle of Kusejr-Amra: Hellenistic in insipration.		717
Mosque el Zeitoun, Tunis.	Iconoclasm.	725
Irish miniatures: Durrow and Kells Gospels.	Death of St. Germanus, patriarch of Constantinople. Works of St. John Damascenus, the greatest Byzantine theologian: *Against the Iconoclasts, Source of Knowledge*.	732
English miniatures: Lindisfarne Gospels, *Codex Aureus*, Canterbury.	Religious poetry: St. John Damascenus, Cosmas of Jerusalem.	740
	Stephen of Alexandria, mathematician and astronomer, teaching at the University of Constantinople. Zacharius (741-752), a Greek Pope.	741
Merovingian illuminated manuscripts: the Gellona Sacramentary. The Grand Mosque of Cordova.	Religious poetry: Gregory and Theodosius of Syracuse. Speculative mysticism: Elias the Ekdikos.	751
		755
		768
		774
	St. Theodore the Studite, defender of icons, poet and theologian.	780
Miniatures, Godescalc Evangeliary.		781
Nestorian frescoes, Tousfân (China).	Nicephorus, patriarch of Constantinople. First flowering of Islamic culture.	786
Palatine Chapel at Aachen. Carolingian frescoes.	Nestorian school, Merv.	787
	St. Theodore the Studite reforms monastic life.	797
Carolingian painting. Illuminated manuscripts: Lothar Gospels; Utrecht Psalter. Byzantinising frescoes, Basilica at Faras in Nubia (Egypt).	Chronicle of George the Syncellus. Theophanes the Confessor (c. 810-814) and patriarch Nicephorus, historians. Nicetas David and Methodius of Syracuse, poets.	**IXth cent.** 813
	Michael II sends a copy of the works of Dionysius the Areopagite to Paris (827).	829
Mosaics showing Byzantine influence, church of Germigny-les-Pres. Frescoes, San Vincenzo al Volturno. The great mosque, Samarra.	Kassia, poetess. Foundation of the 'House of Wisdom', Bagdad. Systematic translation of Greek texts into Arabic.	843
		846
Frescoes, crypt of St. Germain, Auxerre.	University of Constantinople restored. Birth of Al-Hallaj.	853

Dates	Political and other events	Byzantine art
860	Russians attack Constantinople.	
863	Period of Byzantine offensive in Asia inaugurated with a great victory over the Arabs.	
864	Baptism of the Tsar of the Bulgars at Constantinople.	
867	'Photian Schism': breach with the Papacy. Macedonian dynasty: Basil I (867–886). Empire revitalised, wars with Arabs, reconquest of southern Italy.	Mosaics, church of the Dormition, Nicaea (destroyed in 1922). Mosaics, dome of St. Sophia, Salonika.
869	Rurick founds the Russian state.	
880		
886	886–912: Leo the Wise.	Numerous churches and chapels in Cappadocia adorned with frescoes.
894	Empire invaded by Symeon of Bulgaria.	Miniatures, Paris Grec. 510.
Xth cent.	Byzantium allies with the Magyars.	St. Sophia, Constantinople: effigies of bishop-saints notably St. John Chrysostom.
907		Miniatures, *Book of Job*, Marcian Library 538, Venice.
909	909–1171: Fatimids in N. Africa.	
919	Romanus I Lecapenus (919–944), victor over the Bulgars and the Arabs.	Antiquising manuscripts: Joshua Roll; Paris Psalter; Bible of Leo the Patrician.
945	Constantine VII, writer and patron of the arts (944–959). In the West: Otto I, the Great (936–973).	
954		
959	959–963: Romanus II.	
961	Struggle with great landed proprietors.	
962	Formation of a huge Turkish empire in Central Asia with its capital at Ghazna, near Kabul. Otto I crowned emperor.	
963	Nicéphorus II Phocas (963–969) liberates Crete, Cilicia and Cyprus.	Mural paintings, David-Garedja, Ateni and Gelati in Georgia.
969	John I Tzimisces (d. 976): conquest of Northern Palestine and annexation of Eastern Bulgaria. Dissolution of Empire of Bagdad.	Miniatures, Gospels Athens 56 and Gospels Stavronikita 43 (Athos).
976	976–1025 Basil II. Apogee of the Empire.	
989	Russians converted to Christianity. Thirty years' war with Bulgars.	Rock frescoes at Carpignano, near Otranto (Italy).
999	Basil II annexes Georgia.	

ontemporary art	Intellectual life	Dates
reat Mosque of Kairouan.	Byzantines Cyril and Methodius, apostles to the Slavs.	860
		863
	Excommunication of Photius, patriarch of Constantinople, and reviver of study of ancient learning.	864
arolingian ivories. rescoes, Samarra. alace of Balkouvara.	867-872: Pope Hadrian II: forms of Greek hymnography introduced into the Roman church.	867
rescoes, crypt of St. Maximin, Trier.		869
rescoes, St. Benedict, Malles, near Bolzano.	Theodosius: *Tale of the Fall of Syracuse*.	880
1osque of Ibn Touloun, Cairo.	Death of John Scot Erigena, translator of Dionysius the Areopagite and Maximus the Confessor, whose work introduced Byzantine theology to the West.	886
		894
	Arethas of Caesarea edits Plato, Euclid and other ancient authors.	**Xth cent.**
1ausoleum of Ismail, Boukhara.	'Macedonian Renaissance' under Leo VI, the Wise, and Constantine VII Porphyrogenitus.	907
		909
₊bbey of Cluny.	*Palatine Anthology* of Constantine Cephalas; poems of Constantine of Rhodes and John Kyriotis.	919
	Martyrdom of Al-Hallaj. Beginning of Muslim scholasticism with Al-Ash'ari and Al-Farabi. Epic: *Dighenis Akritas*. Constantine VII's *Book of Ceremonies*.	945
	Drama: *The Suffering Christ*.	954
		959
)ttonian painting: Byzantinising frescoes at St. ;eorge, Oberzell (Reichenau).	Speculative mysticism: Paul of Latros (d. 956) and Simeon Eulabes (d. 986). Hagiographical works of Simeon Metaphrastes. Suidas: *Lexicon*.	961
		962
	Foundation of the Great Lavra, Mt. Athos.	963
ᵢirst flowering of Armenian painting (frescoes and ₁iniatures). ₃reat Fatimid mosques at Cairo.	Firdousi, Persian poet: *The Book of Kings*. Several Latin translations of *De Fide Orthodoxa*, by St. John Damascenus.	969
	Foundation of Iviron, the Georgian monastery on Mt. Athos.	976
⅃ozarabic miniatures: Apocalypse of Beatus. ₊pogee of Armenian architecture.	Leo the Deacon, historian. In the West: Gerbert of Aurillac.	989
	John XVI, a Greek Pope. Birth of Avicenna.	999

Dates	Political and other events	Russian and Byzantine art
XIth cent.		Mosaics, St. Sophia, Constantinople. Menologion o emperor Basil II, illuminated manuscript. (Vatica gr. 1613).
1001	Treaty with the Fatimids. Development of Kievan Russia. Russian colonisation in Suzdalia.	Mosaics and frescoes, Hosios Leukas in Phocis (Greece).
1004		
1017	Destruction of Bulgarian power	
1025	Death of Basil II. Seljuk Turks occupy Merv.	Frescoes, St. Sophia, Ochrid (Yugoslavia). Frescoes, St. Sophia, Salonika. Baltimore Menologion.
1040	Byzantines capture Syracuse.	Mosaics and frescoes, St. Sophia, Kiev.
1042	1042–1055: Constantine IX.	
1048	First Turkish invasions of Armenia.	Mosaics, Nea Moni, Chios (Greece).
1054	Death of Jaroslav the Wise, prince of Kiev (1019–1054).	Miniatures, Evangeliary of Ostromir (1056).
1055	Fall of Bagdad to the Turks.	
1066	Conflicts between the civil power and the military aristocracy.	Marginal illustrations, British Museum Psalter. addit. 19352. Miniatures, Paris 74.
1071	Byzantine army crushed at Manzikert. Turks occupy Anatolia. Normans capture Bari and conquer Sicily. Ruin of Greater Armenia, the Armenians driven out by the Turks take refuge in Cilicia.	Frescoes, San Angelo in Formis, near Capua. Miniatures, Vienna Psalter 336 and Coislin 79. Gospels Parma palat 5 Sviatoslav Codex.
1074		
1081	Accession of the Comnene dynasty: Alexius I Comnenus (d. 1118). The Turks occupy Nicaea.	St. Mark's, Venice. Miniatures, Vatican Psalter 320; Pantocrator Psalter 49.
1095	First Crusade: Crusaders in conflict with Byzantium.	Mosaics and frescoes, St. Michael's convent, Kiev.
1099	The Kingdom of Jerusalem.	Mosaics, at Daphni and Vatopedi (Mt. Athos).
XIIth cent.		Mosaics, St. Sophia, Constantinople. Miniatures, *Codex Ebnerianus*, Oxford, Seraglio Octateuch, Istanbul, Baltimore Psalter 733.
1108		Frescoes, St. Sophia, Novgorod.
1118	John II Comnenus (d. 1143).	

Contemporary art	Intellectual life	Dates
Illuminated manuscripts, Reichenau school (Germany).		**XIth cent.**
Ottonian paintings at San Vincenzo, Gravedona, near Como.	Works of St. Symeon, the new theologian, greatest of the Byzantine mystics.	1001
	St. Nilus of Calabria founds the monastery of Grottaferrata, near Rome.	1004
Bronze doors to Hildesheim Cathedral.		1017
Apocalypse of St. Sever. Great Fatimid mosques in Egypt.	John Mauropous teaching at Constantinople, Poems of John Mauropous and Christopher of Mitylene.	1025
	Psellos, first modern. Platonist.	1040
		1042
Romanesque paintings in France and Catalonia.	Important monastic foundations on Mt. Athos. John Xiphilinus, jurist.	1048
	Works of John Kekaumenos, moralist. Translation of Plato into Armenian, by Prince Gregory, pupil of Psellos.	1054
		1055
		1066
	Song of Roland.	1071
Byzantinising frescoes, church of Lambach (Austria).	Death of St. Theodosius of Kiev. John Italus, Neo-Platonist philosopher. Nicetas Stethatos the Studite, mystic, disciple of Symeon.	1074
Bayeux Tapestry.	Eustrates of Nicaea, commentator on Aristotle (d. 1120). In the West: St. Anselm. Foundation of Bačkovo convent. Ethical writings of Theophylactus, archbishop of Ochrid (Yugoslavia). Foundation of monastery on Patmos.	1081
	Russian, Serbian and Bulgarian monks settle on Mt. Athos.	1095
		1099
St. Savin, frescoes at Berzé-la-Ville, Paray-le-Monial, Puy Cathedral, St.-Julien de Brioude, St.-Michel de Rocamadour.	Persian poet, Omar Khayyam. Michael Italicos, continuator of Psellos. Nicephorus of Bryenne: *History of the Emperors.*	**XIIth cent.**
		1108
Mural paintings, St. Maria of Tahull (Spain).	In the West: *Letters* of Héloïse and Abelard. *Treatise on the Love of God* by Bernard of Clairvaux.	1118

Dates	Political and other events	Byzantine and Russian art
1121	Destruction of invaders (Turks of Ukraine). Campaigns against Hungarians.	Mosaics, church of Gelati, Georgia. Miniatures, Paris 533.
1125		Frescoes of St. Antony convent, Novgorod. Cyprus, frescoes of Virgin Forbiotissa, Nikitari, and St. Nicholas near Kakopetria.
1143	Manuel I Comnenus (d. 1180). Successful campaigns against the Turks.	Mosaics, basilica of Torcello, near Venice and at St. Mark's, Venice.
1144		Frescoes, St. Sophia, Novgorod.
1146	Second crusade. Crusaders defeated at Dorylaeum.	(?) Icon of Our Lady of Vladimir.
1147	Norman raid on Greece. Sack of Thebes and Corinth, principal centres of the Byzantine silk industry. Silk-workers deported to Sicily.	Sicily: mosaics of Cefalu Cathedral, Palatine chape and Martorana church at Palermo.
1152	In the West: Frederick I, Barbarossa. Conflict with the Papacy.	
1160		Frescoes, church at Nerezi (Yugoslavia). Frescoes, Mirozhsk convent, near Pskov. Mosaics, Norman palace of Ziza, Palermo.
1169		
1171	Alliance of Byzantium and Amaury I of Jerusalem against Islam.	
1176	Defeat of Myriolephalon. Anatolia lost to Byzantium for good.	Miniatures: Psalter, Vatican 372; Gospels VI 2. Laurentian (Florence); John Climacus, Vatican 394 Paris 550; the two versions of James of Kokkino baphos at Paris and in the Vatican and the Gospe Paris suppl. 27.
1180	Alexius II (d. 1183).	Mosaics, Monreale, near Palermo.
1182	Latins massacred at Constantinople.	Frescoes, convent of Chrysostomos (1180) and th Lavra of St. Neophytos (1183), Cyprus.
1183	1183–1185: Andronicus I.	
1185	1185–1204: Angeli dynasty.	
1186	1186–1393: Second Bulgarian Empire.	In Russia: frescoes of Staraya Ladoga.
1187	Saladin captures Jerusalem.	
1190	Third Crusade. Capture of St. John of Acre. Cyprus occupied by the Crusaders. Orthodox persecuted.	The same artists decorate with frescoes the church St. George, Kurbinovo (Yugoslavia) and the churc of the Anargyroi Saints at Kastoria (Greece). Frescoes at Lagoudhera, Cyprus.
1192	Richard Coeur de Lion halted before Jerusalem.	
1193	Death of Saladin.	
1194	The Hohenstaufen succeed the Normans in Sicily.	
1195	Alexius III Angelus (d. 1203).	In Russia: frescoes of the Cathedral of St. Dimitrius Vladimir. Frescoes at Nereditsa (now destroyed).
1197		

ontemporary art	Intellectual life	Dates
Miniatures showing Byzantine influence: ury Bible.		
lowering of Muslim architecture in Persia.	Nestor's *Russian Chronicle*. Theodore of Smyrna, philosopher.	1121
		1125
		1143
		1144
		1146
	Anna Comnena, historian: *The Alexiad*, Latin translation of the *Commentaries* of Eustrates of Nicaea.	1147
Vork started on Notre Dame, Paris. Vorms Cathedral.	Poetical works of Theodore Prodromus. Zonaras, Manasses and Glykas, chroniclers.	1152
		1160
	Panteleimon, Russian monastery on Mt. Athos.	1169
Byzantinising frescoes, Nonnberg monastery, alzburg.	*Hysminias and Hysmine*, courtly romance by Eusthatius Macrembolites.	1171
	Commentary on Aristotle by Averroes, the Arab philosopher.	1176
		1180
		1182
	Foundation of the New Sion Lavra, Cyprus.	1183
		1185
Building of Canterbury Cathedral.	*Capture of Salonika by the Latins* by Eustathius of Salonika.	1186
Flowering of Seljuk architecture in Asia Minor.	Formation of the *Geste* of Igor in Slavonic and of the Russian epic.	1187
		1190
		1192
		1193
		1194
		1195
	St. Sabas, son of the Serbian king Stephen Nemanja, founds the Serbian monastery of Chilandari on Mt. Athos.	1197

Dates	Political and other events	Byzantine and Russian art
		Deesis mosaics at St. Sophia, Constantinople (date uncertain).
XIIIth cent.	Capture of Constantinople by the Crusaders. Establishment of Latin Empire in the East, Frankish baronies in Greece.	Frankish occupation leads to Byzantine impoverishment. Decline in luxury arts: enamel work, painting on silk.
1204	Partition of Byzantine Empire; in Asia Minor. Empire of Nicaea (1204–1261), Empire of Trebizond (1204–1461); in Greece, Despotate of Espirus.	Illuminated manuscripts for Latin patrons: Iviron 5 Paris 54, Athens 118, etc. Psalters, Stavronikita 46 and Vatican 381.
1206	Accession of Theodore I Lascaris, Byzantine emperor at Nicaea (d. 1222).	Fresco of church of the Mother of God, Studenica (Yugoslavia)
1220	Genghis Khan conquers Persia.	Frescoes at Žiča, Yugoslavia.
1222	John III, emperor at Nicaea (d. 1254). In the West: emperor Frederick II.	Rock frescoes at St. Biagio near Brindisi, St. Lorenzo near Fasano and Santi Stefani near Vasto (Apulia).
1226	In the West: accession of St. Louis. Rise of bourgeoisies, establishment of great national monarchies in France, Great Britain and Spain.	Church of the Forty Martyrs at Tirnovo (Bulgaria) Mosaics, St. Mark's, Venice: Christological scenes in the nave, Biblical scenes in the narthex.
1227	Mongol Empire. Death of Genghis Khan.	
1233	The Tartars invade Russia.	Frescoes, Mileševo monastery, Yugoslavia.
1248		Frescoes, Holy Apostles, Peč (Yugoslavia).
1249	Seventh Crusade.	
1250	Death of Frederick II.	
1254	Theodore II, emperor of Nicaea (d. 1258).	
1258	1258-1282: emperor Michael VIII Palaeologus.	
1259		Frescoes, church at Boiana, Yugoslavia.
1261	Michael VIII delivers Constantinople and founds the Palaeologan dynasty (1261–1453).	Frescoes, St. Sophia, Trebizond. Frescoes, Sopočani monastery, Yugoslavia.
1267		
1268	Angevin dynasty in Sicily.	
1274	Council of Lyons. Byzantium recognised papal authority. Violent opposition from the Orthodox.	Frescoes, Marača and Gradač, Yugoslavia.
1282	Andronicus II (1282–1328) repudiates the Union of the Churches. The Sicilian Vespers deliver Byzantium from the threat from the West.	Mosaics at Porta Panaghia near Trikala and the Virgin Consolatrix at Arta, in Greece. Frescoes, Virgin Moutoulas and the monastery of St. John Lampadistis, Cyprus.
1297	Alexius II Comnenus, emperor of Trebizond,	Frescoes by Michael and Eutychios at church of Peribleptos Virgin (St. Clement), Ochrid (1295); frescoes at Arilje in Yugoslavia.
XIVth cent.	Byzantium in decline. Serbian expansion. Beginnings of Muscovite power.	In Yugoslavia, frescoes by Astrapas at Prizren, by Eutychios and Michael at St. Nikita, at Čučer and Staro Nagoričino. Frescoes at Žiča and Studenica
1304	1304–1377: Popes in exile at Avignon.	

Contemporary art	Intellectual life	Dates
yzantinising frescoes, oratory of St. Sylvester, uattro Santi Coronati monastery, Rome.	Kievan Chronicle.	**XIIIth cent.**
yzantinising frescoes at Anagni Cathedral.	St. Francis of Assisi (1182-1226).	1204
		1206
		1220
		1222
lowering of Muslim architecture in Persia.	Nicephorus Blemmydes (1197-1272) teaching at Nicaea.	1226
		1227
lassical period of Gothic. Bamberg. Sainte-Chapelle.	The romance of *Bethandros and Chrysantza. Callimachus and Chrysorrhoe*, romance by Andronicus Palaeologus.	1233
	Works of George Akropolites, pupil of Blemmydes.	1248
	Foundation of the school of philosophy at Nicaea.	1249
		1250
	Theodore II, emperor, humanist and theologian.	1254
		1258
		1259
hartres Cathedral. lowering of Armenian painting in Cilica.	Nicephorus Blemmydes: *Of Virtue and Asceticism*.	1261
n Italy, the 'maniera greca' predominates in the aintings on wood of the Pisan school. Byzantinising frescoes of the Baptistery of Parma 1260).	George Pachymeres, savant, historian and theologian. The Imperial Academy of Trebizond (astronomy, mathematics, medicine).	1267
		1268
aintings of Cavallini and Torriti at Rome. Duccio nd Cimabue advance beyond the 'maniera greca'.	In the West: apogee of scholasticism.	1274
Rheims Cathedral.	George of Cyprus, patriarch of Constantinople. George Pachymeres (1242-1310) and Maximus Planudes (1260-1310) dominate intellectual life at Byzantium.	1282
Byzantine influence on the miniatures of the Bagdad chool. rescoes of St. Francis at Assisi, frescoes of the hapel of the Arena at Padua by Giotto.	Maximus Planudes translates St. Augustine and St. Thomas Aquinas and edits the last Palatine Anthology.	1297 **XIVth cent.**
		1304

Dates	Political and other events	Byzantine and Russian art
1311	The Catalans ravaging Greece. Expansion of the Serbian Empire under Milutin Byzantium a prey to civil wars.	Mosaics at Holy Apostles, frescoes at St. Nichola Orphanou, Salonika. Frescoes by Panselinos at Karyes (Mt. Athos). Constantinople: mosaics and frescoes of the Chor convent; mosaics at the Virgin Pammakaristos. In Russia: frescoes at the Sneto-Gorski convent Pskov. Frescoes at the church of Christ at Verria (North Greece).
1328	1328–1341: Andronicus III.	In Yugoslavia: frescoes at Dečani, Gračanica, Lesnovo and Marko.
1332	Religious conflicts at Constantinople: the Hesychast dispute.	Golden age of Mistra: frescoes at the Metropolis, th Virgin Peribleptos and Afendiko.
1338	The Turks reach the Bosporus.	
1339	In the West: beginning of the Hundred Years' War.	In Bulgaria: frescoes at the church of Forty Martyr Tirnovo, rock frescoes at Ivanovo, frescoes of th chapels at Trapezica.
1341	Death of Ivan Kalita, 'first consolidator of Russian territories'. Struggle between the supporters of John V Palaeologus and John VI Cantacuzenus (1341–1347).	
1344	Apogee of the Serbian Empire under Dusan. John VI (1347–1355).	Frescoes at Zemen (Bulgaria).
1356	The Turks gain a foothold in Europe and transfer their capital to Adrianopolis. Emperor John V (1355–1376).	
1365	Tamburlaine embarks on the conquest of his empire.	
1370	The Ottoman Sultan Murad subjugates Bulgaria, occupies western Thrace and imposes his suzerainty on John V.	Novgorod: frescoes by Theophanes the Greek at the church of the Transfiguration; frescoes at St. Theodore Stratilates and the church of the Nativity.
1378	In the West: the Great Schism (1378–1429).	Frescoes at the church of the Dormition, Volotovo and the church of the Nativity, Kovalyovo.
1379	1379–1391 Emperor John V (restored).	
1380	Battle of Kulikovo. Dmitri Donskoi victorious over the Tartars.	In Yugoslavia: frescoes of the Moravan school at Ravanica, Ljubostinia; frescoes at St. Andrew on th Tresca, near Skopje.
1389	The Turks crush the Serbs at Kossovo. Bajazet succeeds Murad.	Frescoes at St. Nicholas (Curtea des Arges) in Rumania. The Khitrovo Gospels, masterpiece of Byzantino-Russian miniature.
1391	Tamburlaine penetrates into Russia. 1391–1425: Manuel II Palaeologus.	
1392	Conquest of Serbia and Bulgaria by the Turks.	
1395	Tamburlaine leaves Russia.	
1396	Bajazet defeats the Crusaders at Nicopolis.	
1397	The Turks besiege Constantinople.	
1399	1399–1403: Voyage of Manuel II to the West.	
XVth cent.		Golden age of Russian painting, Andrey Rublev iconostasis of the Cathedral of the Dormition Zvenigorod, near Moscow.
1402	Byzantium saved by Tamburlaine's victory over the Turks at Ankara.	Theophanes the Greek working on the iconostas of the Cathedral of the Annunciation, Moscow.

Contemporary art	Intellectual life	Dates
Triumph of Gothic art in the West. 'Proto-Renaissance' in Italy: Duccio, Giotto, Simone Martini, Ambrogio and Pietro Lorenzetti, Orcagna.	Dante, *Divine Comedy*.	1311
	St. Peter, metropolitan of Moscow (d. 1326). Theodore Metochites, humanist, statesman. Nicephorus Gregoras, first reformer of the Julian calendar.	
	A Greek, Theognostus, metropolitan of Moscow (1326-1353). Barlaam the Calabrian (1290-1348) and Demetrius Kydones (d. 1400) oppose Hesychasm.	1328
		1332
		1338
	The great mystics St. Gregory Palamas (d. 1360) and Nicholas Kavasilas (d. 1371), contemporaries of Meister Eckhart (b. 1260).	1339
The Alhambra of Granada.	St. Sergius of Radonezh (d. 1391) founds the Troitse monastery (1340).	1341
	Theological works of the emperor John VI Cantacuzenus. The metropolitan Alexis, spiritual guide of the Russian state. *Lybistros and Rhodamne*, romance. In the West: Ruysbroek, Boccacio, Petrarch, Chaucer and Froissart.	1344
		1356
Beginning of the flamboyant style: Amiens Cathedral.		1365
	Foundation of the Pantocrator and Dionysiou monasteries, Mt. Athos. Foundation of the Meteora monasteries.	1370
	The Chronicle of the Morea: narrative of the conquest of the Peloponnese by Frankish knights.	1378
		1379
	Apostolate of St. Stephen of Perm (d. 1396). St. Catherine of Siena (1347-1380).	1380
	Birth of Plethon.	1389
	In Russia, death of St. Sergius of Radonezh.	1391
Miniatures of the *Book of Hours* of the Duc de Berry.	*Pesma* Serbian popular poem.	1392
	Solemn translation of the icon of Our Lady of Vladimir to Moscow.	1395
		1396
		1397
		1399
Flowering of Muslim architecture in Central Asia (Samarkand).	Manuel II Palaeologus: *The Emperor's One Hundred Royal Precepts: Letters.*	**XVth cent.**
	Definitive version of the *Thousand and One Nights.*	1402

Dates	Political and other events	Byzantine and Russian art
	Heyday of the Moldo-Wallachian principalities.	Icons by Rublev and Prokhos of Gorodetz.
1408	Moscow besieged by the Tartars.	Rublev and Chyorny: fresco of the *Last Judgment* in the Cathedral of the Dormition, Vladimir.
1413	1413–1420: Sultan Muhammed I.	Frescoes at St. Sabas, Trebizond.
1419	Hussite rising in Bohemia.	Frescoes of the Morava school at the monasteries of Manassija, Kalenič and Rudnica (Yugoslavia).
1420	1420–1451: Sultan Murad II.	
1425	1425–1448: John VIII Palaeologus.	Frescoes of the bell tower at St. Sophia, Trebizond. Church of the Pantanassa Virgin, Mistra, decorated with frescoes. Byzantino-Moldavian miniatures at Graviluric.
1439	John VIII at the Council of Florence. Violent opposition from the Orthodox.	
1448	Constantine XI Dragases, last emperor of Byzantium.	Miniatures of the Morozov Gospels.
1453	29 May: Sultan Muhammed II captures Constantinople. End of the Byzantine Empire. In the West: end of the Hundred Years' War.	
1460	Fall of Mistra.	
1461	Capture of Trebizond. In Rumania: Stephen the Great (1457–1504).	
1462	Accession of Ivan III in Russia.	St. Mamas, Louvaras, Cyprus.
1467	Growth of the Muscovite state: annexation of Rostov.	Iconostasis of the Cathedral of Kargopol.
1469	First Greek rising against the Turks of the Peloponnese (lasted until 1479).	
1472	Marriage of Ivan III and Sophia Palaeologus.	Frescoes by Dionysi of church of Dormition in the Ferapontov Monastery. Frescoes at Bačkovo, Kalotino and Dragilevči in Bulgaria.
1480	Ivan III throws off the Tartar yoke and extends his rule to Novgorod.	Defensive walls of the Kremlin built.
1482		
1492	Discovery of America. Capture of Granada by the Catholic kings.	The Italian Marco Ruffo builds the Gate of the Redeemer at the Kremlin. The Moldavian painter Gavril.
1494		
1496	War of Russia against Sweden.	
1497	Voyage of Vasco da Gama.	

Contemporary art	Intellectual life	Dates
	Manuel Chrysoloras, humanist (d. 1415). Epiphanes the Wise, biographer of St. Sergius.	
	St. Cyri l of the White Lake founds the Kirillov monastery in Northern Russia.	1408
	The Greek Pope, Alexander V, defender of Platonism.	1413
Dome of Cathedral of Florence by Brunelleschi.		1419
Fra Angelico: *The Madonna and the Musician Angels.*	Plethon teaching at Mistra.	1420
Van Eyck: *The Mystic Lamb.* The golden age of Persian miniature.	The heresy of the 'Judaisers' in Russia. John Cananos, John Anagnostis and Ducas, historians.	1425
	John Argyropoulos teaching Greek at Padua (1434-1444).	
	Sojourn of Plethon in Italy.	
	The philosopher and historian Ibn-Kaldoun at Tunis.	1439
	Western Neo-Platonism: Marsilio Ficino. Death of Plethon. Invention of printing by Gutenberg.	1448
	Patriarch Gennadios Scholarios. Works of John Bessarion, theologian in Latin and Greek.	1453
	Tver Chronicle.	1460
	Chronicle of Constantinople, by George Phrantzes.	1461
Van der Weyden: *Triptych of the Magi.*	Numerous monasteries founded in Russia.	1462
The Legend of the Cross, fresco by Piero della Francesca.	Bessarion bequeaths his library to the Signoria of Venice (Marcian Library). Bessarion: *Against the Calumniators of Plato.*	1467
		1469
Filippo Lippi: *Coronation of the Virgin.* Hans Memling: *The Seven Sorrows of the Virgin.*	*History of the Decline of the Greek Empire* by Laonikos Chalkokondylas. *History of Mahomet* by Critobulus of Imbros. Death of George of Trebizond and of Theodore of Gaza, Aristotelian philosophers. Works of Joseph of Volokolamsk (1439-1518).	1472
Frescoes of Sistine Chapel at Rome.		1480
	Birth of Luther.	1482
	The Byzantine humanists, Hermonymus of Sparta and John Argyropoulos, teaching at Paris.	1492
	Death of Pico de la Mirandola.	1494
		1496
Last Supper by Leonardo da Vinci.		1497

Dates	Political and other events	Byzantine and Russian art
	National monarchies in France, England and Spain.	Frescoes in Rumania.
XVIth cent.		
1500	Ivan III occupies the left bank of the Dnieper.	
1502	1502–1736 Sevefid dynasty in Persia.	Frescoes at Poganovo, Yugoslavia.
1506	Accession of Vassily III.	
1518	Revolt against the Turks in Epirus.	
1520	Suleiman the Magnificent. Apogee of the Turkish Empire.	
1521	Conquest of the Balkans.	
1522	Capture of Rhodes. Revolt against the Turks in Greece. Smolensk reunited to Moscow.	The Cretan school: frescoes by Theophanes of Crete at the Great Lavra and Stavronikita, Mt. Athos.
1526	Hungary becomes a vassal-state of the Turks.	Building of Church of Our Lady of Smolensk, Moscow.
1529	Siege of Vienna by the Turks.	Post-Byzantine frescoes at Suczava, Humor, Arbora, Moldovitsa and Voronets in Rumania.
1533	Accession of Ivan IV, the Terrible, unifier of Russia.	Frescoes by Catelanos at the chapel of St. Nicholas, the Great Lavra, Mt. Athos.
1543	Massacre of the Chouisky by Iran IV.	
1547	Ivan IV takes the title of Czar (Caesar), heir to the emperors of Rome and Byzantium. Moscow ravaged by fire.	Decoration of the Mt. Athos monasteries of Koutloumou, Philotheou, Dionysiou, and Xenophon.
1550	The Mongol Khan of Siberia recognises Russian suzerainty.	Mural paintings at Kastoria and the Mavriotissa monastery, Greece. Frescoes of Theophanes of Crete at the church of the Transfiguration, Great Meteora.
1552	Ivan IV seizes Kazan.	Building of the church of St. John Baptist at Dyakovo, near Moscow.
1556	Ivan IV defeats the Mongols at Astrakhan.	Frescoes by Catelanos to the monastic church of Varlaam, Meteora.
1561	Defeat of the Teutonic Order by the Russians.	Postnik and Barma building the Cathedral of St. Basil the Blessed at Moscow.
1564	The Turks occupy Cyprus.	
1571	The Turks defeated at the battle of Lepanto.	Icons by Michael Damaskinos, painter of the Cretan school.
1573	Rising of the Croats under Matija Grubec, the 'peasant king'.	
1576		
1577		
1579	The Turks occupy the Cyclades.	
1581	Russia occupies western Siberia.	Frescoes of the church of St. Basil the Blessed, Moscow.
1589	The metropolitan of Moscow is raised to the dignity of patriarch.	

Contemporary art	Intellectual life	Dates
Dürer: *Apocalypse.*		
Leonardi da Vinci: *Mona Lisa.*		**XVIth**
Dürer: *Self-Portrait.*		**cent.**
		1500
Michelangelo: statue of *David.*		1502
Bramante starts on the building of St. Peter's, Rome.		1506
Giorgione: *Venus in repose.*		
Mathias Grünewald, *Isenheim Altapiece* (1513).		1518
Dürer: *Death and the Knight.*	Philotheus, theorist of Moscow as the 'third Rome'.	1520
Holbein: *The Dead Christ.*		
	John-Andrew Lascaris and Francis I draw up plans for the Collège de France.	1521
	The metropolitan Maximus the Greek, champion of ecclesiastical liberty against Czarist autocracy.	1522
Titian: *Martyrdom of St. Peter.*	Vassian Patrikiev and Fedor Karpov, reformers.	1526
Titian: *Portrait of Charles V.*	Death of Machiavelli.	1529
Michelangelo: frescoes of the *Last Judgment* in the Sistine Chapel.	Birth of Montaigne.	1533
Birth of Domenikos Theotokopoulos, 'El Greco', in Crete.	Nicholas Sofianos, humanist.	1543
Tintoretto: *Presentation in the Temple.*	Literary flowering in Crete (theatre, epic, lyric). Birth of Cervantes.	1547
Apogee of Ottoman architecture.	The *Council of Hundred Chapters* (Moscow) proclaims its loyalty to the Byzantine canons.	1550
Veronese: *Coronation of the Virgin.*	The metropolitan Macairius (d. 1563) opens the first printing works, Moscow, and issues a universal	1552
	history (*Carstvennaia Kniga*) in several volumes, illustrated with thousands of miniatures and also a monumental collection of religious texts.	1556
Breughel: *Massacre of the Innocents.*		1561
Veronese: *The Marriage at Cana.*		
El Greco in Italy.	*The Acts of the Apostles*, first printed book.	1564
Veronese: *Battle of Lepanto.*	Ostrog Bible, first book printed at Moscow.	1571
		1573
Death of Titian.		1576
El Greco settles at Toledo.	Correspondence of Ivan IV with Prince Kurbski.	1577
		1579
	Montaigne's *Essais.*	1581
El Greco: *Burial of the Count of Orgaz.*	Jeremiah II, patriarch of Constantinople (1572-1595).	1589

Dates	Political and other events	Byzantine and Russian art
1596		Frescoes at Sucevitsa in Rumania.
1598	Accession of Boris Godunov.	Icons by Prokop Tchirin.
XVIIth cent.	1595–1601: in Wallachia, Michael the Brave at war with the Turks.	Istoma Savin: icon *The life of Peter the Metropolitan*. Mercurius and Daniel, painters of the Cretan school, decorate the refectory of the Dionysiou monastery, Mt. Athos; apocalyptical cycle after the engraving of Dürer and Cranach.
	1598–1605: Czar Boris Goudonov.	
1605	Death of the false Dmitri and accession of Basil Chouiski.	
1611	Greek rising under Dionysius the Philosopher.	Icon painters of the Cretan school: Lampardos, Tzanes, Theodore Poulakis.
1613	Romanov dynasty in Russia. Czar Michael: 1613–1645.	
1614		
1625	Philaret, patriarch of Moscow, regent of Russia.	
1627		Iconostasis of the church of the Consecration, Kremlin, Moscow.
1642		
1644	The Russians reach the frontiers of Manchuria on the Amur.	Frescoes at the church of the Prophet Elisha at Jaroslavl.
1645	Czar Alexis.	
1646	The Russians occupy the whole of Northern Asia as far as the Pacific.	Simon Ushakov (d. 1686): iconostasis and frescoes at the church of the Virgin-of-Georgia, Moscow. The Danilov monastery, Moscow.
1654	Ukraine annexed to Russia.	Icons of the 'Stroganov' school. Jacob Kasanets and his staff decorate with frescoes the Arkhanelsk Cathedral, Kremlin.
1669	Crete occupied by the Turks.	
1670	Revolt of the Don Cossacks suppressed.	
1672	Birth of Peter the Great (d. 1725).	
1676	Czar Feodor (d. 1682).	
1682		
1689	Accession of Peter the Great. The Turks complete the conquest of Crete.	Frescoes showing baroque influence in the churches of St. John Chrysostom and St. John Baptist, Jaroslavl.
1697	Peter the Great visits Europe.	
1698		
XVIIIth cent.		
1703	Foundation of St. Petersburg, new capital of Russia.	
1725	Death of Peter the Great.	

Contemporary art	Intellectual life	Dates
	Birth of Descartes.	1596
		1598
	Giordano Bruno burned as a heretic.	**XVIIth cent.**
Rubens: *Descent from the Cross.*	Religious writings of Ivan Vychenski, monk and Slavonic author, from the Ukraine.	1605
El Greco: *Assumption of the Virgin.*	The Ukrainian philologist and hellenist Pavma Berinda compiles a Greek dictionary.	1611
		1613
Death of El Greco.	Abraham Palitsyne: account of the siege of the Troitse-Sergiev-Lavra by the Poles. Death of Shakespeare.	1614
	Cyril Loukaris, reformer, patriarch of Constantinople (1620-1638).	1625
	Simon Ushakov: writings on painting.	1627
	Death of Galileo.	1642
Rembrandt: *The Anatomy Lesson.*		1644
		1645
	Works of the Russian writer Simeon of Polotzk and of the Ukrainian preacher Lazarus Baranovitch.	1646
	The council of Moscow defends the traditional art against westernisation.	1654
	Nikon, reforming patriarch (d. 1681).	1669
	St. Dmitri of Rostov: spiritual writings. Autobiography of Avvakum the arch-priest, inspirer of the Old Believers. Schism of the Old Believers (1666).	1670
		1672
		1676
	Avvakum burned as a heretic.	1682
		1689
		1697
	Dosithaeus, patriarch of Jerusalem.	1698
		XVIIIth cent.
	Russia enters the European 'koiné'.	1703
	In his *Guide to Painting*, Dionysius of Fourna attacks modernism and advocates a returh to the style of Panselinos (XIVth century).	1725

Austria

Vienna

National Libral: manuscripts, amongst them the "Genesis" (5th century?) "Dioscorides (6th Century)
Museum: jewellery

Belgium

Brussels

Cinquantenaire Museum: pavement mosaics from Apamea (4th-6th century)
Royal Museums: textiles
Stoclet Collection: enamel, icons

Chimay

College Treasure: mosaic icon

Liège

Diocesan Museum: textiles
St. Paul's Cathedral Treasure

Bulgaria

Boiana

Beautiful 13th century frescoes

Sofia

Museum: rich collection of icons

Egypt

Sinai

Monastery of St. Catherine: Church mosaic of the Transfiguration (6th century). Treasure: richest collection of icons of all periods
Library: 10,000 manuscripts

France

Auxerre

St.-Eusèbe (church): textile with eagles

Lyons

Musée des Tissues: textiles

Paris

Bibliothèque Nationale: fine collection of manuscripts, every period
Louvre: mosaics from Antioch, goldsmiths' work, Byzantine and Russian icons
Musée de Cluny: Byzantine and Coptic textiles
Collection Schlumberger, comtesse de Béarn Martin Leroy

Poitiers

St.-Radegonde (church): reliquary, cloisonné enamel

Sens

Cathedral Treasure: one of the richest collections of Byzantine textiles

Germany

Aix la Chapelle (Aachen)

Cathedral Treasure: textiles
Church of St. Jean Baptiste: mosaic icon

Bamburg

Cathedral Treasure: textiles

Berlin

Kaiser-Friedrich-Kunstgewerbemuseum: mosaics from Ravenna
Staatliche Museen: icons, manuscripts, enamel
Library: manuscripts

Düsseldorf

Kunstgewerbemuseum: Coptic and Byzantine textiles

Freising

Cathedral: mosaic icon

Limburg

Cathedral Treasure: admirable staurotek with cloisonné enamel

Munich

State Library: manuscripts, amongst them the "Serbian Psalter" (14th century)

Recklinghausen

Icon Museum: rich collection of Coptic, Byzantine and Russian icons

Tübingen

University Library: manuscripts

Great Britain

Edinburgh

Talbot Rice Collection

Holkham

Earl of Leicester's Collection: icons, manuscripts

London

British Museum: icons; rich collection of manuscripts including the "Cotton Bible", "Psalter of 1066"

Victoria and Albert Museum: icons, enamel, embroideries

Oxford

Bodleian Library: manuscripts
Ashmolean Museum: icons

Greece

Athens

Byzantine Museum: very rich collection of icons from the 12th-17th centuries; fresco fragments from ruined churches of Attica; liturgical textiles including the "Epitaphios of Salonika"
Benaki Museum: important collection of icons from the 14th-17th centuries; Coptic and Byzantine textiles
National Library: 3000 manuscripts
Paul Kanellopoulos Collection, Stathatos (icons, frescoes, manuscripts)
Daphni, convent church: mosaics from late 11th or early 12th century
"Omorphi Ecclesia" church: 14th century frescoes
Convent church at Kaisariani on Hymettus: post-Byzantine frescoes

Chilandari (Mount Athos)

14th century frescoes, 14th-16th century icons, 800 Byzantine and Slav manuscripts

Chios

Nea Moni convent: 11th century mosaics

Corfu

Museum: pavement mosaics (4th-6th century); frescoes of ruined churches

Dionysiou (Mount Athos)

Frescoes from 16th century (Cretan school). Rich collection of icons; 800 manuscripts

Heraklion (Crete)

St. Menas Church: icons by Michael Damaskenos (16th century)

133

Historical Museum: frescoes from ruined churches

Hosios Leukas

11th century mosaics and frescoes

Iviron (Mount Athos)

Very rich collection of icons and manuscripts

Karyes (Mount Athos)

Frescoes by Panselinos (14th century) in Protaton

Kastoria

The town is itself a small Byzantine museum: 70 churches, including that of the Anargyroi (12th century), Mavriotissa convent (12th century), Archangels (1360)

Kyrenia (Cyprus)

Metropolitan palace: rich collection of icons

Lavra (Mount Athos)

Great Lavra: frescoes of the Cretan school (16th century). Very rich collection of icons; 1,536 manuscripts

Meteora

Group of 14th century convents. Frescoes of the Cretan school in the convents of St. Nicholas and St. Barlaam (16th century); fine collection of icons in the Transfiguration convent

Mistra

The town is a small Byzantine museum illustrating the Palaeologue era
Churches: Metropolis, Brontochion, Peribleptos, S. Theodore (14th century), Pantanassa (1430)
Museum: 14th century frescoes from ruined churches

Nicosia (Cyprus)

Archbishopric: rich collection of icons: manuscripts
Maronite bishopric: icons

Paphos (Cyprus)

St. Neophytos monastery: 12th century frescoes; rich collection of icons

Patmos

Monastery of St. John: frescoes; very rich collection of icons; very important library
Convent of the Annunciation: icons
Convent of the Virgin "the source of life"; icons

Rhodes

Metropolitan palace: rich collection of icons

Stavronikita (Mount Athos)

Frescoes by Theophanes of Crete (1546); fine collection of icons: important collection of manuscripts

Salonika

The second city of the Empire
Churches:
St. George: mosaics (early 5th century)
Hosios David: mosaics (c.450)
Acheiropioctos Basilica: mosaics (5th century)
St. Demetrius: mosaics (5th-7th century) and frescoes in chapel of St. Euthymius (14th century)
St. Sophia: mosaics (8th-9th century)
Chalceon Virgin: frescoes (1028 and 14th century)
Holy Apostles: mosaics and frescoes (early 14th century)
St. Nicholas Orphanou: frescoes (1310-1320)
Vlatadon convent: icons
Archaeological Museum: mosaics from Serres

Vatopedi (Mount Athos)

Mosaics (1090), 14th century frescoes; very rich collection of icons and manuscripts

Xenophon (Mount Athos)

Frescoes of the Cretan school (16th century), icons, manuscripts

Hungary

Budapest

Museum: enamels from the crown of Constantine IX

Israel

Jerusalem

Museum: pavement mosaics from Beth-Shean, Targa, Beth-Guvain, Tiberia, Caesarea, Khirbet el Minya

Italy

Brixen (Bressanone)

Cathedral treasure: textiles with eagles (chasuble) of St. Albuin, c.1000)

Castell' Arquato

Museum: textile, 'Communion of the Apostles'

Castelseprio

St. Maria: antiquising paintings, 7th-10th century

Cefalù (Sicily)

Cathedral: 12th century mosaics

Cosenza

Cathedral treasure: cross with cloisonné enamels

Florence

Gallery of the Academia: icons
Opera del Duomo: mosaic icon
Uffizi Gallery: icons
Bargello: icons
Laurentian Library: rich collection of manuscripts, including 'Rabulensis' (6th century), 'Cosmas'

(11th century)
Ricardiana Library: manuscripts

Galatina

Municipio: mosaic icon

Grotta Ferrata

Convent treasure: icons and manuscripts
Convent church: 11th and 12th century mosaics

Milan

Ambrosian Library: rich collection of manuscripts, all periods

Monreale (Sicily)

Cathedral: 12th century mosaics

Palermo (Sicily)

Martorana: mosaics (12th century)
Palatine Chapel: mosaics (12th century)
Ziza Palace: mosaics (12th century)
National Library: manuscripts

Parma

Palatine Library: manuscripts

Pisa

National Museum: Byzantine icons; Byzantinising Pisan paintings

Ravenna

The town is a complete Byzantine museum of the 5th and 6th centuries
'Mausoleum of Galla Placidia'; mosaics (450)
Baptistery of the Orthodox: mosaics (485)
Baptistery of the Arians: mosaics (c. 500)
Archbishop's Chapel: mosaics (c. 500)
Sant' Apollinare Nuovo: mosaics (6th century)
San Vitale: marvellous 6th century mosaics
Sant' Apollinare in Classe: mosaics (6th century)
Museum: rich collection of Italo-Cretan icons (16th-17th century)

135

Rome

Byzantine or Byzantinising mosaics in churches as follows:
St. Sabina (422-432), Santa Maria Maggiore (5th century), SS. Cosmas and Damian (526-530), St. Theodore (550), St. Lawrence-outside-the-walls, St. Agnes (625-640), St. Stephen-Rotondo (642-649), St. Peter-in-Vincoli (7th century), St. Prassede (817-824), St. Mark (827-844), Santa Maria-in-Domenica (817-824), St. Cecilia (840) Byzantine or Byzantinising frescoes: catacombs of Domitilla, Generosa, St. Calixtus, churches of Santa Maria Antiqua (6th-9th century), St. Nereus and Achilles (late 8th century), St. Chrisogonus (9th century)
Treasure and Library of the Vatican: sizeable collection of objects in goldsmith's work (enamels), textiles, illustrated manuscripts (Joshua Roll, Cosmas, Menologion of Basil II, Homilies of Jacob the Monk)
Pinacotheca: Byzantine and Italo-Cretan icons
Vatican Grottoes: 8th century mosaics
Lateran Museum: treasure of the Sancta Sanctorum chapel: icons
Kircher Museum: enamels
Barberini, Sterbini, Stroganov Collections

Rossano

Archiepiscopal Museum: 'Codex Purpureus' (5th-6th century)

Sassoferrato

Museo Civico: mosaic icon

Venice

Down to the 13th century, Venice was virtually an artistic colony of Byzantium
Basilica of St. Mark (11th century): Byzantine or Byzantinising mosaics (11th-14th century); Pala d'Oro: masterpieces of Byzantine enamel work; Treasury: very rich collection of goldsmiths' pieces and cloisonné enamel icons
Marciana Library: rich collection of manuscripts and enamels
Correr Museum
Gallery of the Academia: icons, Reliquary of the Cross belonging to Bessarion
Church of San Giorgio dei Greci: Cretan and Creto-Italian icons
Hellenic Institute of Byzantine and Post-Byzantine Studies: icons
Venice, vicinity of

Torcello: 11th and 12th century mosaics
Murano: 14th century mosaic

Jordan

Jerusalem

Greek Orthodox Patriarchate: collection of icons, manuscripts and textiles
Mosque of Omar: Byzantine mosaics, 7th century

Netherlands

Maastricht

St. Servais (church): textiles

Rumania

Curtea des Arges

St. Nicholas: 14th century frescoes

Bucharest

National Library: manuscripts
Museum: icons, manuscripts, textiles

Putna

Monastery contains a rich collection of Byzantine and Post-Byzantine embroideries; manuscripts

Voroneje

Post-Byzantine frescoes (16th century)

Spain

Cuenca

Cathedral: 14th century icon

Madrid

National Library: manuscripts, including "Chronicle of Skylitzes" (14th century)

Vich

Episcopal Museum: textiles

Sweden

Stockholm

National Museum: enamels, manuscripts

Syria

Damascus

Mosque of the Ummayads: 8th century mosaics
Museum: frescoes from Dura-Europos; Graeco-Roman and Byzantine pavement mosaics

Turkey

Antioch (Antakya)

Museum: pavement mosaics from Antioch,

Seleucia, Tarsus (4th–6th century)

Constantinople (Istanbul)

St. Sophia: mosaics of the 6th, 9th-12th centuries
St. Irene: iconoclast mosaics
St. Theodore (Kilise Djami) mosaics of the 14th century
Chora Monastery (Kahrie Djami): mosaics and frescoes of 14th century
Virgin Pammakaristos: (Fetiye Djami) 14th century mosaics
Museum of Mosaics: pavement mosaics from the Great Palace (5th century)
Topkapi Saray: illuminated manuscripts including the 'Octateuch' (12th century)
Museum of Antiquities: pavement mosaics
Oecumenical Patriarchate: rich collection of icons, manuscripts.

Göreme (Cappadocia)

Numerous rock churches: Tokali kilise; Kiliçlar; Elmali kilise (11th-13th century frescoes)

Trebizond (Trabzon)

Capital of a Greek Empire 1204-1461
Churches:
St. Sophia (c.1260): frescoes
Virgin Theoskepastos (14th century): frescoes
St. Savas (1411)
Convent of Sumela: frescoes 14th-16th century

U.S.A.

Baltimore

Walter's Art Gallery: manuscripts, enamels

Chicago

University Library: manuscripts including the New Testament Rockefeller-McCormick 2400 (13th century)

Cleveland

Museum of Art: manuscripts

New York

Metropolitan Museum: enamels
Pierpont-Morgan Library: manuscripts

Washington

Dumbarton Oaks Collection: manuscripts, enamels, icons, etc.

U.S.S.R.

Kiev

St. Sophia: 11th century mosaics and frescoes
Convent of St. Michael: 12th century mosaics
Museum: rich collection of Byzantine and Russian icons

Kostroma

Ipatiev Monastery: Russian icons

Leningrad

Hermitage Museum: objects from the treasures of Vladimir, Chernigov and Kiev (12th century); fresco of St. Nicholas (12th century); mosaic from the convent of St. Michael, Kiev; Byzantine and Georgian enamels; Byzantine and Russian icons
Russian National Museum: very rich collection of Byzantine and Russian icons, including the *Angel with Gold Hair* (12th century); icons from Novgorod, Pskov, Tver and Moscow; icons by Andrey Rublev (*St. Peter* and *St. Paul*, the *Prophet Sophonios*, *Presentation in the Temple*), by Dionisy (*Life of St. Cyril*, *Trinity*) and by Ushakov (*Trinity*, *Holy Face*)
Saltikov-Chtchedrin Library: rich collection of

manuscripts; Greek manuscripts nos. 101, 1393, 1397

Moscow

Cathedral of the Annunciation: monumental iconostasis (1405) with icons by Theophanes the Greek and his pupils
Cathedral of the Archangel: 16th century frescoes
Cathedral of the Dormition: frescoes by Simon Ushakov and others (17th century); Monumental iconostasis
Church of the Virgin of Georgia (Ushakov Museum): frescoes of Simon Ushakov
St. Andronic monastery (Andrey Rublev Museum): frescoes by Rublev (15th century)
The Virgin of Smolensk: 17th century frescoes; monumental iconostasis; the refectory of the Novodevichi monastery has also been converted into a museum
Tretiakov Gallery: exceptionally rich collection of Byzantine and Russian icons; the *Virgin of Vladimir* (12th century); icons from Novgorod; iconostasis of Kargopol; schools of Tver and Pskov; Muscovite school; icons by Rublev, Dionysius, Ushakov, Savins, Tchirin
National Historical Museum: copies of frescoes and mosaics from St. Sophia, Kiev; rich collection of Byzantine and Russian icons of the 14th and 15th centuries, 12th century manuscripts: paintings by Ushakov; enamels. Reserve collections: Greek and Russian manuscripts (9th-14th centuries)
Pushkin Museum of Art: Byzantine and Russian icons, inluding the fine 'Morozov Gospel' (14th century): Byzantine and Russian textiles

Novgorod

Antoniyev monastery: frescoes (1125)
St. Sophia (cathedral): frescoes (12th century)
Skovorodsky monastery: church of the Archangel Michael: 14th century fresco
St. Theodore-Stratelates (church): frescoes (1380)
Church of the Transfiguration: frescoes by Theophanes the Greek (1378)
In the vicinity of Novgorod:
Volotovo: church of the Dormition: frescoes (1380)
Museum: rich collection of icons from Novgorod and the Northern School

Vologda

Museum: Russian icons

Zagorsk

Troitse-Sergieva-Lavra, Cathedral of the Trinity monumental iconostasis (42 icons), by Andrey Rublev, Daniil Chyorny and their pupils.
Museum: icons and textiles

Yugoslavia

Belgrade

National Museum: pavement mosaics and frescoes from Stobi (4th–6th centuries); fragments from frescoes of ruined churches and copies of 12th–15th century frescoes; 'Miroslav Evangeliary' (c. 1190); embroideries, 14th-16th century
Gallery of Frescoes: copies of frescoes showing the evolution of medieval painting in Yugoslavia
National Library: manuscripts
Museum of the Orthodox Serbian Church: icons, manuscripts, embroideries of the 14th-19th centuries

Čučer

St. Nikita (church): frescoes (1310)

Dečani

14th century frescoes; rich collection of icons and manuscripts

Gračanica

14th century frescoes

Manasija

15th century frescoes

Mileševo

13th century frescoes

Ochrid

Church of St. Sophia: frescoes (c. 1046)
St. Clement: frescoes by Eutychios and Michael (late 13th cent.)
Museum of Historical Monuments: icons

Peč

Seat of the Serbian Orthodox Patriarchate
Church of the Holy Apostles: 13th century frescoes
Church of St. Demetrius: 14th century frescoes
Church of the Virgin: 14th century frescoes
Library: manuscripts of the 13th-18th centuries

Poreč

Euphrasian Basilica: mosaics (535-543)

Prizren

Church of Our Lady of Ljeviška: frescoes by Astrapas (1307)

Skoplje

Art Gallery: important collection of icons (14th-16th century)

Sopočani

Jewel of Serbian Byzantine art, 13th century frescoes

Staro Nagoričino

Frescoes by Eutychios and Michael (c. 1314)

Studenica

The richest monastery in Yugoslavia
Church of the Virgin (1191); frescoes of the 13th-16th century
Treasure of the church of the King (1314): frescoes from the beginning of the 14th century
St. Nicholas: 13th century frescoes

BALTIC

Lindisfarne

Kells

York

Breedon

Hereford

Stratford-on-Avon   St. Albans

Langfort   Winchester

Romsey

Hildesheim

Aachen   Cologne

Ingelheim

Rheims   Lorsch

FRANCE   Regensburg

Dan

Fontevrault   St. Gallen

St.-Savin

Poitiers   Vézelay

Angoulême   St. Jean-de-Côle

St.-Avit-Sénieur   Périgueux   Como   Venice   Torcello

Souillac   Monza   Parenzo

Moissac   Cahors   Parma   Ravenna

Toulouse   Genoa   Salona

Lucca   Florence

Pisa   Assisi

SPAIN   Corsica   Siena

Viterbo   Anagni

Rome   ITALY

Monte Cassino   Bari

Amalfi

Rossano

Palermo   Cefalù

Monreale   Sicily

Piazza Arme

Announa   Carthage

Timgad

Tébessna   Haïdra

Important monuments of Byzantine art

◆ Pre-Byzantine

◆ Time of Justinian (527–565)

▲ Macedonian period (867–1057)

▲ Palaeologue period (1258–1453)

Ⓘ Monuments of secondary importance

○ Influence of Byzantine art

1 Ravaniča
2 Ljubostinja
3 Sofia
4 Nagoričino
5 Bačkovo

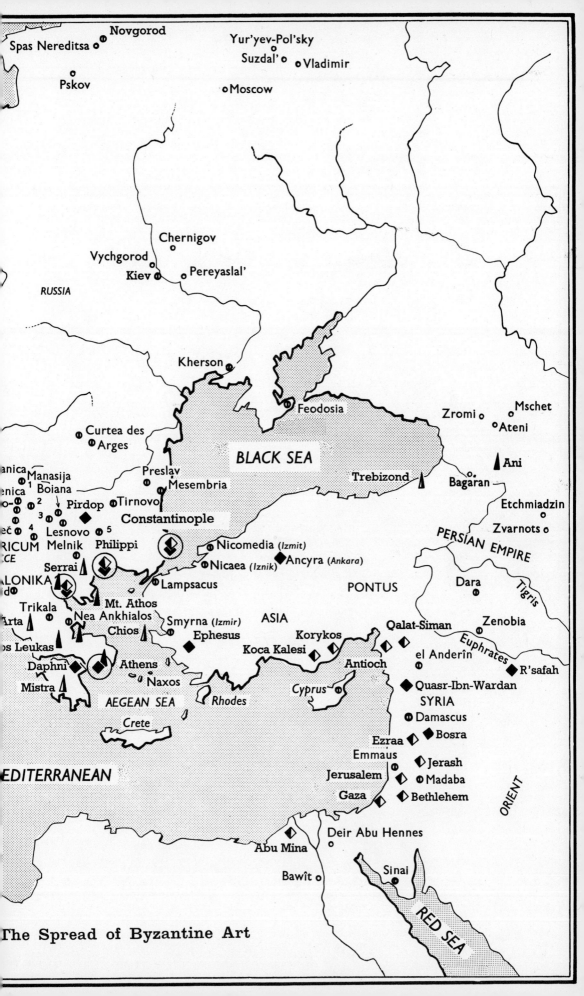

Spas Nereditsa ⊙ Novgorod

Yur'yev-Pol'sky
Suzdal' ⊙ Vladimir

Pskov ⊙

⊙ Moscow

⊙ Chernigov

Vychgorod ⊙
Kiev ⊙ ⊙ Pereyaslal'

RUSSIA

⊙ Kherson

⊙ Feodosia

BLACK SEA

Zromi ⊙ Mschet ⊙
⊙ Ateni

▲ Ani

Curtea des ⊙
Arges ⊙

⊙ Preslav
⊙ Mesembria

Trebizond ▲
Bagaran ⊙

Etchmiadzin ⊙

anica
Manasija ⊙
1 Boiana
enica

⊙ ⊙ Tirnovo
2 ⊙ ⊙ Pirdop

Zvarnots ⊙

⊙ 3
4 ⊙ ⊙ Lesnovo
eč

Constantinople

Nicomedia *(Izmit)* ⊙
Ancyra *(Ankara)* ◆

PERSIAN EMPIRE

Tigris

RICUM
CE
LONIKA
d

Melnik ⊙ 5
Philippi ◆

Nicaea *(Iznik)* ⊙

PONTUS

Dara ⊙

Serrai ▲
ALONIKA

Lampsacus ⊙

Zenobia ⊙

Trikala ▲
Nea Ankhialos
arta ▲
os Leukas ▲

Mt. Athos ▲
Chios ▲

Smyrna *(Izmir)* ⊙

ASIA

Ephesus ◆

Korykos ◆
Koca Kalesi ◆

Qalat-Siman ◆

Euphrates

el Anderîn ⊙

R'safah ◆

Daphni ◆
Mistra ▲

Athens ◆
⊙ Naxos

Rhodes

Cyprus ⊙

Antioch ◆

Quasr-Ibn-Wardan ◆

SYRIA

AEGEAN SEA

Crete

Damascus ⊙

Bosra ◆

Ezraa ◆

EDITERRANEAN

Emmaus ◆
Jerusalem ◆
Gaza ◆

Jerash ◆
Madaba ⊙
Bethlehem ◆

ORIENT

Abu Mina ◆
⊙ Deir Abu Hennes

Bawît ⊙

Sinai ⊙

RED SEA

The Spread of Byzantine Art

Ravenna

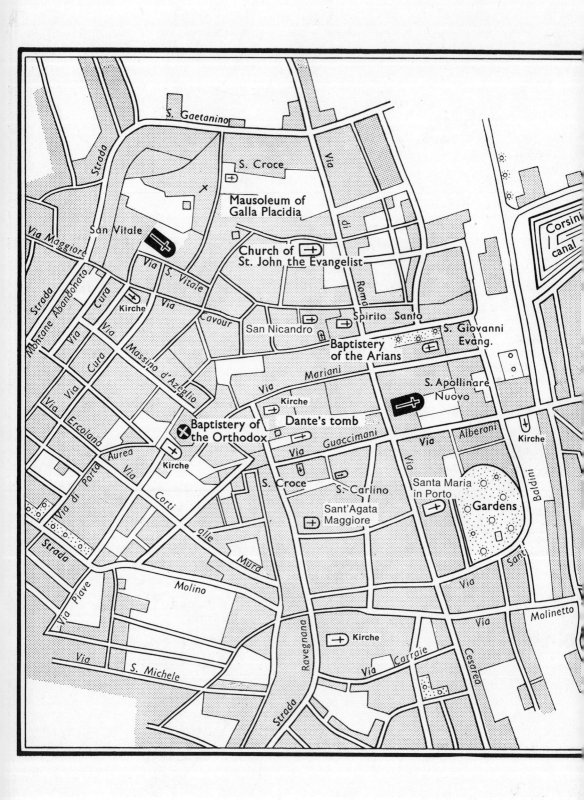

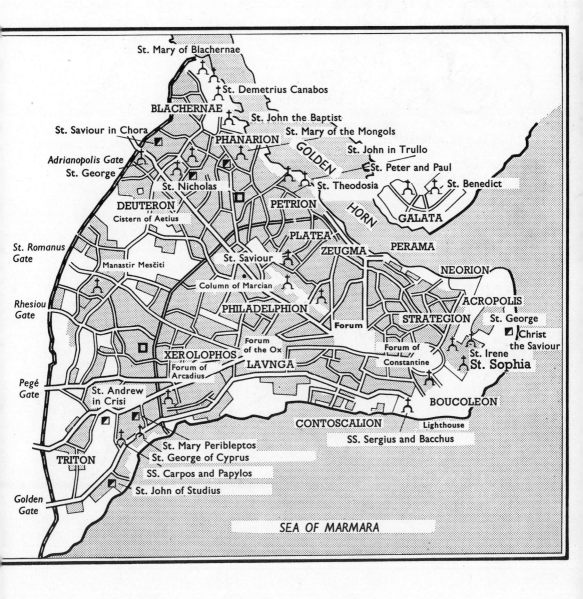

Walls of Constantine
Walls of Theodosius
Byzantine churches
Monasteries
Cistern

St. Mary of Blachernae
† St. Demetrius Canabos
BLACHERNAE
St. John the Baptist
St. Saviour in Chora
St. Mary of the Mongols
PHANARION
St. John in Trullo
Adrianopolis Gate
St. George
St. Peter and Paul
St. Nicholas
St. Theodosia
St. Benedict
DEUTERON
PETRION
GALATA
Cistern of Aetius
GOLDEN
St. Romanus
Gate
PLATEA
PERAMA
St. Saviour
ZEUGMA
Manastir Mesčiti
HORN
NEORION
Column of Marcian
Rhesiou
Gate
PHILADELPHION
ACROPOLIS
Forum
STRATEGION
St. George
XEROLOPHOS
Forum
of the Ox
Forum of
Constantine
Christ
the Saviour
Pegé
Gate
Forum of
Arcadius
LAVNGA
St. Irene
St. Sophia
St. Andrew
in Crisi
BOUCOLEON
CONTOSCALION
Lighthouse
TRITON
St. Mary Peribleptos
St. George of Cyprus
SS. Sergius and Bacchus
SS. Carpos and Papylos
Golden
Gate
St. John of Studius
SEA OF MARMARA

Dictionary

Acheiropoietos

'Not made with human hands.' Name given to icons by tradition, ascribed to St. Luke or to supernatural intervention. From the fourth century an icon alleged to have been executed by St. Luke was venerated at Constantinople. It disappeared at the moment when the city was captured by the Turks in 1453, having been exposed by the Byzantines at the most vulnerable points on the city's defensive walls. The cult of acheiropoietos icons scored a triumph when the miraculous icon of Edessa was translated to Constantinople in 944.

Acheiropoietos Basilica

Church at Salonika, fifth century. Fine ornamental mosaics (garlands of fruit, vases, arabesques) in the soffits of the nave arches.

Adam of Bremen

German traveller (twelfth century) whose writings contain valuable information on Kievan Russia.

Afendiko

Church at Mistra in Greece, built about 1290, decorated with frescoes in the fourteenth century. The church proper contains large figures of saints and Church

fathers, also episodes from the life of Christ and of the Virgin.

Ahnas

Egypt, large sanctuary of the fourth century. Its sculptural decoration pinpoints the transition from Graeco-Roman to Coptic art.

Alpatov, M. V.

Historian of Russian art. His study *La Trinité dans l'Art byzantin et l'Icône de Roublev* was published at Paris in 1927. With N. Brunov and O. Uruff, the author of numerous works on old Russian art.

Amari, Michel

(1806-1889) Italian historian of Muslim Italy.

Ambrosian Library

The Ambrosian Library at Milan contains about 1000 Greek manuscripts.

Andronicus II Palaeologus

(1258-1332) Byzantine emperor 1282-1328. During his reign Byzantine humanism, progenitor of the Renaissance, found its wings. Andronicus formed a palace academy, over which he himself presided, where literary men gathered on fixed days to discuss all kinds of topics, scientific subjects in particular. It was to this gathering that Nicephorus Gregoras presented his plan for reforming the Julian calendar. The academy was the model for the Italian academies of the Renaissance.

Angeloktistos

Church on Cyprus, whose name signifies 'built by the angels'. Contains sixth century mosaics representing the Virgin between two angels.

Annunciation, Cathedral of

Kremlin, Moscow. History relates that Theophanes the Greek worked there about 1405, also the monks, Prokhor of Gorodetz and Andrey Rublev. On the iconostasis, magnificent icons executed by Theophanes and his pupils (icons of the *Archangel Michael* and *St. Peter*) and by anonymous masters of the Moscow school (*St. Demetrius, St. George*).

Anthemius of Tralles

Mathematician and architect; sixth century. Invited by Justinian to direct the building of the Basilica of St. Sophia, Constantinople. His work, begun in 532, was completed in 537 by Isidore of Miletus.

Antinoë

Metropolis of the Thebaid (Egypt), founded in 132 by Hadrian; built round two principal streets 14.61 m. wide, which crossed at right angles and were bordered by vaulted porticoes with fine Corinthian columns. Excavations conducted between 1890 and 1900 by Grayet brought to light numerous very wealthy burials from the Byzantine period, funerary portraits and figured textiles. Antinoë had a large number of churches.

Antioch

An impressive number of cities founded by the Seleucids were given this name in honour of their founders, Antiochus I (280-262), Antiochus II (262-237) and Antiochus Epiphanes (174-163). The most important was Antioch on the Orontes, capital of the Seleucid Empire. Built by Seleucus I in 300 B.C., enlarged by Seleucus II (246-226) and Antiochus IV (174-163), embellished by the Byzantine emperor Theodosius II (408-450), Antioch was for a thousand years a city of great importance, both for its intellectual and for its mercantile activity. The population, reckoned at 500,000 in the Roman period, is thought to have declined to 200,000 after the sack of the city by the Persians in A.D. 260, climbing to 300,000 in the sixth century. The cult of St. Peter, who founded the church of Antioch before that of Rome, was observed with great fervour and the

147

Antiochenes were proud to recall that the adjective 'Christian' was born in their city. The theological school of Antioch played a large part in the religious controversies of the fourth and fifth centuries and the patriarchs, less powerful than those of Alexandria, enjoyed great authority. The only witnesses to the Antiochene school of painting are the fine mosaics preserved at the museum in Antioch, at the Louvre and in Baltimore.

Apamea

A large number of the Hellenistic cities scattered between Iran and Asia Minor bore this name, in honour of Apama, the daughter of a Persian satrap, who became the wife of Seleucus I (312-281). The most considerable was Apamea on the Orontes, in Syria. Mosaic pavements with mythological scenes decorated pathways running beneath porticoes. Sizeable fragments of these are exhibited in the Musée du Cinquantenaire, Brussels.

Arianism

Heresy preached about 323 by Arius, which denied the divinity of Christ, regarding him merely as a perfect man. The heresy disappeared from the East after the Council of Constantinople, 381. In the West it survived for several centuries as the national religion of the Goths.

Astrapas

Important Byzantine painter of the late

thirteenth and early fourteenth centuries. With his sons (?) Eutychios and Michael, decorated a large number of churches at Ochrid, Prizren, Čučer, Žiča, etc.

Athens, Byzantine Museum of

The Byzantine Museum at Athens contains a large collection of icons, textiles (including the celebrated 'epitaphios' of Salonika) and frescoes, originally in churches of Attica, now in ruins. 'Athens' designates manuscripts preserved in the National Library, Athens.

Bačkovo

(Bulgaria) The Petritzos monastery at Bačkovo, near Philippopolis, was founded in 1083 by a Georgian nobleman, Gregory Pakourianos, general of the Byzantine army under Alexius Comnenus, who was killed fighting the Petchenegs in 1086. The foundation was supplemented by a hospice for old men, a school and three guest-houses; it was reserved exclusively for Georgians. The church is decorated with frescoes of the late eleventh century

Bactria

A country of ancient Asia, whose capital was also called Bactria. For nearly three centuries after Alexander, his successors, the Graeco-Bactrian kings, kept alive at the cross-roads of the Afghan valleys, as far as the region around Lahore, an astonishingly faithful version of Greece. The greatest of these kings was Menander (175-150), who mounted a victorious expedition into the heart of India.

Baptistery of the Arians

(Ravenna) Octagonal structure built in the time of Theodoric, adjacent to the Cathedral of the Arians (now the church of the Holy Spirit), towards the end of the fifth century. The dome is adorned with a mosaic representing the baptism of Christ, surrounded by the twelve apostles.

The decoration takes its inspiration from the Baptistery of the Orthodox.

Baptistery of the Orthodox

(Ravenna) Octagonal structure built at the beginning of the fifth century and decorated with mosaics about the year 455. The interior has two registers of superimposed arcades, ornamented with mosaics figuring prophets and green acanthus leaves highlighted with gold on a dark blue ground. The dome is entirely covered with mosaics.

Barlaam and Joasaph

Hagiographical romance falsely attributed to St. John of Damascus. It is in fact a Christian version of the legend of the Buddha. The romance enjoyed great success and was translated into several languages: sixty versions of it are known. Its exotic imagery inspired both miniaturists and frescoists. The finest illustrations are found in the manuscripts preserved at the Iviron Monastery (No. 453) and at Paris (No. 1128).

Basil, St.

Church Father, bishop of Caesarea 329-379. Created a form of monastic life suited to the climate and genius of Hellenic countries: he has always been regarded by the Orthodox Church as the supreme monastic legislator. His ideas spread through all the western provinces of the Empire. St. Benedict (480-543) drew inspiration from his rule.

Beisan

(Israel) Recent excavations have uncovered splendid mosaic pavements from a Byzantine convent founded in 567.

Benaki, Museum

(Athens) Important collection of icons from the fourteenth-sixteenth centuries and of Coptic and Byzantine textiles.

Bessarion

(1390-1472) Formerly archbishop of Nicaea, became a cardinal of the Roman Church: has been called the most Greek of the Latins and the most Latin of the Greeks. Pupil of Plethon, he tried to reconcile the revived Platonism of his day with the Aristotelianism of the Middle Ages. The bequest of his rich library to the Signoria of Venice in 1467 was the last service rendered by this illustrious representative of Byzantium to European humanism.

Bethlehem, Basilica of the Nativity

Built by Constantine the Great. The texts praise the splendour of its mosaics, which also covered the external wall of the church, the earliest date from the seventh century. They were restored about 1169 on the orders of the emperor Manuel Comnenus by the mosaicist Ephraim. According to Father Quaresimus, who saw the mosaics at the end of the sixteenth century when they were almost all intact, the west wall of the church was covered with mosaics representing the Tree of

Jesse, bearing medallions of the prophets who foretold the Nativity. The wall of the nave carried a long frieze of half-length figures representing Christ's ancestors; inscribed above, between architectural decoration, were summaries of the acts of the seven oecumenical councils. The transept and the choir had scenes from the Gospels, three of which, *The Entry into Jerusalem*, *The Doubting of Thomas* and the *Ascension*, have escaped destruction.

Bible of Leo the Patrician

Tenth century manuscript preserved in the Vatican Library. The work is adorned with eighteen full-page miniatures. Two artists seem to have been at work: one favours a linear style, the other is more of a colourist and develops the ornamentation of the ground to greater effect.

Blachernae, Palace of

At Constantinople. The first Blachernae palace was built by the emperor Anastasius I (reigned 491-518) to serve as a place of retreat at times of pilgrimages to the nearby church which contained the Virgin's mantle. A new palace was built towards the end of the twelfth century by Alexius I Comnenus. Under Manuel I Comnenus (1143-1180), the court officially abandoned the Great Palace and in 1150 installed itself at Blachernae.

Bodleian Library

Oxford; has a rich collection of manuscripts.

Boiana

Place near Sofia (Bulgaria). The church dates from the thirteenth century. Its mural paintings, dating from 1259, rank among the finest creations of the thirteenth century. Apart from scenes illustrating the life of Christ (including an admirable *Christ among the Doctors*) and the Festivals, the decoration to the church consists of eighteen scenes from the life of St. Nicholas, a large number of saints' figures (including the beautiful St. Theodore Tiro) and portraits of the founders.

Bréhier, L

(1868-1951) Eminent French Byzantinologist. His main publications are: 'L'Art byzantin', 1924; 'L'art chrétien', 1928; 'Le Monde byzantin', 3 vols., 1950.

Cappadocia

Territory of Asia Minor whose capital was Caesarea. In the fourth century Basil, Gregory of Nazianzen and Gregory of Nyssa made Cappadocia the classic home of eloquence and Christian thought. In the fifth and sixth centuries an important monastic colony became established to the west of Caesarea in the volcanic region of Urgüp. At first the hermits lived in mere caves dug out of the tufa, but the existing remains reveal the presence of true monasteries, with external façades often ornamented with blind arcades, made out of a labyrinth of chambers and churches. The monks undermined the rock and then literally sculpted it, carving out arches and leaving free-standing pillars and columns. The earliest frescoes go back to the sixth and seventh centuries; others betray iconoclast influence. The enormous mill-stones, two metres high, which were rolled into the entry of the monasteries to seal them against any attack date from the time of the Arab invasions. In the tenth century, thanks to the Byzantine victories of the Macedonian era, the region was freed from the Arab danger. Most of the Cappadocian frescoes date from the tenth to the thir-

teenth centuries. This powerful centre of monastic life was abandoned after the Turkish invasions.

Carthage

(Tunisia) In the time of Justinian I ranked as one of the capital cities of the Empire. Carthage had not suffered under Vandal rule (433-538) and retained the splendours of its Roman past.

Castelseprio

(Italy) Formerly a fortified place between Milan and Varese, destroyed by the Milanese in 1287. The small church of Santa Maria Fuori Porta, which dates from the seventh-eighth centuries, contains fine antiquising frescoes of uncertain date.

Catelanos, Francos

Francos Catelanos of Thebes was a leading disciple of the Cretan school of the sixteenth century. With his brother George, he decorated, c. 1566, the narthex of the convent church of Barlaam at Meteora

(Greece) and about 1564 the monastery of the Transfiguration at Veltsista. He was also responsible for the frescoes in the chapel of St. Nicholas in the Great Lavra on Mount Athos.

Cefalù

(Sicily) The Cathedral, built by Roger II of Sicily between 1101 and 1154 has preserved in its interior a noteworthy ensemble of Byzantine mosaics. Those in the apse, *Christ Pantocrator*, *Virgin and Archangels*, *Apostles*, date from 1148 and are among the finest works of the twelfth century.

Chalcedon

City of Asia Minor, at the entrance of the Thracian Bosporus. The Monophysite heresy was condemned by the Fourth Oecumenical Council, held at Chalcedon in 451.

Chilandari

Serbian convent on Mount Athos, founded in 1197 by the Serbian king Stephen

Communion of Six Apostles (details)
'Codex purpureus', 6th-7th cent.
Rossano, Cathedral

Nemanja. Contains frescoes of the four-teenth century and a fine collection of 14th-16th century icons, including the *Tricheroussa Virgin* or *Virgin with Three Hands*. The library possesses eight hundred Slav and Greek manuscripts. Molyvok-lissia, a dependency of Chilandari close to Karyes, is adorned with frescoes by Zorzis executed between 1536 and 1541.

Chludov Psalter

Preserved at the Historical Museum, Moscow; belongs to the category of psalters with marginal illustrations, known as 'monastic psalters', in opposition to the 'aristocratic psalters', with full-page illus-trations. It is ornamented with over two hundred marginal vignettes which are lively in execution and illumined in flat tints, harmoniously blended.

Chora

Monastery at Constantinople, now a museum. The church of St. Saviour-in-Chora is of several periods. Its mosaic and frescoes are contemporary with one another and were executed between 1305 and 1320 under the patronage of Theodore Metochites. The mosaics in the two narthexes, recently cleaned by the Byzan-tine Institute of America, comprise two cycles illustrating the life of the Virgin and of Christ. The decoration is completed by the Deesis and a panel representing Metochites offering a model of the church to Christ. The frescoes in the south side-chapel are dominated by two huge com-positions representing the *Descent into*

Hell and the *Last Judgment*. The Chora mosaics and frescoes are among the masterpieces of Christian art.

Chronicle, Alexandrian

Written in Coptic, fourth century. A kind of popular almanac giving the allegorical figures for the Roman and Jewish months, lists of the prophets and of the kings of Rome, and a chronicle of events between 382 and 393. The illustrations, in a sort of earthy gouache of brilliant colours, are distributed at random in the middle of the text or in the margin.

Chyorny, Daniil

With Andrey Rublev painted the frescoes of the Cathedral of the Dormition, Vladimir (1405).

Clement of Alexandria

(c. 150-215) Church Father; effected the first synthesis of Christianity and Greek philosophy.

Codex Rossanensis

Codex purpureus Rossanensis. Gospels written in gold on purplish parchment, preserved in the archbishop's palace at Rossano, Italy; probably sixth century. The master responsible for this major work has reproduced, in the few square centimetres of his miniatures, the vast expanse of an apsidal hemicyle or of a lengthy basilical frieze.

Codex Sinopensis

Codex purpureus Sinopensis. Fragments of St. Matthew's Gospel written in gold on purplish parchment, probably sixth century, preserved at the Bibliothèque Nationale, Paris. Adorned with five paintings, among them the admirable *Healing of the Blind Men.*

Coislin

As heir to chancellor Pierre Séguire (died 1672), the Duc de Coislin, bishop of Metz, requested Dom Bernard de Montfaucon, the illustrious founder of Greek palaeography, to draw up a detailed description of the 416 Greek manuscripts which constituted the most valuable portion of Séguier's library. The Coislin collection was removed to the Bibliothèque Nationale at Paris in 1795, where the volumes were left in the order Montfaucon had assigned to them.

Comneni

Great Byzantine family which produced a considerable number of emperors to form the Comnene dynasty (1057-1185).

Constantine the Great

(274-337) Roman emperor from 306 to 337. Constantine was initially a pagan and a believer in the solar cult. The date of his conversion to Christianity is uncertain. However that may be, he proclaimed liberty of conscience by his edict of 313 (Edict of Milan) but only showed a clear preference for Christianity from the beginning of 320. In 324 he decided to transfer the capital of the Roman Empire to Byzantium. The solemn inauguration of the 'New Rome' (Constantinople) took place on 11 May 330. The numerous churches built by Constantine include St. Peter's Basilica at Rome, St. Sophia, St. Irene and the Holy Apostles at Constantinople, the great octagonal church at Antioch, the Basilica of the Holy Sepulchre and the rotunda of the Resurrection at Jerusalem and the church of the Nativity at Bethlehem.

Constantine Monomachus, Crown of

Crown of cloisonné enamel, preserved in the National Museum at Budapest. It was perhaps sent to the Hungarian king Andrew I, a friend of Byzantium, who reigned from 1046 to 1060.

Constantine VII Porphyrogenitus

Byzantine emperor from 913 to 959; contributed to the splendours of the Empire by his literary and artistic tastes and his reorganisation of state education.

Constantinople

When Diocletian abandoned Rome in 284 and instituted a new capital in the East, at Nicomedia, he confirmed the indubitable primacy the Hellenistic East had already acquired in the Empire. The East contained the great centres of economic life: Alexandria, Antioch, Ephesus, Salonika, Trebizond. The best schools of law, rhetoric and philosophy were those of Beirut, Alexandria, Gaza and Caesarea. Papinian and Ulpian, the master minds of late Roman jurisprudence, were Syrians. The Gregorian and Hermogenian codes, which gathered together the great legal work accomplished by Diocletian, were compiled at Beirut. It was again in the East that the great spiritual questions, indicative of the new world coming to birth, were being tackled: the majority of the earliest Church Fathers, the Neo-Platonist philosophers and the great Gnostics were Egyptians, Syrians or Cappadocians. Lastly, it was in the East too that the iconography of the new art was being formed.

The foundation of Constantinople in 330 set the seal on this displacement of the centre of gravity to the East. The movement was hastened by the economic crisis and the barbarian invasions: while in the West the monetary economy and urban life were disappearing and the inhabitants of old Rome were taking refuge in antique ruins transformed into fortresses, in the East urban civilisation was taking on a new lease of life. Less than a century after its foundation, Constantinople and its suburb had nearly a million inhabitants. As the rhetor Themistios, who was writing at this time remarked 'the city grows without ceasing, like a vigorous animal'.

Constantinople, Lost Monuments of

Almost nothing remains of the countless churches and palaces which were the ornament of the Byzantine capital in its heyday under the Macedonian dynasty. The sumptuous New Palace of Basil I has disappeared without trace. Gone too are the Pentakouvouklon with its five cupolas, the Triclinium of Nineteen Couches (remodelled by Constantine VII) and the Bucoleon Palace of Nicephorus Phocas, of which William of Tyre has left us an enthusiastic description. Constantine VII mentions by name forty-three churches in Constantinople alone, which were built or restored through the efforts of his grandfather Basil I, but we know little about their decoration. It is known that Romanus III (1028-1034) was inordinately proud of the decoration to his favourite church, Peribleptos. Psellos relates that Michael (1034-1041) loaded the church of the 'anargyroi' saints (SS. Cosmas and Damian) with gold mosaics 'of what one would have said were living images'. Constantine IX Monomachus, emptied the State Treasury to build a sumptuous monastery in the Manganese quarter. But all these have disappeared, above all, the 'Nea', the 'New Church' of Basil I (881), which was the key monument to the art of this period. Equally irreparable is the loss of the mosaics, remade towards the end of the ninth century, in Justinian's church of the Holy Apostles. For it was in these two churches that the iconographic programme was established which was to last, with variants, to the end of the

Byzantine era and is perpetuated in Orthodox churches into our own day. Likewise, practically nothing remains of the palaces and churches built by the emperors of the Comnene dynasty.

Copts

Name originally given to the inhabitants of Egypt. Historically, the Coptic period is the time during which Monophysitism developed in Egypt, that is to say between the Council of Chalcedon (451) and the Arab conquest (641).

Cosmas

Byzantine traveller and geographer, native of Alexandria; his famous *Christian Topography* was written towards the middle of the sixth century. The work has come down to us in several manuscripts, one at the Vatican which is probably ninth century, two of later date preserved at the Laurentian and at Sinai. The illustration consists of maps, representations of the earth, exotic animals and plants, monuments of Alexandria and numerous scenes drawn from Christian history.

Crete (Cretan school)

Between 1500 and 1669 Crete was the principal centre of Byzantine art. Cretan painters, some of whom sign their work —Theophanes, Antony, Zorzis—founded a school which worked in the monasteries of Mount Athos and the Meteora and was the guiding spirit in the last flowering of Byzantine painting in the sixteenth century. Fifteen large ensembles of mural painting were realised at Mount Athos between 1535 and 1568 by artists of the Cretan school. Theophanes, its leading light,

decorated the churches of the Lavra (1535), and probably also its refectory (1546), and of Stavronikita and of Xenophon (1563). His pupils Euphrosynos, Zorzis and Antony, his sons Neophytes and Symeon, and other anonymous pupils, decorated the churches of the convents of Dionysiu (1543 and 1547), Xenophon (1544), Molyvoklissia (1536), Koutloumousi (1540), Philotheou (1540) and St. Paul (1555). The most considerable and original disciple of the Cretan school is Francos Catelanos; the paintings of the refectory of Dïonysiu (1603?) are the last important productions of the school.

Icon painters of the Cretan school include Michael Damaskenos (16th century), Andrea Ricco (c. 1600), Lampardos Tzanes (17th century), Theodore Poulakis (1622-1692). The island ceased to be an artistic centre after it was occupied by the Turks in 1669. 'The tendencies of this school in the last resort go back to the Hellenistic traditions of Byzantine painting, but the immediate models for its compositions belong to Palaeologue art, though they also participate in the other artistic movement of the day, the Macedonian school, which is at once more dramatic and more realistic' (M. Chatzidakis).

Cučer

The monastery of St. Nikita was founded by King Milutin at the beginning of the fourteenth century and contains frescoes by Michael and Eutychios, as attested by their signatures on the shield of one of the warrior saints, to be seen on the south wall. The frescoes include a cycle dealing with the miracles of Christ, the Passion and the great festivals.

D

the cycle of the festivals of Christ and the Virgin.

Damaskenos, Michael

The most considerable painter of the Cretan school; his known works date from 1571 to 1591. Icons by Damaskenos are scattered throughout the Orthodox world, at Mount Sinai, the Stavronikita convent on Mount Athos, Hosios Leukas, Zante (museum, church of St. Catherine-of-Sinai, St. Spyridon-Flambouriaris), Venice (Collection of the Hellenic Institute, San Giorgio dei Greci) and Candia (St. Menas church). The westernisation of the Byzantine icon starts with Damaskenos.

Daphni

Church in Greece situated on the Sacred Way between Athens and Eleusis. Built in the middle of the eleventh century for a convent. Its mosaics, executed about 1100, represent the maturity of the Byzantine classical style. The huge bust of the Pantocrator in the dome is one of the greatest creations of Byzantine art. The essence of the decoration consists of thirteen large compositions representing

Dečani

The monastery of Dečani in Yugoslavia, begun in 1327, was completed in 1335 by Dušan, who in 1348 had the interior decorated with frescoes remarkable for the superabundance of the narrative cycles. The monastery treasure is a collection of 14th-16th century icons worthy of a museum. The library contains manuscripts from the 13th-16th centuries.

Deesis

The theme of the Deesis ('Supplication') belongs to the apocalyptical cycle: Christ, the supreme judge, is represented between the Virgin and John the Baptist, both of whom intercede for mankind.

Demus, Otto

Eminent Austrian Byzantinologist. His writings on the Venetian and Sicilian mosaics are authoritative. His essay *Byzantine Mosaic Decoration* (1947) is the best introduction to the Byzantine aesthetic.

157

Dionisy

The most important Russian painter after Rublev. About the year 1500 he decorated, together with his sons, the church of the Nativity of the Virgin at the Ferapontov Monastery in Northern Russia, near the White Lake. His paintings are totally lacking in dramatic sense; but his figures, disproportionately elongated, are ethereal and appealing by reason of their lightly applied and delicate colouring.

Dionysiu

Monastery on Mount Athos built in 1389, rebuilt after a fire in 1535. The convent church was decorated with frescoes by the Cretan painter Zorzis in 1547. The refectory was decorated in 1603 by Mercurius and Daniel, painters of the Cretan school, who used engravings by Dürer and Cranach to illustrate the Apocalypse. This is the first full-length apocalyptical cycle to appear in Byzantine art.

Dionysius the Areopagite

(Fifth century) His mystical theology, systematised in the East by Maximus the Confessor and translated in the West by Hilduin in 835, was of first importance as an influence on Christian thought.

Dioscorides

Celebrated physician of the Graeco-Roman period. The oldest surviving edition of his book on plants was executed at Byzantium for the princess Juliana Anicia and is now at Vienna. The general style is Hellenistic, but certain elements of oriental origin can be detected in the details of the decoration.

Dormition, Church of, at Nicaea, Turkey

Seventh or eighth century domed basilica, destroyed during the Graeco-Turkish war of 1920-1922. The four archangels grouped in pairs on each side of the apse dated from the ninth century. In the apse, on a gold ground, was a standing Madonna, entirely enveloped in a dark blue mantle and pressing the infant Christ, in a gilded tunic, with both hands to her breast. The mosaics of the narthex, the four evangelists between four medallions representing Christ, the Virgin, two saints and a Virgin orans, dated from the middle of the eleventh century.

Dormition, Cathedral of

Vladimir, U.S.S.R. Frescoes by Daniil Chyorny and Andrey Rublev, including *The Last Judgment*, executed c. 1408.

Droysen, Johann Gustav

(1808-1884) German philologist, historian and statesman; author of a remarkable *History of Hellenism*.

Dsromi

In Georgia (U.S.S.R.). The church contains seventh century mosaics.

Dura-Europos

City on the Euphrates founded about 300 B.C. by Nicanor under the name Dura, later given the name Europos by Seleucus I. The monuments of Dura, all before the capture and abandonment of the city by the Persians in A.D. 260 (temples of the Palmyrene deities, synagogue and Christian church) demonstrate the existence of an art more or less foreign to the Hellenistic tradition, and in which features encountered in Byzantine art are already discernible. The frescoes from the synagogue and the Palmyrene temple are preserved in the museum at Damascus.

Duthuit, Jean

Living French art historian and writer on aesthetics. Principal publications: *Byzance*, 1926; *La Sculpture copte*, 1931; *L'Art byzantin* (in collaboration with Georges Salles and W. F. Vollbach); *Le Musée inimaginable* (Vols. I-III); *L'Image en Souffrance*, 1961; *L'Image et l'Instant*, 1961: *Le Feu des Signes*, 1963.

Edessa

(Turkey) Capital of Osrhoëne, populated by Syrians, from the end of the second century B.C. under the rule of the Abgar dynasty. King Abgar VIII (179-214) was converted to Christianity after a journey to Rome. Edessa was one of the first states to make Christianity an official religion.

Elkomenos

Church at Monemvasia in Greece. Noteworthy icon of the crucifixion.

Elvira

City in Spain. A decree of the Council of Elvira in 300 provides the earliest testimony to the iconoclastic tendency of the early Christians.

Enamel cloisonne

One of the most delicate of all techniques; gold laminations, which sketched out the strokes, contours and folds in the drapery of the personages represented, were soldered on to thin plates of gold or electron. The compartments thus marked out were then filled with vitreous pastes made from

lead and borax mixed with metallic oxides which produced the various colours. Lastly, the surface was polished with goat-skin to make the cloisonné design stand out and to give the enamel its indestructible sheen. Byzantine enamel work was in its heyday between the ninth and the twelfth centuries.

Epitaphios

Liturgical veil borne solemnly in the procession 'of the great entry', during which the holy elements are carried to the altar at which Mass is being celebrated.

Eudocia

(421-460) Wife of Theodosius II. This empress, who continued an ardent Christian without renouncing the cultural ideal of her native city of Athens, is a living example of the co-existence at Byzantium of Christianity and antique culture.

Eusebius

(c. 265-340) Bishop of Caesarea (Cappadocia). Author of a valuable *Ecclesiastical History* and father of this genre of historical writing.

Evangeliarium of Ostromir

Russian manuscript executed 1056-1057 for Ostromir, governor of the city of Novgorod. Regarded as the oldest work of the Russian language.

Ferapontov, U.S.S.R.

The celebrated monastery of Ferapontov, in northern Russia, was decorated with frescoes about the year 1500 by master Dionysius and his son.

Galla Placidia

(c. 386-450) Empress of the West, daughter of Theodosius, wife of the barbarian king Athaulf and afterwards of Constantius III (died 421). She ruled the Roman Empire during the minority of her son, Valentinian III. A magnificent mausoleum was erected for her at Ravenna.

Gandhara

Former province of North-West India, part of the Empire of Alexander the Great. Source of the finest specimens of Graeco-Buddhist art.

Georgia

Situated on the eastern frontier of the Byzantine Empire, Georgia presents the image typical of an artistic province of Byzantium. In the eleventh century Georgia was the centre of a brilliant civilisation linked with the reigns of David the Restorer and of Tamara. If Georgian architecture owes nothing, or practically nothing to Byzantium, the frescoes and mosaics decorating the churches at David-Garedja, Ateni, Ihari, and Gelati (10th-12th centuries) are thoroughly Byzantine in iconography and style. The Gelati monastery was the repository of the celebrated triptych of the Virgin of Khakouli (now in the museum at Tiflis), one of the masterpieces of Byzantine goldsmiths' and enamel work. The frescoes of the convent of Tsalendikha executed by a Greek, Manuel Eugenikos, about 1384-1392 are one of the last great creations of Byzantine painting.

Gerasa

Town in Jordan (Jerash). Gerasa enjoyed great prosperity during the Byzantine era down to the time of the Arab conquest in 632. Exploration of its ruins has revealed the existence of eleven Christian monuments and a large synagogue. The Cathedral dates from the end of the fourth century. The church of St. Theodore and its baptistery date from 496. The ensemble formed by the rotunda of St. John the Baptist, the church of St. George and the church dedicated to SS. Cosmas and Damian dates from c. 529-533. The last church to be built at Gerasa was probably that of bishop Genesios, 610. The town was demolished by an earthquake in 746 and from the eighth century disappears.

Göreme

(Turkey) The ancient town of Korama (Cappadocia). It is in the region of Göreme that the most important group of the Cappadocian rock churches is to be found.

Grabar, André

Eminent French Byzantinologist. Principal publications: *La peinture religieuse en Bulgarie*, 1928; *L'Empereur dans l'Art byzantin*, 1936; *La Peinture byzantine*, 1953; *L'Iconoclasme byzantin*, 1957; *L'art byzantin du Moyen Age*, 1957.

Gračanica

(Yugoslavia) Monastery founded in 1321 by King Milutin. The church contains frescoes which rank among the finest creations of the fourteenth century.

Great Lavra

Convent on Mount Athos founded in 963 by St. Athanasius. The catholicon, completed in 1004, was adorned in 1535 with frescoes executed by Theophanes of Crete. Other artists of the Cretan school (Francos Catelanos in particular) decorated the refectory, the phiale and the St. Nicholas chapel. The Koukouzelissa chapel contains fine frescoes of popular inspiration dating from 1712. The convent is the repository of enamels, textiles and fine icons from the 14th-16th centuries. The library contains 2200 manuscripts.

Great Mosque of Damascus

Founded by the Ummayad Caliph Al-Walid, who ruled at Damascus from 707 to 715. A very ancient cult centre already existed at the very heart of the city. A temple of Jupiter, of which traces remain, had replaced the sanctuary of a Syrian god and in turn given way to a basilica dedicated to St. John the Baptist. Al-Walid summoned artists from Constantinople; the materials and labour force both came from Egypt. The texts comment favourably on the richness of the sculpted and mosaic decoration executed by the specialists from Constantinople.

Gregoras, Nicephoras

(1296-1350) Byzantine historian and savant; author of a *Byzantine History*.

Gregory of Nazianzen, St.

(329-389) Owes his title 'the Theologian' to a group of five among the forty-five sermons of his that we possess, written in 380 and known as the 'Theological Discourses'. They contain an exposition of the Trinity which has become classic in Christian theology.

Gregory of Nyssa, St.

(335-394) Brother of St. Basil, bishop of Nyssa (Cappadocia), one of the greatest Byzantine theologians. His work had a strong influence on medieval thought.

Grotta Ferrata

Abbey of Basilian monks near Rome, founded in 1004 by St. Nilus of Calabria. There is an eleventh century Deesis in mosaic on the tympanum of the door. The mosaics of the triumphal arch (Pentecost) and the Byzantine frescoes are thirteenth century. The abbey possesses a rich library and a small gallery of Byzantine paintings.

Hesychasm

From a very early date the Byzantines gave the name Hesychasts to monks following a rigorously hermitical life in holy solitude. In the fourteenth century the term Hesychasm was applied in particular to a form of ascetic mysticism. Its distant origins go back to the great eleventh century mystic, Symeon the New Theologian, with whom it has great affinities in doctrine and practices. Its immediate origins are connected with Gregory of Sinaï, who wandered through the Byzantine provinces around the year 1330. The Hesychasts took as their supreme ideal attainment of the vision of divine light, and adopted a method appropriate to this end. In his solitary retreat, the Hesychast had to squat in a bent position, his chin wedged against his chest, his gaze fixed on his navel, and repeat the prayer 'Lord Jesus Christ, Son of God, be gracious unto me', holding his breath each time he recited it: little by little a sense of ineffable bliss stole over the supplicant, he saw himself enveloped in the rays of a supraterrestrial divine light, that same divine light which the witnesses to the transfiguration of Jesus beheld on Mount Tabor. The belief in the perpetual visibility of the light of Tabor aroused some opposition, and the method practised by the Hesychasts in particular came in for ironic criticism. The campaign against the Hesychasts was launched by Barlaam, a monk from Calabria.

Holy Apostles, Constantinople

Begun in 536, completed in 546, the five-domed church of the Holy Apostles was the second church of Constantinople. It was destroyed by the Turks to make room for the mosque of Mahomet II, and to form an idea of it we have to look to monuments such as St. Mark's at Venice which were copied from the Holy Apostles. From the descriptions of Constantine the Rhodian and Nicholas Mesarites, we know it contained a mosaic executed by Eulalios showing the complete cycle of episodes from the life of Christ. In the scene of the 'Women at the Tomb', the painter introduced himself, under the figure of one of the soldiers guarding the Holy Sepulchre: this is the only known example from Byzantine art of the portraits of the author so much favoured by the Renaissance.

Holy Apostles, Salonika

The five-domed church of the Holy Apostles at Salonika was built about 1312-1315 and is decorated with mosaics and frescoes of great quality. The style of the mosaics presents a compromise between the idealism of the contemporaneous mosaics in the Chora monastery (Constantinople) and the realism of the late thirteenth century Macedonian school.

Homilies of St. Gregory of Nazianzen

The Homilies (Sermons) of St. Gregory of Nazianzen enjoyed great popularity at Byzantium: hence the vast quantity of illustrated manuscripts in which they survive. The most beautiful is 'Paris 510', illustrated in c. 880 for the emperor Basil I.

163

Its forty miniatures exhibit all the tendencies which characterise Byzantine painting just after the iconoclastic crisis. Some of the illustrations (cross with foliage) are wholly iconoclast; another group of images, unfurling in long friezes and superimposed registers, is reminiscent of Cappadocian frescoes; lastly a magnificent sequence of pictures with landscape and depth confronts us with the antiquising school responsible for the 'Paris Psalter'. The same lyricism is found in 'Paris 533' (eleventh century), Coislin 239 (late eleventh century), the fine manuscript belonging to the Greek Orthodox Patriarchate of Jerusalem (No. 14) and the superb 'Paris 550' (twelfth century).

mosaics from the Macedonian era. The noteworthy frescoes in the crypt date from the eleventh century.

Hosios David

Oratory at Salonika. The apse is adorned with fifth century mosaics representing Christ Emmanuel surrounded by symbols of the Evangelists and contemplated by two Old Testament prophets.

Hosios Leukas

(Phocis, near Delphi, Greece). Monastery founded near the end of the tenth century. The church of Hosios ('Blessed') Leukas is magnificently decorated with multicoloured marbles and mosaics on a gold ground (compositions include a 'Pentecost' and an admirable 'Nativity'; there are also 147 isolated figures). Spared both by time and the restorers, the mosaics of Hosios Leukas are the largest ensemble of

Hymn, Acathist

Hymn 'chanted standing', one of the finest pieces of Byzantine melodic poetry, sung on the Saturday of the fifth week in Lent in gratitude to the Virgin for saving Constantinople during the sieges of 626, 678 and 718. In the splendour of its language and depths of mystical feeling, the Acathist is unique in Byzantine literature and has inspired fresco and icon painters throughout the Orthodox world.

I

Icon

The cult of the icons (images), a characteristic feature of the Orthodox confession, in the seventh century seems to have been even more fervent than that of relics. Icons derive from the Graeco-Egyptian funerary portraits which were placed on sarcophagi containing mummies, portraits whose artistic object was not to exalt the body, but to express the presence of a soul.

Prior to the sixth and seventh centuries, icons did not receive the extraordinary veneration they would later attract. Hence the earliest icons, preserved in the monastery on Sinai and in the museums of Kiev and Moscow, still appear to be influenced by fluctuations in the prevailing aesthetic. The sixth century saw in circulation portraits of Christ and the Virgin, declared to be authentic on the basis of apocryphal texts such as the letter of Lentulus to the Roman Senate describing the appearance of the Saviour. It was at this time that acheiropoietos icons started to proliferate.

Iconoclasm

The period 726-843 is dominated by the iconoclast movement (the word means 'icon-breaking'). The iconoclast movement unleashed by the emperor Leo III (717-741) seems to have been directed first against the adoration of the icons, then against certain practices judged idolatrous, for example, the lighting of candles and burning of incense, and finally, at times, even against the cult of the Virgin and the saints, especially the cult of relics. The movement rapidly acquired a political and social significance, since it was aimed at the Church and at monasteries whose growing power rested on possession of the holy icons. The first iconoclastic measure was of Arab origin, the edict of Caliph Yezid (723) ordering the destruction of images in Christian churches and dwellings. Byzantine iconoclasm met with some success in Asia Minor and among the soldiers, who in general came from the eastern provinces of the Empire; but it also met impassioned resistance, above all in Europe, during the anti-iconoclast revolt in Greece of 727. A council summoned at Constantinople in 730 condemned the images, but a counter-council held at Rome in 731 anathematised those who opposed them. Constantine V (740-775) convoked a council at Constantinople in 753 which was followed by measures such as the destruction or white-washing of images, the dispersal of relics, the confiscation of monastic possessions and the secularisation of convents.

Orthodoxy was restored between 787 and 813 during the reign of Irene the Athenian, the cult of images being reinstated by the Seventh Oecumenical Council, held at Nicaea in 787. After Irene's time the quarrel over the images flared up again in the period 813 to 842, especially during the reign of the iconoclast emperor Theophilus (829-842). On his death in 842 his widow Theodora became regent and in 843 restored the cult of the images.

Iconoclast hostility was directed not at all against art as such, but exclusively against religious art and the 'idolatrous' cult to which it gave rise. In place of the sacred iconography, the iconoclasts favoured decoration with plant or animal subjects and above all secular images: images of the emperor and, in his honour, representations of battle and hunting scenes, chariot races and scenes from the hippodrome. Fire and sword thus brought into being a secular art of unprecedented luxury, in which the influence of the art of the Caliphs is discernible.

Iconostasis

Wood-work covered with icons and pierced by three gates which in Orthodox churches separates the altar from the congregation.

Irish Art

The heyday of Irish art was the eighth century. The characteristic feature of Irish miniatures (*Durrow Evangeliary*, *Book of Kells* at Trinity College, Dublin *Evangeliary of St. Gall* at the monastery of St. Gallen), is the reduction of organic

shapes to a simple ornamental sign and the abundance of abstract ornament.

Isidore of Miletus

Sixth century Byzantine architect who in 537 completed the building of St. Sophia at Constantinople, begun in 532 by Anthemius of Tralles. Isidore's nephew Isidore the Younger, reconstructed the dome in 554.

Iviron

Monastery on Mount Athos founded towards the end of the tenth century by three Georgian noblemen. It was destroyed by fire in 1865 and retains none of its original decoration. The miraculous icon of the *Portaitissa Virgin* is preserved in a small chapel. The library contains 1500 manuscripts including an eleventh century gospel, gospels of the thirteenth to fourteenth centuries and the romance of *Barlaam and Joasaph* all richly illustrated.

J

John of Damascus, St.

(673-749) Of Arab origin (his name was Mancour), St. John of Damascus (Damascinus) was the greatest Christian theologian of the eighth century. His principal work *The Source of Knowledge*, translated into Latin in 1151 under the title *De fide orthodox*, enjoyed an immense success. An ardent champion of the icons during the iconoclast crisis, St. John saw the icon as a degree in the ascent towards the divine.

John II Comnenus

John, who has been called 'the greatest of the Comneni', was among the most splendid of the Byzantine emperors; he reigned from 1118 to 1143. Thirty years old at the time of his accession, he had married in 1108 Irene, a Hungarian princess, by whom he had four sons and four daughters. He associated with himself as ruler his eldest son Alexis, who predeceased him. The reign of John II is marked by magnificent religious foundations, the most important being the Pantocrator monastery at Constantinople, to which was attached a hospital, a guest house and an asylum for old men.

John VI Cantacuzenus

(1293-1383) Byzantine emperor from 1341 to 1355, theologian, and one of Byzantium's best historians. After his abdication in 1355 he retired to Vatopedi on Mount Athos, where he wrote most of his works. He also employed himself in copying, and the magnificent manuscript of his minor theological works ('Paris 1241'), with its striking portrait of himself as basileus and monk on the frontispiece, is thought to be an autograph.

John VIII Palaeologus

Byzantine emperor from 1425 to 1448. Faced with an Empire in desperate straits, John, like his predecessors Manuel II and John V, journeyed to the West, and like them agreed to recognise the Papal supremacy, in the hope of obtaining practical help from the Latins: at the Council of Florence in 1439, John VIII, supported by Cardinal Bessarion, and Pope Eugenius IV, proclaimed the union of the Churches, which met all the demands of the Vatican. But the union remained a dead letter; in the East it was resisted by the people, in the West no effort whatsoever was made to defend Christendom against the Turks.

Joshua Roll

Preserved in the Vatican Library. It consists of a parchment, about 10·50 m. long, 31 cm. high, on which the exploits of Joshua are set out in uninterrupted sequence. The date of the work is the

167

Portrait of Justinian
Copied from Ravenna, San Vitale
Chartres, Musée des Beaux-Arts

St. John the Almoner and St. Nicholas
Fresco, 15th cent.
Church of the Kalenic monastery
(Yugoslavia)

subject of controversy (fifth century?
tenth century?). Profoundly penetrated
by Hellenistic traditions, the work perhaps evinces the antiquising taste prevalent
at Constantinople in the tenth century.

Justinian I

The reign of Justinian I, 527-565, marks
the culmination of the first period of
Byzantine history. Thanks to the genius
of his generals, Belisarius and Narses, and
the skill of his diplomats, the eastern
frontier of the Empire was held against
Persian attacks, Africa was reconquered
from the Vandals, part of Spain was
liberated from the Visigoths and the
lengthy resistance of the Ostrogoths in Italy
was broken. The Mediterranean was
once again a Roman lake.

Justinian collected and revised the existing
codes of law and in 534 promulgated his
own great Code, a monument of jurisprudence. An indefatigable builder, Justinian filled the Empire with churches,
fortresses, palaces, aqueducts and giant
cisterns. Most of his constructions survive
only as a memory. Apart from St. Sophia
at Constantinople, only St. Sergius and
St. Irene have escaped ruin.

Kairouan

Town in Tunisia, west of Susa. The famous
Great Mosque contains Byzantine capitals
taken from ruined buildings at Carthage.

Kalenič

(Yugoslavia) Monastery in the wooded
gorge of the river Kalenič. The church was
founded by Bogdan about 1415. It is on
the trefoil plan and its façades are characterised by a polychrome effect. The frescoes
are sentimental and lyrical in inspiration.

Kanakaria

The church of the Kanakaria-Virgin on
Cyprus contains fine seventh century
mosaics.

Kargopol

Town of Northern Russia, on the Onega,
region of Arkhangelsk. The iconostasis of
the Cathedral was adorned with late
fifteenth century icons, now in the Tretia-

kov Gallery at Moscow and the museum at Kiev, which rank among the masterpieces of Russian painting.

Karyes

Capital of Mount Athos. Its principal church, the Protaton, possesses noteworthy frescoes by Panselinos from the beginning of the fourteenth century. Near Karyes is the Rabdouchu chapel, ornamented with fourteenth century frescoes.

Kastoria

(Greece) Kastoria, with an admirable situation on the lake of the same name, still retains its Byzantine character. It possesses seventy-two churches, among them the church of the Taxiarchs (1352), ornamented with frescoes; the metropolitan church, which contains an iconostasis; St.Stephen's an eleventh century church with numerous frescoes; the basilica of the Anargyroi Saints, eleventh century, containing twelfth century paintings. The church of St. Nicholas has fifteenth century frescoes. The Panaghia, Koubelidiki, a church of the late eleventh century, with chequer decoration round the cupola, is a jewel of Byzantine architecture. The Mavriotissa monastery, east of Kastoria, has a chapel ornamented with twelfth century frescoes.

Kavasilas, Nicholas

(Died 1371) His books *On the life of Jesus* and *Interpretation of the Divine Liturgy* are landmarks in the history of Christian mysticism.

Kazanets, Yakov

(Died c. 1660) Icon painter who belonged (about 1648) to the studio of the Palace of Arms at Moscow. In 1652 he directed the band of artists who decorated the Cathedral of the Annunciation in the Kremlin at Moscow with frescoes. He is known to have worked with Ushakov and Kondratev on the decoration to the church of the Virgin of Georgia at Moscow. His icon of *The Annunciation with the Acathist Hymn* (c. 1659, church of the Virgin of Georgia, Moscow) reflects the taste for baroque which was beginning to invade mural and icon painting.

Kievan Russia

In the tenth century, while the West was sunk in the torpors of feudalism, a closed economy and serfdom, a brilliant urban civilisation was developing along the great commercial route which linked Byzantium and the Baltic. In the North, the bourgeois republic of Novgorod, with its satellite towns of Pskov and Staraya Ladoga, and in the Ukraine the towns of Kiev and Tchernigov, were the principal staging posts on this great highway of international traffic. Eventually Russian colonisation created a third centre of urban civilisation in Suzdal' in the North, with the towns of Vladimir-Suzdal' and

Yaroslavl'. These towns formed a federation which gave birth to the first national Russian state. In the eleventh century they issued customaries, codes of private and mercantile law, directly inspired by the law of Justinian and of Rhodes. Kiev, with its white walls, 400 churches and dazzling palaces, to which Persian and Byzantine architects contributed, was the capital and enjoyed great renown in Europe and Asia.

Kirillov

Famous monastery in Northern Russia founded by St. Cyril of the White Lake at the beginning of the fifteenth century.

Koine

Language common to the Greek and Hellenised world of the Hellenistic and Roman periods. By extension: common language, multinational culture.

Kokkinobaphos

Convent close to Constantinople. The homilies of James, monk of Kokkinobaphos, were copied in two identical illustrated manuscripts of the twelfth century, both remarkably well preserved, one at the Bibliothèque Nationale, Paris, the other at the Vatican. The decorations transport the reader to the gate of Paradise and its four rivers, before the throne of God in limbo, where the just await the coming of the Messiah, to the church of the Holy Apostles at Constantinople with its mosaics of the Ascension. The miniatures appear to be inspired by the dramatic representations and pageants enacted in churches. The paintings, which follow one another in a strictly logical order, represent a dramatic action which centres on the Virgin.

Kurbinovo

(Yugoslavia) The church of St. George is ornamented with noteworthy frescoes dating from the late twelfth century. Among the scenes preserved, mention should be made of those representing the great festivals and the Passion, also the angel of the *Annunciation*. The band of artists responsible for this decoration perhaps also worked at the church of the Anargyroi, Kastoria (Greece).

Kusejr' Amra

(Jordan) Ummayad palace of the seventh century, decorated with frescoes of Hellenistic inspiration.

Kydones, Demetrius

(1320-1400) Byzantine philosopher. Through his translations of St. Thomas Aquinas and St. Augustine and his journeys to Italy, where he made a prolonged stay, he contributed to closer intellectual understanding between East and West. His Platonism presages the Renaissance.

Kyriaki, St.

Church on the Greek island of Naxos, whose frescoes date from the iconoclast period (ninth century).

Laodicaea

A large number of the Hellenistic towns founded by the Seleucids in Syria, Asia Minor, Mesopotamia and Persia were given this name.

Lagoudhera

The frescoes in the church of Lagoudhera, Cyprus, rank among the masterpieces of the twelfth century.

Laurentian Library

The Laurentian Library at Florence possesses a rich collection of Byzantine manuscripts.

Lavra

Originally a group of tiny cells whose monks lived in isolation but under the authority of an abbot, assembling in the church to say the offices. When conferred on certain of the great monasteries, the title assigned them first rank in the hierarchy. A surviving example is the Great Lavra on Mount Athos, founded in 963 by St. Athanasius.

Lesnovo

The monastic church was built in 1341 by Oliver, the reigning despot. Frescoes in the interior dating from 1349 represent scenes whose inspiration is often drawn from folk-lore.

171

Detail of a miniature
From a Macedonian monastery
Princeton N.J. University Library

Limburg-on-the-Lahn

(Western Germany) The cathedral treasure contains a reliquary which is among the masterpieces of Byzantine enamel work.

Ljubostinja

(Yugoslavia) Monastery founded by the wife of King Lazarus. Fragments of late fourteenth century mosaics, including numerous portraits, to be seen on the walls of the narthex.

Macedonian Dynasty

Under the Macedonian dynasty (867-1025) Byzantium entered on its 'Second Golden Age'. The offensive was resumed on every front. Southern Italy, Crete, Cyprus, Cilicia, Antioch and northern Syria were each in turn reconquered from the Arabs; the power of Bulgaria, neutralised in 926, was finally demolished after thirty years of warfare (986-1018); when Basil II died in 1025, the territory of the Empire had more than doubled. During the ninth and tenth centuries, while the European continent, ravaged by the Normans and the Magyars fell into a state of semi-barbarism, Byzantium, vis-à-vis with Islam, remained the only truly civilised Christian state. Its resources were vast. It has been reckoned that at the end of the tenth century they amounted to 600 million gold francs.

The economic and political revival of the Empire was accompanied by a splendid intellectual renaissance. The foundations for the revival of classical studies in the ninth century were laid by the circle centring on the patriarch Photios (820-891). In the tenth century the movement broadened in scope, thanks to the imperial patronage of Leo VI, the Wise, and above all of Constantine VII Porphyrogenitus (912-959). In the eleventh century the intelligentsia came to power: in order to keep the military aristocracy in check, Constantine IX Monomachus (1042-1054) entrusted the direction of affairs to a ministry of savants—a unique event in Byzantine annals.

Michael Psellos is the figure who best represents this early Byzantine humanism.

Manasija

(Yugoslavia) Fortified monastery built between 1407 and 1418. The fifteenth century frescoes are in the style of the Morava school.

Manuel II Palaeologus

The emperor Manuel II, who reigned from
1391 to 1425, was not only the protector
of humanists such as Plethon and Bessarion, but also himself one of the last and
most remarkable of Byzantine writers. On
10 December 1399, accompanied by
Boucicault, Marshal of France, Manuel
set out for the West. He went first to Venice
visited several other Italian cities and from
there made his way to Paris and afterwards
to London. He was received everywhere
with honour, and his visit and his personality, which commanded respect, left
their mark. The sojourn of the emperor
and his retinue in the Western capitals
made a great contribution to the circulation of ideas, since it permitted closer
contact between the Byzantine and Western worlds in the early renaissance period.

Marko

(Yugoslavia) Monastery founded in 1371.
The work of two painters can be distinguished. One group is characterised by
its linear technique, the other by its intense
colouring.

Matejič

(Yugoslavia) The monastery church was
built c. 1356. The frescoes are now somewhat effaced and faded, but one can still
see, in addition to portraits of the founders
and anonymous people, illustrations of
entire cycles: the cycle of the great festivals, Christ's miracles and parables, the
Passion, the cycle of the Virgin and the
Acathist Hymn, the acts of the Apostles,
the miracles of the archangel saints, the
cycle of the oecumenical councils, scenes
from the Old Testament, etc.

Mavriotissa

Monastery near Kastoria, Greece, ornamented with fine late twelfth century
frescoes.

Menologion of Basil II

Vatican Library. Eight artists supervised
the teams who collaborated in this work;
contrary to Byzantine custom, their names
are inscribed in the margins.

Meteora

(Greece) The Meteora occupy one of the
most remarkable sites in Greece, formed
like a forest of gigantic rocks hewn into
the shapes of tables, needles and pillars.
It was here that the last monastic republic,
formed prior to the fall of the Empire,
established itself in the fourteenth century.
Between 1356 and 1372 the monk Athanasius founded the convent of the Trans-

173

figuration on the Great Meteor. In 1388 his disciple the hermit-king Ioasaph, son of the Serbian king Symeon, enlarged the monastery. Following their example, other ascetics established wealthy monasteries (twenty-four in all) on the summits of neighbouring rocks.

Mileševo

The monastery was founded c. 1234 by King Vladislav. There are splendid frescoes painted on a yellow ground which was formerly gilded, in imitation of mosaics. The *Resurrection* is one of the finest creations of Byzantine art. The signatures of the authors of these frescoes have recently come to light: Demetrius, George and Theodore. Another group, less talented, painted the frescoes of the narthex, which unlike those in the church have been executed on a blue ground.

Millet, Gabriel

(1867-1953) Eminent French Byzantinist. Principal publications: *L'Art byzantin* in A. Michel, *Histoire de l'Art*, Vols. I and III, Paris; *Recherches sur l'Iconographie de l'Evangile aux XIVe, XVe et XVIe siècles*, Paris 1916; *Monuments byzantins de Mistra*, 1910; *Les Monuments de l'Athos*, 1927; *L'Art byzantin chez les Slavs*, 2 vols. 1930.

Milutin

Serbian king, reigned from 1282 to 1321, founder of several churches and monasteries. His marriage to the Byzantine princess Simonida was an important factor in the development of Byzantine influence in the Serbian kingdom.

Mistra

Mistra, near Sparta in Greece, presents a unique picture of a Byzantine town of the fourteenth and fifteenth centuries, with its tortuous alley-ways running between churches, monasteries and palaces and its two concentric walled enclosures, the whole being protected by a massive fortress built by Guillaume de Villehardouin in 1249. In 1259 Guillaume was taken prisoner by Michael Palaeologus and in 1263, after three years in captivity, surrendered Mistra to the Greeks. After half a century of warfare with the Frankish barons, the Greeks reconquered the greater part of the Peloponnese, which from 1349 formed a kind of appanage, governed under the title of Despot by sons or brothers of the emperors: Manuel Cantacuzenus from 1349 to 1380; his brother Matthew from 1380 to 1383; then, from the house of Palaeologus, Theodore I, 1383-1407, Theodore II, 1407-1443, Constantine, 1443-1448, Demetrius, 1448-1460. While the core of Byzantium was slowly decaying, the despotate of Mistra was bursting with life. It was here, in the twilight of the Byzantine Empire, that Hellenism showed its will to live and to renovate the state. It seems as though Hellenism found in the despotate of Morea a place of refuge from which it was not merely content to maintain its position but looked capable of extending them.

Moldavia-Wallachia

The Moldo-Wallachian principalities of Rumania were formed at the beginning of the fourteenth century. Since the end of the thirteenth century, the Vlachs, vassals of Hungary, had been struggling without success for independence. Their efforts were finally successful in the time of Bassarab I (1310-1352), the 'great Bassarab'. His tomb has been discovered in the princely church of Arges, which one of his successors, Radu Negru, had ornamented with frescoes, with the help of Byzantine masters, about the period 1375-1387. Despite the heroic resistance of Stephen the Great (1457-1504) and Michael the Brave (1593-1601), Rumania fell under the Turkish yoke. But Byzantine influence survived in Wallachian art after the fall of Constantinople and spread to all the arts, though not without some contribution from the Catholic West and the Asiatic East. In Moldavia, whose princes long hesitated between Catholicism and Orthodoxy, Byzantine art made its appearance in iconography and the luxury arts. Very extensive cycles in painting of the post-Byzantine style covered the interior, and even the exterior, of Moldavian churches at Voronets (1547-1550), Homor (1530), Vatra-Moldovitsei (1537) and Suczava (1522).

Monophysitism

Monophysitism, which recognises only the divine nature of Christ, is the opposite of Nestorianism and Arianism which stress his human nature. The ancient East saw Christ only as the emissary of the transcendent being: a man inhabited by the divine spirit (Nestorianism) or a God clothed in human appearance (Monophysitism). Mary gave birth to a man: she is the mother of Christ, not the progenetrix of God. Christ is merely a man, the vehicle of God, or, on the other view, he is a God who did not 'really' suffer on the cross. Hence the Christ of the Council of Chalcedon, at which Orthodoxy imposed its conception of the union 'without mixture' of the two natures, was described by the Monophysites as 'the two-faced idol'. When attempts were made to enforce the decisions of the council, fierce revolts broke out in Egypt and Syria, and it was from this time that the East started to detach itself from the Hellenistic and Byzantine 'koiné'.

Monreale

Sicilian city, close to Palermo. The cathedral was founded in 1174 by the Norman king, William II, shown in a mosaic offering the church to the Virgin. The interior is ornamented with Byzantine or Byzantinising mosaics dating from the twelfth and thirteenth centuries and representing cycles of the Old and New Testaments. It is the largest mosaic ensemble extant, covering 6340 square metres.

Morava, School of the

The school of the Morava marks the last phase in medieval Serbian art. After the disaster of Kossovo in 1389, the Serbs, driven back by the Turks, were forced to retreat towards the north, to Kruševac, which became the last bastion of national independence. It was in the region of the Morava that the great monasteries of Ljubostinija (1402), Ravanica (1381), Manasija (1407-1418) and the church of Kalenič were founded, last off-shoots of Serbian art.

Moscow

The name of Moscow is mentioned for the first time in 1147: as a capital it is thus a late arrival, much less ancient than Kiev or Novgorod. Moscow became the seat of a principality in 1275, but its greatness begins only with Ivan Kalita (1328-1341) 'the first amalgamator of Russian territory' and Dmitri Donskoi, vanquisher of the Tartars (1378-1380). For a long while the princes of Moscow were unable to profit from the decline of the Tartar power. But in the reign of Ivan III (1462-1505) Moscow went over to the offensive again and became the capital of an empire. At the accession of Ivan III, Muscovite terri-

tory had covered scarcely 15,000 square miles. The annexation of the principalities of Yaroslavl', Perm, Rostov, Tver (between 1463 and 1486) and the territory of the city of Novgorod, the destruction of the Tartar Empire in 1502, the acquisitions made by Vassily III between 1506 and 1533, increased the area of the Muscovite Empire to at least 40,000 square miles. Thus, at the time when the Byzantine Empire was fading away, the Muscovite state, whose princes took their name of czar (Caesar) from the basileus, was engaged in what amounted to a holy war with Islam, driving it back from Russia.

Moscow, School of

Muscovite painting of the fourteenth century began by adopting the traditions of Vladimir-Suzdal', though with greater fidelity to the Byzantine canons. The school of Moscow found its fullest expression in the works of Rublev. The icons of the Muscovite school between the time of Rublev and Dionisy represent the classical period of Russian painting.

Mosque of Omar

Large Ummayad mosque at Jerusalem, also known as the Dome of the Rock, built by the Caliph Abd al-Malik in 691. Above the Rock—venerated by Jews, Christians and Muslims—rises up a splendid dome resting on a circle of sixteen columns and pillars, which are surrounded by two galleries on the octagonal plan. This first great Ummayad sanctuary, which later became the temple of the

Templars and progenitor of the churches of this military order, was the work of Greek architects; its walls were decorated by Byzantine mosaicists.

Mount Athos

Northern Greece. It was between the tenth and the twelfth centuries that Mount Athos became the centre of Orthodox monasticism. The earliest convents (the Great Lavra, Vatopedi, Zographou, Philotheou, Xenophon) were Greek houses. About 972-979 three Georgian noblemen built the Iviron monastery, reserved for their fellow-countrymen. At the beginning of the eleventh century, the colony of Amalfi merchants established at Constantinople founded a Benedictine monastery on Mount Athos; in 1030 some Russian ascetics settled in the Esphigmenou monastery; towards the end of the century, Serbian and Bulgar monks founded the convent of St. Paul. The Koutloumoussiou convent owes its Turkish name to a Seljuk prince converted to Christianity, who was its founder in the first half of the twelfth century. From that time the number of foreign elements continued to increase. In 1169 Russian monks established the Russikon. In 1186, Ratsko, son of the Serbian kral Stephen Nemanja, became a monk at Karyes. In 1197, Nemanja himself abdicated and came to join his son on Mount Athos: in 1198 they rebuilt, at their own expense, the Chilandari monastery and populated it with Serbian monks. It was Ratsko, the future St. Sava, who brought Serbia back to Orthodoxy. In the fourteenth century the monastic republic of Athos increased in size through new foundations and acquired considerable influence in Church and State. Several of these foundations were beneficiaries of the generosity of the Serbian kings, then at the height of their power. In 1293 Stephen Milutin carried through a magnificent restoration of Chilandari, which had become a Serbian national sanctuary. In 1447 George Brankovič built the catholicon of the monastery of St. Paul at his own expense. Two Wallachian princes, Bassarab (1352-1364) and John Vladislas (1364-1374) rebuilt the Koutloumoussiou monastery. Other foundations on Athos include the Pantocrator (1363), Dionysiu (1385) and Stavronikita (1542).

The Threnos,
Fresco, 1164
Nerezi church (Yugoslavia)

Narthex

Elongated gallery preceding the naves in a basilica and placed perpendicular to them. It was originally used by catechumens and penitents, people forbidden to be present at the whole of the Mass. Some basilicas had two.

Nea Moni

(Island of Chios, Crete) The convent was founded between 1042 and 1056 by Constantine Monomachus, after the miraculous discovery of an icon by some shepherds. The mosaics of the Nea Moni represent the summit of Byzantine classical art.

Nerezi

(Yugoslavia) The monastery of St. Panteleimon near Nerezi, in the neighbourhood of Skoplje, was founded in 1164 by Prince Alexius Comnenus. The frescoes in the church, executed about the same date, are a landmark in the history of European painting; through the discriminating distribution of the voids and the intense expressivity of the countenances they belong to the majesty of the monumental order, and at the same time show awareness of the nuances and secrets of the life of the psyche. A profound life, at once personal and ideal, radiates from the array of saints and lights their faces with disturbing, phosphorescent gleams. But the new sensibility expresses itself with greatest force in the two immense compositions of *The Descent from the Cross* and the *Threnos.*

Nicaea

One of the largest cities of Asia Minor, founded 316 B.C. Two oecumenical councils were held there, in 325 and 787. When Constantinople was captured by the Crusaders in 1204, Theodore I Lascaris took refuge in Nicaea, where he founded an empire of which Nicaea was to remain the capital until the recapture of Constantinople by Michael Palaeologus in 1261. Nicaea was taken by the Turks in 1326.

Apart from a few fragments of mosaic pavement, nothing now remains of the magnificent Basilica of St. Sophia (reconstructed four times between the fifth century and the age of the Palaeologi). The church of the Dormition was destroyed in 1922.

Nicopolis

(Greece) Some fine pavement mosaics representing hunting scenes, trees, founders' portraits, and geometrical motifs

Georgian Virgin. 16th cent.
Paris, Louvre

in infinite variety have been discovered among the ruins of the basilicas of Doumetios and Alkyson (sixth century).

Niš

(Yugoslavia) Birthplace of Constantine the Great. Rebuilt by Justinian I under the name Naissopolis. A large tomb dating from the end of the fifth century or the beginning of the sixth has recently been discovered. Another tomb contains an ensemble of Byzantine frescoes which date from the late fourth and early fifth centuries and are admirably well preserved.

Nonnos

Alexandrian poet of the fifth century. He wrote a fantastical epic poem on the voyages of Dionysos to the Indies and later, after his conversion, a poetic paraphrase of the Gospel according to St. John.

Novgorod

The city was the earliest of Russian republics, and its political and social regime presents many analogies with that of western communes. From the tenth century Novgorod was one of the most important industrial and mercantile centres of eastern Europe. The city traded with Byzantium, the East, Scandinavia and the Hanseatic towns.

From the thirteenth century Novgorod starts to break away from the Byzantine 'koiné': in both architecture and painting, specifically regional features become more marked. It is true that the oldest Novgorod icons (twelfth century) are still within the Byzantine orbit; on the other hand, it seems that some of these icons should be attributed to the studio of Petrovitch the Greek, mentioned under the year 1196 in the first Novgorod chronicle. But in the thirteenth century, the occupation of Russia by the Tartars and the isolation of Novgorod and Northern Russia favoured the development of a regional school of painting independent of Byzantium. In the Novgorod icons of the thirteenth century 'the purely negative distortions, the clumsiness of the drawing, the passion for vivid but often clashing colours, offer a striking contrast to Greek words, or works which could be described as Greek by adoption'. But these 'stammerings' were a sign that a new language was in gestation, and towards the beginning of the fourteenth century we witness the birth at Novgorod and its satellite town of Pskov, as also in central Russia, of a purely Russian school of painting. The finest Novgorod icons were painted towards the end of the fourteenth century and in the fifteenth century.

O

Ochrid

(Yugoslavia) Formerly a Greek colony, from the end of the third century Ochrid was the seat of a bishopric. Towards the end of the ninth century, Clement and Naum, disciples of Cyril and Methodius, apostles to the Slavs, founded churches and monasteries at Ochrid. In the tenth century the Bulgar tsar Samuel made it the seat of a Slav patriarchate. Recovered by the Byzantines in 1020, Ochrid became the seat of a Greek archbishopric: archbishop Leo (1037-1057) was the donor of the Cathedral of St. Sophia, the most remarkable of the city's monuments. Mention may also be made of the Peribleptos church (thirteenth century frescoes) and the small church of SS. Constantine and Helena (fourteenth century frescoes).

In the neighbourhood of Ochrid are the monastery of St. Erasmus (fourteenth century frescoes), the church of the Ascension at Leskovac (fifteenth century frescoes), the beautiful monastery of St. Naum and the monastery of the Holy Virgin of Zaum (1361, fourteenth century frescoes). The Museum at Ochrid contains a noteworthy collection of icons from the fourteenth to sixteenth centuries.

Octateuch

The first eight books of the Old Testament. Five illustrated examples have come down to us. Another, exceptionally rich and dating from the twelfth century, was probably destroyed in the great fire of Smyrna in 1922.

Okunev, N.

Living Russian Byzantinist, specialising in Serbian art. Principal publications: *Monumenta artis serbicae*, 4 vols., Zagreb-Prague, 1928-1932.

Omorphi Ecclesia

Church at Athens containing fourteenth century frescoes.

Oppian

Poet of the third century A.D. Author of a book on hunting. The Marciana Library at Venice possesses a fine tenth century manuscript of this work. Although inspired by an antique original, now vanished,

180

the miniatures resemble representations of tenth century Byzantine art.

Origen

(184-253) Church Father, born at Alexandria. His work constitutes the earliest original synthesis of Neo-Platonism and Christianity and has exercised a decisive influence over Christian thought.

Pala d'Oro

(St. Mark's, Venice) The Pala is a retable, 3·15 m. by 3·10 m., entirely composed of eighty enamels set in gold and silver mounts picked out with precious stones. The whole repertory and development of Byzantine enamel work can be studied in this monument, unique of its kind. Begun at the end of the eleventh century, refashioned and extended in 1105, augmented after 1204 with spoils from the Pantocrator convent at Constantinople, the retable was completed in the fourteenth century with enamels manufactured at Venice. The eighteen medallions affixed to the lower border of the Pala (imperial hunts, orientalising scenes), belong to the tenth century. The three rows of medallions which frame the Pantocrator date for the most part from the late eleventh and early twelfth centuries. Lastly, the six large enamel plaques representing the festivals

of the Church and the marvellous quadrilobate icon of the archangel Michael which adorns the upper volet of the Pala make it possible for us to imagine what the iconostasis of the Pantocrator convent must have been like: together with the affecting Cross of Cosenza (cathedral treasure), they rank among the masterpieces of Comnene painting.

Palaeologi, Dynasty of

Under the Palaeologi (1261-1453), the Byzantine Empire was the 'sick man' of medieval Europe. Nevertheless, the last two centuries of the Empire, in many ways very deceptive, saw a magnificent intellectual and artistic flowering which is often compared with the Italian Renaissance. The most remarkable features are Hesychast mysticism and the return to the spirit of ancient Hellenism.

Palamas, St. Gregory

(1296-1360) The leading figure of Hesychast mysticism, canonised shortly after his death. His doctrine of the uncreated light which emanates from God and places the Hesychast in communion with Him,

181

is at once a continuation of the Neo-Platonist tradition, dear to the Greek fathers, and the forerunner of modern mysticism.

Palatine Chapel

Palermo. Begun in 1132 by the Norman king Roger II, the Palatine Chapel of the Norman kings was consecrated in 1140. The lower portion of the walls is coated with marble, the upper portion with magnificent Byzantine mosaics of the twelfth century. In the sanctuary there are scenes from the New Testament and lives of the saints, dated 1143. The mosaics of the central nave were executed between 1154 and 1166.

Pammakaristos (Fetiye Djami)

The church of the Pammakaristos-Virgin at Constantinople was a dependency of a convent for women, destroyed in 1586. The south nave of the church terminates in a lateral chapel decorated with important early fourteenth century mosaics. The Byzantine Institute of the University of Boston has recently brought to light a 'Deesis' and several mosaics, whose style recalls that of the Chora church.

Panaghia Chalceon

'Virgin of the blacksmiths', Salonika, Greece. The church was ornamented in 1028 with frescoes whose style is reminiscent of those of St. Sophia, Ochrid.

Panopolis (Chemmis)

In Upper Egypt, known chiefly for its necropolis, which has yielded evidence of a very flourishing tapestry industry, together with numerous funerary portraits, indicative of a wealthy population.

Panselinos, Manuel

According to the eighteenth century *Manual of Painting* by Dionysius of Fourna, Panselinos was the grand master of Byzantine painting in northern Greece. 'He rises above all other painters, ancient and modern, as is attested by his paintings on walls and on wood,' Dionysius declares. For a long time it was thought that he lived during the first half of the sixteenth century. But after the researches of Professor Xyngopoulos of the University of Salonika there can be little doubt that he worked between 1300 and 1320 on the decoration to the Protaton church on Mount Athos.

Pantanassa

(Mistra, Greece) The church of the Pantanassa Virgin (Queen of the World) was built about 1430 by John Frangopoulos and its frescoes are the last manifestations of the art of Mistra. Their style, however, is inferior to that of the other Mistra churches (Peribleptos, Afendiko).

Pantocrator

Epithet denoting Christ in triumph, and in Byzantine art applied specifically to half-length representations of Christ in all his power, situated in the apses or cupolas of churches.

Parigoritissa

(Arta, Greece) The church of the Parigoritissa Virgin (Consolatrix) was built towards the end of the thirteenth century. The mosaics of the dome are remarkable for their bold colouring.

Paris (Parisinus)

Denotes Greek manuscripts preserved in the Bibliothèque Nationale, Paris. The original collection comprises 3900 Greek manuscripts, and 1400 Greek manuscripts which have entered the Library since 1740 are located in the Greek Supplement with one important exception, the Coislin collection (400 manuscripts), which is kept together as a separate group.

Paris Psalter

Ornamented with 14 miniatures, this famous manuscript (Bibliothèque Nationale No. 139) belongs to the category of psalters with frontispieces, known as aristocratic; its full-page pictures illustrate the life of David and the canticles. The sumptuous paintings of this manuscript take us back ten centuries: in its Pompeian landscapes, architectural features, and beautiful allegorical figures we meet again the whole picture of the Alexandrian ideal and notably the plastic quality of the human body, the terrestrial beauty of the faces and the naturalistic treatment of the extension in three dimensions.

Patmos

(Greece) The monastery of St. John the Evangelist was founded by John Christodoulos, monastic reformer in the time of Alexius Comnenus. The monastery possesses numerous icons and a rich library of 330 manuscripts.

Peč

(Yugoslavia) Peč became the holy city of the Orthodox Serbs when archbishop Arsenus I transferred the patriarchate there in the thirteenth century. The patriarchate, in an imposing setting outside the city, has three churches: the church of the Holy Apostles (beginning of the thirteenth century), adorned with magnificent frescoes (1250), some of which are preserved under the dome and at the altar; the frescoes of the fourteenth century are of inferior quality; the church of St. Demetrius, adorned with fine fourteenth century frescoes; the church of the Virgin (fourteenth century), with fourteenth century frescoes and in the narthex, sixteenth century frescoes of lesser importance.

Peribleptos, Mistra

The church of the Peribleptos Virgin at Mistra, in Greece, contains the finest frescoes from the middle of the fourteenth century (1350): for example, the *Dormition of the Virgin*, the *Divine Liturgy* celebrated by Christ and the angels, the *Nativity*, the *Ascension*, the *Transfiguration* and finally episodes from the *Childhood of the Virgin*.

Peribleptos, Ochrid

The church of the Peribleptos-Virgin at Ochrid was decorated with frescoes by Michael and Eutychios about 1295. Recently cleaned, these frescoes (600 square metres) have disclosed the existence of a tendency to realistic and dramatic painting which blossomed in Macedonia and Serbia between 1290 and 1330.

Pisa

In the thirteenth century, Pisa was an important centre of Byzantine influence in Italy, and the Museum there possesses three pieces of Byzantine origin or inspiration: a large painted crucifix (293 × 233 cm.) from the Cathedral of Lucca, a small icon of the archangel Michael, in which the elongated and ethereal shapes prefigure the mystical quality of fourteenth century icons, and a noteworthy Crucifix, perhaps to be attributed to the Greek master Apollonios, mentioned by Vasari. The Greeks who, according to Vasari, presided over the beginning of Italian painting in the thirteenth century, passed on the

Byzantine art of the icon to Giunta Pisano (Assisi, S. Maria of the Angels, Bologna, S. Domenico, etc.), the master of San Francesco (Pisa S. Francesco), Enrico and Ugolino (Pisa S. Martino and S. Pierino) the painters of the history of St. Francis (Perugia, Vanucci Gallery, Assisi, S. Chiaro). The maestro del Bigallo (Florence, Bigallo) Coppo di Marcovaldo (San Gimignano, Duomo), Salerno di Copo (Pistoia, Duomo) and even Vigoroso da Sienna (Perugia, Vanucci Gallery) express in varying degrees the penetration of Byzantine art into Italy, which is also evident in the paintings of the Baptistery of Parma (1260).

Piscator

(1546-1625) Humanist and theologian. Supported the Reformation, partisan of Calvin. Published a German version of the Bible (1601-1604).

Pisides, George

Byzantine poet of the early seventh century, contemporary with Heraclius, whose victorious campaigns against the Persians he celebrates in his poetry.

Plethon

The last half century of Byzantium is characterised by the triumph of humanism and its extension to Italy and the rest of the West. Plethon is the key figure of this movement. Born at Constantinople (1352?-1360?), he withdrew about the year 1410 to Mistra, where he became the director of a school of philosophy; he died at Mistra in 1452 or 1464. In 1475 his remains were removed by Sigismund Malatesta to .Rimini, where they still rest today, in the church of San Francesco.

Poreč

Once a Roman colony, Poreč in Yugoslavia still has the fine Byzantine basilica built by bishop Euphrasius about 535-543. Originally, all the principal parts of the basilica were covered with mosaics. The fragments which still survive evince an art influenced by that of Ravenna. The scenes of the Annunciation and the Visitation are especially fine. The ciborium dates from the thirteenth century; its mosaics were executed by Venetian artists.

Prizren

(Yugoslavia) The church of Our Lady of Ljeviška was built in 1307 by King Milutin. It is ornamented with about 600 square metres of frescoes, considered among the finest of the fourteenth century.

The monastery of St. Saviour, on the hill which dominates the town, has some interesting frescoes from the middle of the fourteenth century.

Proconnesus

Small island of the Propontis, occupied about 670 by the Milesians. Its rich marble quarries were exploited throughout antiquity. In Roman times it took the name Marmara.

Procopius

Byzantine historian of the sixth century, contemporary of Justinian I. His treatise *De aedificiis* gives a list of buildings erected, renovated or ornamented, thanks to the efforts of Justinian and Theodora.

Protaton

The oldest church on Mount Athos, at Karyes. Fine frescoes by Manuel Panselinos, executed between 1290 and 1320.

Psalter of Basil II

Preserved at the Marciana Library, Venice; contains two illuminated pages showing the emperor in triumph and eight pictures representing scenes from the life of David.

Pskov, School of

(U.S.S.R.) Originally a satellite town of Novgorod. The school of Pskov, (14th-15th century), affiliated to that of Novgorod, nevertheless presents features of its own. If the paintings of the Mirozhsky Monastery (1156) are still faithful to Byzantium, the frescoes of the Snetogorsky monastery, close to Pskov, which were executed about 1313, and the icons of Pskov, are characterised by markedly popular traits and by their acid colouring, in which an intense green and orange-red predominate.

Qasr el-Lebia

Town in Libya. In the time of Justinian I given the name Theodorias, in honour of the empress. Excavations conducted in 1959 brought to light the beautiful mosaic pavements of two churches built in 539, through the efforts of Justinian.

Rabulensis, Codex

Syriac Gospel preserved in the Laurentian Library at Florence, illustrated in 586 by the monk Rabula at the convent of Zagba in Mesopotamia. The first twelve leaves contain a calendar. The text is richly decorated. Miniatures are shown in the margins. The Evangelists are pictured beneath arcades; and there are large full-page compositions, framed in the fashion of mosaics with geometrical or inscribed motifs beneath arcades, which represent the Crucifixion, Resurrection, Ascension, Pentecost, the Virgin and Child and the seated Christ.

Ravanica

The Ravanica monastery in Yugoslavia, built about 1381 by Prince Lazar, is

Christ appearing to the Apostles and
The Doubting of Thomas
Mosaic
Ravenna, Sant' Apollinare Nuovo

situated not far from Cuprija (on the Ravaniča). The frescoes inside the church, which are the work of Constantine, represent amongst other things Lazar with his wife Milica and his two sons Stefan and Vuk.

Ravenna

Capital of the emperors of the West from the time of Honorius (384-423) and Galla Placidia to that of Romulus Augustulus (476); capital of the Ostrogothic kingdom of Theodoric the Great (455-526) capital of a Byzantine exarchate from the reconquest of Italy in 540 by Belisarius, general of Justinian I, until 754. Ravenna thus presents a unique example of a Byzantine city of the fifth to seventh centuries. The Mausoleum of Galla Placidia, the Baptistery of the Orthodox, the Baptistery of the Arians, San Apollinare Nuovo, the Archbishop's Chapel, San Vitale and Sant Apollinare in Classe are the principal monuments of Byzantine art as found at Ravenna.

Ravenna, Archbishop's Chapel

Otherwise the chapel of St. Andrew, in the archbishop's palace, Ravenna. A cruciform oratory, preceded by a small vestibule. In the mosaic to the cupola, the medallion bearing the monogram of Christ is borne by four angels surrounded by symbols of the Evangelists. The arches show Christ and male and female saints.

Red Church (Perustica)

Church near Philippopolis (Bulgaria). Its frescoes, dating from the sixth century, are unfortunately becoming increasingly effaced with time.

Ricco, Andrea

We have no precise information about this famous icon painter, one of the best representatives of the Cretan school (his works are dated c. 1600). It seems that he worked in Italy and at the convent of Patmos. Most of his icons are to be found in Italy and are preserved at the Uffizi Gallery in Florence, at the Pinacothek in Turin and at San Giorgio dei Greci, Venice.

Riegl, Alois

(1858-1905) Historian of Austrian art. His *Die spatrömische Kunstindustrie* is the authoritative work in this field.

Romanus the Melode

The greatest Byzantine poet. Born at Emesa (Homs, Syria), he was deacon at one of the churches of Berytos (Beirut) and lived at Constantinople under Justin and Justinian I.

Rome, Byzantine

'Towards the middle of the seventh century,' writes Charles Diehl, 'Rome was a semi-Byzantine city. Since the restoration of imperial authority in the time of Justinian, the East had invaded it as never before. In the period from 606 to 741, the Roman Church was governed successively by thirteen Greek or Syrian Popes.'

It was at this time that the European mission of Byzantium first became manifest. In 668 a Byzantine, Theodore of Tarsus, was consecrated archbishop of Canterbury, and it was on the foundations he laid that the Church in England was to be built up. Theodore was also at the source of the first 'renaissance' of classical studies in Europe. It was in one of the schools he founded that Alcuin, the moving spirit in the Carolingian renaissance, received his education.

Byzantine influence did not fail to make itself felt in the Roman art of this period. If the mosaic of the church of SS. Cosmas and Damian (c. 526-530) was the last composition to manifest the Roman classical tradition, the mosaics of St. Agnes, St. Venantius and the oratory of the Greek Pope John VII (705-707), together with the frescoes in Santa Maria Antiqua bear witness to the Byzantine character imprinted on Roman art between the sixth and eighth centuries.

Next there was the influx to Rome of a large number of artists fleeing the iconoclast persecution; Rome, together with the monastery of Studius, formed the chief centre of resistance to iconoclasm, as a fresh sequence of monuments bears witness; the frescoes of SS. Nereus and Achilles (795-816), the mosaics of St. Prassede and Santa Maria-in-Domenica (817-824) and of St. Cecilia and St. Mark (827-844). A certain unease can be sensed in these paintings, whose value is uneven: they show a tendency towards schematisation for which there is scarcely any equivalent in the Byzantine world. It is perhaps permissible to regard this as an early indication of northern stylisation, a first quickening of the nascent Romanesque spirit.

Rossanensis (see under Codex)

Rublev, St. Andrey

(c. 1370-1430) The greatest painter of medieval Russia. He probably served his apprenticeship in the icon workshop of the Troitse monastery at Zagorsk. In 1400 he was working at Zvenigorod. In 1405 he collaborated in the decoration to the Cathedral of the Dormition in the Moscow Kremlin. In 1408, with Daniil Chyorny, he decorated the Cathedral of the Dormition at Vladimir. Either about 1411 or 1422, he decorated the Troitse church at the monastery of Zagorsk, and it was there he painted his masterpiece, the famous icon of *The Trinity*. Rublev was beatified by the Russian Church. His works are assembled at the Andrey Rublev Museum, Moscow.

Sacred Palace

The Sacred Palace of Constantinople, built by Constantine the Great, contained within the same enclosure the private apartments of the imperial family (palace of Daphne) and, separated from them by walls, a fabulous complex of audience rooms, churches, oratories, whose numbers increased over the centuries and which were resplendent with marble, mosaics, and figured and gold-embroidered fabrics. The architecture of the great halls, the Tribunal of the Nineteen Couches, the Chrysotriclinium built by Justin II (565-578), the long gallery of Justinian II (685-695, 705-711), resembled that of churches in their ground plans, imposing proportions, vaults and magnificent decoration. In 1081 Alexius Comnenus abandoned the Sacred Palace and removed his court to the more congenial and comfortable quarters of the Blachernae palace.

The sack of 1204 was a fatal blow to the Sacred Palace, and the neglect of the Crusaders, who occupied it for sixteen years, completed its ruin. In the fourteenth century the palace became a grazing ground and a cemetery for the poor was also established there. The only surviving remnants of its past marvels are the pavements now contained in the Museum of Mosaics.

St. Agnes outside the Walls, Rome

A seventh century Byzantine mosaic in the apse.

St. Catherine, monastery of

The monastic colony of Mount Sinai, which occupies so prominent a place in medieval history, was first set on a regular basis in the sixth century, when Justinian at great expense built a monastery dedicated to the Virgin. From the twelfth century under the patronage of St. Catherine, the convent possesses an admirable mosaic, thanks to the liberality of Justinian I. The chapel of St. James contains frescoes of the thirteenth century. The convent of Sinai is a veritable museum of Byzantine art. Its library contains 2291 Greek manuscripts, 600 Arabic, 257 Syriac, 88 Georgian, 40 Slavonic and 6 Ethiopian. The convent also possesses a very important collection of icons (over two thousand, representative of all epochs of Byzantine painting from the fifth century).

St. Demetrius, Salonika

The basilica of St. Demetrius, dating from the fifth century, was the finest in Salonika. Destroyed in the terrible fire which ravaged the town in 1917, it has been rebuilt, partly from fragments found among the ruins and partly from entirely new

189

materials. The mosaics which adorned the interior were almost completely destroyed in the fire. Those that remain in the sanctuary and the crypt spread over several centuries, from the fifth to the seventh.

St. George, Naxos, Greece

Chapel on the island of Naxos, with noteworthy antiquising frescoes of the ninth century.

St. George, Salonika

Formerly a Roman rotunda which has by turns served as Christian church, Turkish mosque, Christian church and museum. Together with the mosaics of the mausoleum of Galla Placidia, the mosaics of St. George's are indisputably the masterpieces of fifth century painting.

St. Irene

The church of St. Irene, Constantinople, was one of the first Christian sanctuaries of Byzantium. Embellished by Constantine, it was rebuilt by Justinian in 546. Nothing survives of its decoration, apart from a large cross in the eastern apse, which must have been executed in the iconoclast period.

By a cruel stroke of irony, the church of St. Irene was converted into a museum of Ottoman artillery.

St. John of Ephesus

The basilica of St. John—one of the most magnificent sanctuaries built by Justinian I—was built on the site of the apostle's tomb. Converted into a mosque in 1330, the sanctuary was destroyed when the city was captured by the troops of Tamburlaine.

St. John of Studius

The convent of Studius was the largest in Constantinople and for centuries played a decisive role in the religious life of the Orthodox world. The monastic church of St. John the Baptist—one of the most beautiful churches in the capital—is now a ruin. It is known that the walls were once decorated with mosaics, and there are still remnants of a fine mosaic pavement.

St. Mark, Venice

Completed between 1071 and 1095, the five-domed church of St. Mark at Venice follows the general plan of the Holy Apostles church, Constantinople. The marble decoration (13th-15th century) and the mosaics (4,000 square metres, 12th-17th century) make the church so glorious an ensemble that it was given the name 'Chiesa d'Oro'.

The three cupolas with representations of the *Ascension*, *Pentecost* and *Christ Emmanuel* date from the twelfth century. Like the mosaics in the apse and in the niche of the centre portal, as also the scenes from the life of Christ and the Virgin (13th century), they are a local reflection of the Byzantine painting of the Comnene period. On the other hand, the mosaics of the narthex (13th century) seem to be inspired by sixth century miniatures, such as those in the Cotton Bible. The *Madonna* of the St. Zeno chapel (13th century) and the *Crucifixion* of the baptistery (14th century) give the impression of being a last effort by the Byzantine school, but as a whole the remainder of the decoration to St. Mark's represents a more or less provincial synthesis of Byzantine and late Roman Western art. Behind the altar is the gold retable known as the 'Pala d'Oro'. In the left transept is displayed the 'Nikopeia Virgin' (Our Lady of Victories), a Byzantine icon brought from Constantinople in 1204.

The treasure contains a very important collection of Byzantine works of art (300 pieces of goldsmiths' work, 110 reliquaries) and a few icons, including the admirable icon in enamel of the archangel Michael.

St. Michael (with-the-Roof-of-Gold), Kiev

Known as 'roof of gold' because of its gilded domes; decorated with mosaics in the purest Comnene style.

St. Nicholas Orphanou, Salonika, Greece

The frescoes, recently cleaned, are among the finest productions of Byzantine painting of the fourteenth century.

St. Paul, Mount Athos

Monastery founded in the eleventh century by Serbs and Bulgars. Frescoes by Theophanes of Crete (1355) in the chapel of St. George. The monastic library contains 250 manuscripts.

St. Sophia, Constantinople

St. Sophia was built by Justinian to replace an earlier basilica, destroyed in 532. He entrusted the task to Anthemius of Tralles and Isidore of Miletus, and placed enormous funds at their disposal. The work was completed within the astonishingly short space of five years and six months (532-537).

Preceded by a huge narthex, the church proper occupies an area of 7000 square metres, being 77 m. long by 71 m. 70 broad. The existing dome, rebuilt in 562, rises 54 m. above the ground with a diameter of 31 m., surpassing in height that of the Pantheon at Rome (43 m.) and the vaults of Gothic cathedrals.

Communion of the Apostles
Christ officiating (detail) 11th cent.
Ochrid (Yugoslavia), St. Sophia

Today the floor is covered with great marble flagstones. In the time of Justinian, the Great Church was adorned with a pavement of mosaics combined with polychrome marbles, a description of which has come down to us. The lower portion of the walls was ornamented with marble facings, carefully polished. Above these marbles, the walls, vaults, dome and pendentives were decorated entirely with mosaics. These were either destroyed or covered with plaster when the church was converted into a mosque in 1453. The Byzantine Institute of America has removed the plaster and restored a large number of mosaics from the time of Justinian, but most of the mosaics are of post-iconoclast date, between the middle of the ninth and the end of the twelfth centuries. It is possible that other mosaics survive in the dome, beneath the Turkish repaint. St. Sophia was used as a mosque until 1935. Today it is a museum.

St. Sophia, Kiev

The Cathedral of St. Sophia at Kiev—the doyen of Russian churches—was built between 1017 and 1037 by Yaroslav the Wise, in commemoration of a victory over the Petchenegs. It consisted of five naves, later increased to nine, leading up to five apses and surmounted by thirteen cupolas tiered in pyramid fashion. At either end of the façade were two round towers containing spiral staircases which gave access to the tribunes and the palace adjacent to the church. These staircases were decorated with frescoes representing secular subjects drawn from the life of the Byzantine court and festivals held

192

in the hippodrome at Constantinople. The mosaics of St. Sophia lie stylistically between those of Hosios Leukas and of Daphni.

St. Sophia, Novgorod

Cathedral, built between 1045 and 1052, containing a few remnants of twelfth century frescoes.

St. Sophia, Ochrid, Yugoslavia

Cathedral, which contains the most important Byzantine frescoes from the early eleventh century. In the lower range, saints and patriarchs of East and West. In the vault an *Ascension*, surrounded by a splendid frieze of prostrate angels with veiled hands.

St. Sophia, Salonika, Greece

The date of construction is disputed (sixth to seventh century). In the apse, remnants of a mosaic cross, dating from the iconoclast period, which was replaced about 886 by a monumental mosaic representing the *Virgin and Child*. In the

Adoration of the Magi
Mosaic
Rome, Santa Maria Maggiore

cupola, admirable mosaic decoration of the same period, representing the *Ascension*.

St. Sophia, Trebizond

Church of St. Sophia, the best preserved of the Byzantine monuments at Trebizond; probably built shortly after the accession of the Comnene dynasty of Trebizond in 1204. Enlarged and ornamented with frescoes about 1260. These frescoes, recently cleaned, rank among the finest creations of thirteenth century Byzantine painting.

St. Venantius, Rome

Chapel, baptistery of St. John Lateran. The mosaic in the apse (c. 640) represents the Virgin, Christ and saints, some of whom wear the costume of Byzantine dignitaries.

San Angelo in Formis, Italy

The basilica of San Angelo, near Capua, contains Romano-Byzantine frescoes of the eleventh to twelfth century.

Santa Costanza

(Rome) A circular edifice, erected at the beginning of the fourth century. In the vaults of the ambulatory are fourth century mosaics. In the small apses, mosaics of the fifth to seventh centuries.

Santa Maria Antiqua

(Rome) The church was restored and decorated with frescoes through the efforts of the Greek Pope John VII (705-707) and embellished by Popes Zacharias (741-752) and Paul I (757-767). It now possesses a very remarkable sequence of several layers of superimposed frescoes from the sixth to tenth centuries. The antiquising frescoes of the presbytery date from the time of John VII; the frescoes in the chapel of SS. Julitta and Quiricus, executed in the time of Pope Zacharias, belong to the Byzantinising art of the region.

Santa Maria in Cosmedin or in Schola Graeca

(Rome) The sacristy of the church has a fragment of mosaic representing the adoration of the Magi (705-7), formerly in the oratory of John VII at St. Peter's.

Santa Maria Maggiore, Rome

Also known as Santa Maria delle Neve, the basilica was built by Pope Liberius

(352-366); it was remodelled and ornamented with mosaics through the efforts of Pope Sixtus III (432-440), immediately after the Council of Ephesus had affirmed the dogma of Mary's divine maternity. The mosaics of the central nave, barely visible in the place they occupy, belong stylistically to the tradition of Graeco-Roman painting. The mosaics of the triumphal arch are less fine than those of the nave, but give a more precise indication of the path later taken by this art.

In the Pauline chapel, a noteworthy Byzantine icon of the Virgin (ninth century?) is displayed on a costly altar decorated with lapis lazuli and agates.

Sant' Apollinare in Classe

The basilica of Sant' Apollinare in Classe at Ravenna was consecrated in 549. The date of the splendid mosaics which cover the triumphal arch is disputed. At all events, their style and iconography permit us to ascribe them to the middle of the sixth century. The decoration of the conch of the apse belongs to the same period, and is probably a symbolic representation of the Transfiguration. On the other hand, the two panels at the sides of the apse were composed a century later (668-685?). These mosaics have been more or less destroyed and as they appear today have been almost wholly remade.

Sant' Apollinare Nuovo

The basilica at Ravenna now known as Sant' Apollinare Nuovo was built between

493 and 526 by the Ostrogothic king Theodoric, and was originally destined for Arian worship. After the reconquest of Ravenna by the Byzantines, archbishop Agnellus converted the basilica to orthodox worship, between 556 and 565.

The interior is divided into three naves by two rows of twelve columns in Greek marble, sent either from Greece or Constantinople. The mosaic decorations can be divided into three horizontal zones.

The topmost zone comprises a sequence of decorative panels alternating with twenty-six compositions illustrating on the left wall Christ's miracles and on the right the Passion; this is the most ancient Gospel cycle to have come down to us. We find here again the iconographical duality, Hellenistic and Oriental, of early Christian art.

The second zone of mosaics develops in the intervals between the windows and presents thirty-six figures of prophets, apostles and saints, seen full face. These parts of the decoration to the church belong definitely to the time of Theodoric. But the mosaics of the bottom zone (trains of martyrs and virgins preceded by the three Magi) were executed after the Byzan-

194

St. Maximian
6th cent. Detail, apse mosaic
Ravenna, San Vitale

tine reconquest. A fragment of mosaic representing a personage crowned with a diadem and wearing a nimbus was long thought to be a portrait of Justinian. Today it is thought more likely to be a portrait of King Theodoric.

San Vitale, Ravenna

The church was begun by bishop Ecclesius some time after his return from a journey to Byzantium in 525, in company with Pope John. It was finished about 547-548. The choir is adorned with marvellous mosaics executed between 525 and 547. Two distinct bands of painters collaborated in them. One group, nourished on Hellenistic-Roman naturalism, has executed on the lateral walls of the choir *Scenes from the Life of Moses*, the *Visitation of Abraham* the *Sacrifice of Abel and of Melchizedek*

and the *Evangelists*. These are accompanied by a complicated decoration of arabesques, acanthus and horns of plenty, in the midst of which can be seen a whole host of birds and beasts, reminiscent of the ornamental style of the fifth century. Another band of artists, however, has decorated the apse and apsidal vault of the church in the hieratic style of the sixth century. In the conch the young and beardless Christ is seated on the orb of the world, surrounded by angels and saints. On either side, two celebrated compositions show on the left Justininian and on the right Theodora, followed by their court, and bearing presents for the church. The mosaics of San Vitale are beyond any doubt the masterpiece of Byzantine painting from the century of Justinian.

Savin

Family of icon painters (late 16th-first quarter of 17th centuries) belonging to the school of Stroganov. Ustoma Savin (end of 16th century) worked for the Stroganovs and towards the end of his life was made 'master of the Czar's workshop'. The *Virgin of Bogoliubsk* and the triptych of the *Metropolitan Peter*, which is now in the Tretiakov Gallery at Moscow, may be mentioned as among his finest icons. The icons of his son Nazair (died 1621) are distinguished for their studied drawing and great wealth of ornament. His brother Nicephorus was the rival and colleague of Prokop Tchirin, with whom he painted a *Deesis*, now at the Russian Museum, Leningrad.

195

Seleucia

Numerous Hellenistic towns in Aria Minor, Syria, Mesopotamia and Iran were given the name Seleucia in honour of the Seleucid kings. Seleucus and his dynasty dreamed of Hellenising Asia; their Empire was to have as its base a vast network of more or less Greek cities and colonies. The work of urbanisation accomplished by the Seleucids is one of the most astonishing feats of history.

Sergius of Radonezh

(1314-1393) St. Sergius of Radonezh exerted a capital influence over the spiritual and moral life of ancient Russia. Born of an important Boyar family, whose name, however, is unknown, he withdrew about 1340 to the banks of the little river Kantchoura, north of Moscow. There he built a little cell and church out of wood, which was to become the nucleus of the Troitse-Sergieva lavra, the most famous of all Russian convents. His life continued to be one of manual labour and renunciation: wooden torches lit the church for the morning and evening offices, the priest's books were written on birch bark. After Sergius' friend and protector, the metropolitan Alexis, had taken charge of the affairs of the Muscovite principality, the small convent of the Troitse became the chief religious centre of the country. Dmitri Donskoi made a pilgrimage to the Troitse to receive the saint's blessing before his decisive victory over the Tartars at Kulikovo in 1380.

Sinai, Codex Sinaiticus

Denotes manuscripts preserved in the library of the convent of St. Catherine on Mount Sinai.

Skoplje

(Yugoslavia) The museum has a noteworthy collection of icons of the thirteenth to fifteenth centuries from the churches of Ochrid.

Soghanli, Cappadocia

After Göreme, the region in Cappadocia with the most important group of rock churches. The most important is the church of St. Barbara, which has tenth and eleventh century frescoes.

Solovetski

Celebrated monastery on an island in the White Sea, founded in the fourteenth century by St. Zosimus and St. Sabatios, disciples of St. Sergius. A charming icon from the beginning of the seventeenth century (Tretiakov Gallery) shows the two saints and the white churches which fill the island, surrounded by waves and blessed by Christ, who appears in a richly ornamented aureole.

Sopočani, Yugoslavia

Monastery near the town of Novipazas, built by King Uros I (1242-1276). Ravaged

Dormition of the Virgin (detail)
Apostles, Fresco, 1260-1265
Church of Sopočani monastery (Serbia)

in 1689, it has just been restored. Most of the frescoes date from the middle of the thirteenth century; they rank among the masterpieces of European art.

Split

(Yugoslavia) The palace of Diocletian (c. 295 A.D.); the magnificent structure in which the emperor installed himself after the burning of his palace at Nicomedia formed the nucleus of the town of Split.

Staro Nagoricino

(Yugoslavia) Monastery, above the village of the same name, founded in 1314 by King Milutin. The frescoes to the interior are the work of the sons of Astrapas, Michael and Eutychios, who decorated a large number of monuments in Serbia and Macedonia.

Stavronikita, convent of

On Mount Athos, founded 1542. Here is kept the miniature mosaic of *St. Nicholas* (13th-15th century) and in the monastic library manuscripts from the eleventh and twelfth centuries, Theophanes of Crete decorated the catholicon with frescoes (c. 1546). The convent has numerous icons apart from the mosaic *St. Nicholas*. The library contains 170 manuscripts.

Stobi

(Yugoslavia) In the third century a defence post, in the fourth Stobi became the capital of Macedonia Secunda. Excavations have brought to light a Greek theatre, a basilica dating certainly from the sixth century and the so-called Parthenius palace, whose pavements are adorned with mosaics.

Stroganov

Wealthy merchants of Novgorod who resided in the late sixteenth and early seventeenth century at Solvytchegodsk, in northern Russia, where they had immense landed estates on both sides of the Urals.

Stroganov, School of

The group of icon painters who worked for this family towards the end of the sixteenth and in the first half of the seventeenth century used to be known by this

197

name. But most of these painters—Tchirin, Kassanets, the Savins, Borojain—were employed even more regularly by the Czar and his immediate entourage. Their works have no resemblance in manner, but nevertheless possess certain traits in common: reduced dimensions, studied and elegant poses, a colouring dominated by half-tones and golds.

Studenica

(Yugoslavia) The largest and wealthiest monastery of Serbia, standing in the valley of the same name.

The church of the Holy Virgin, completed about 1191, is Stephen Nemanja's finest monument. The interior is adorned with pictures dating from 1209, including a poignant crucifixion. Some of the decoration to the apse belongs to the same period. The frescoes of the chapels of the exonarthex date from 1234. Two other churches are to be found in the precincts of the monastery: the church of the King, built by Milutin in 1314 and containing noteworthy frescoes illustrating the *Life of the Virgin*; and the church of St. Nicholas, which contains fragments of a thirteenth century fresco.

Suzdal'

Vladimir-Suzdal' was at its height during the second half of the twelfth century and the first third of the thirteenth, and is characterised by great fidelity to the Byzantine spirit.

In the twelfth century, Kiev ceased to be an important artistic centre, ravaged as it was by disputes between the princes and the invasions of nomadic Turks and Mongols; the centre of Russian life was displaced towards the north, to Novgorod, its satellite town Pskov and the towns of Suzdal' (Vladimir, Suzdal', Yaroslavl', etc.) sheltered from the nomads by their impenetrable forests. At Novgorod and in Suzdal' one can already see the originality of the Russian genius unfolding, manifest in the bulbous shape given to cupolas and above all in the marvellous sculpture-embroideries of the Suzdal' churches. But while sculpture presents an original synthesis of Armenian, Romanesque and Scandinavian elements, the painting remains entirely Byzantine. Unfortunately the frescoes of Nereditsi (1199) were totally destroyed during the last war. The Mirozhsky convent at Pskov preserves a cycle of frescoes dating from 1156. Like those of the church at Arkazhi (1189), they offer us a provincial, if not rustic, version of the Byzantine painting of the twelfth century. The frescoes of the Cathedral of Vladimir (1189) are vastly superior in style.

Symeon

The writings of Symeon of Salonika (fourteenth century) contain a mystical and symbolical interpretation of the structure of the Church.

Tabor, Mount

The scene of Christ's Transfiguration, as described by Matthew, Luke and Mark. In Byzantine iconography the Christ appears in a circular glory between Elijah and Moses. Peter, John and James turn

aside or fall backwards. 'The solitude, the height, the calm, the dizzying transfiguration, the bursting light, the spreading cloud; all these things filled them with dread, they fell, seized and prostrated with fear.' (St. John Chrystostom.)

Tchirin, Prokop

Died about 1621-1623. The leading light of what used to be called the 'Stroganov school'; his name figures under the year 1620 in the list of painters working for the Czar in the studio of the Palace of Arms, Moscow. His style is dominated by a striving after costly effect and a passion for ornamentation set off by goldsmiths' work.

Theodore the Studite, St.

(759-826) Monk, writer and Byzantine politician; reformer of orthodox monasticism.

Theodore II Lascaris

(1222-1258) Theodore II Ducas Lascaris, was Byzantine emperor from 1254 to 1258. Regarded as the incarnation of the Platonic ideal of the philosopher-king, Theodore II was as learned in philosophy as he was in mathematics and physics. His discourses are among the finest pieces of Byzantine rhetoric.

Theodore Metochites

(1260-1332) Theodore Metochites, first minister of Adronicus II, philosopher, astronomer and musicologist, represents the Byzantine humanism of the thirteenth and fourteenth centuries. He was the donor of the mosaics to the Chora church at Constantinople and had his own likeness represented on the tympanum of the Royal entry, which gives access to the church, in the rich costume of grand logothete, offering to Christ the model of the church he had had restored.

Theophanes of Crete

Leader of the Cretan School (16th century) began his career at Meteora where he decorated the convent of St. Nicolas-Anapavsa with frescoes, in 1527. His masterpiece is the decoration of the

199

catholicon (and probably the refectory) of the Great Lavra of Mount Athos in 1535. Helped by his son, Symeon, Theophanes also decorated the catholicon and refectory of the Stavronikita convent with frescoes. His son Neophytus painted the frescoes in the metropolis of Kalambaka (Thessaly) in 1573. One is inclined to attribute to Theophanes the great icons dating from 1542 which ornamented the iconostasis of the Protaton church.

Theophanes the Greek

Theophanes the Greek, the Russian El Greco, started his career at Constantinople. Around the year 1360, he visited in turn Feodosia, Nizhniy-Novgorod and Novgorod. According to the chronicle, he decorated forty churches and a considerable number of palaces before coming to Moscow in 1405, where he decorated the church of the Nativity and the Virgin, and the Cathedral of the Annunciation at the Kremlin, as also the palace of Prince Andrew, nephew of Ivan Kalita. Today all that survive are the frescoes in the church of the Transfiguration (1376) at Novgorod and the fine icons to the iconostasis of the Cathedral of the Annunciation in the Kremlin.

Torcello

The basilica of Torcello, near Venice, has admirable mosaics of the eleventh and twelfth centuries.

Transfiguration, Church of, Novgorod.

The frescoes of the church of the Transfiguration, executed about 1378 by Theophanes the Greek, are among the most original creations of Byzantine painting. The full-length portraits of patriarchs and of other biblical figures, the Pantocrator treated as a mask, the *Visitation of Abraham*, the figures of apostles and stylite saints are rendered in a manner at once expressionist and impressionist, which recalls the boldest ventures of the Byzantine miniaturists of the thirteenth to fourteenth centuries.

Trebizond

(Turkey) Formerly Trapezus, Trebizond enjoyed great prosperity during the Byzantine era. Between 1204 and 1461 it was the capital of an independent Greek empire and one of the main intellectual centres of Hellenism. Among the numerous churches of Trebizond may be mentioned St. Sophia (13th century), the Virgin-Theoskepastos (14th century frescoes), the Virgin-Chrysokephalos, St. Eugenius, St. Sava (frescoes dated 1411).
Forty kilometres south-south-east of Trebizond, at a height of 1200 m. stands the monastery of the Virgin of Sumela, one of the high places of Orthodoxy. Now abandoned, the monastery contains frescoes from the fourteenth century.

Troitse-Sergiev Monastery

(U.S.S.R.) The most famous of the Russian monasteries, founded by St. Sergius of Radonezh. The Troitse Cathedral was built by St. Nikon, successor of St. Sergius, about 1422. Several of the icons on the iconostasis of the cathedral are the work of Andrey Rublev; the finest, that of the Trinity, now in the Tretiakov Gallery, is indisputably the most elevated expression of orthodox spirituality.

Tver

(U.S.S.R.) Town on the Volga, in the fourteenth and fifteenth centuries the centre of a school of icon painters whose importance Soviet researchers are just beginning to appreciate. To this forgotten school is ascribed the fine *Blue Dormition* (15th century), in the Tretiakov Gallery, Moscow.

Tzanes, Emmanuel

Important icon painter of the Cretan school. Left Crete about 1649(?); resided at Corfu until 1659, at which date he left for Venice, where he worked until his death in 1690.

Ummayads

Arab dynasty which reigned at Damascus from 661 to 750. Dethroned by the Abbasids, the dynasty removed to Spain and founded the caliphate of Cordova (756-1031). The most striking feature of Ummayad rule is the place held under it by Syrian Christians. The caliphs retained the Byzantine administration, and the highest offices of state were occupied by Christians. In the same way, Greek remained the only language to figure in the registers kept by the state, and the current coinage, imitated from Byzantine types, never ceased to carry the Byzantine cross. The Ummayad Empire only started to become distinctively Arab in the time of the Caliph Abd al-Malik, who ruled from 685 to 705.

Ushakov, Simon Fedorovitch

(1626-1686) The last great painter of old Russia. Icon painter, engraver, frescoist, theorist about painting, in 1664 Ushakov was appointed accredited master of the royal painting studio established at the Palace of Arms, Moscow. His finest icons were executed for the church of the Troitse-Nikitniki (Moscow), for the monasteries of Novodevitchi (Moscow) and the Troitse-Sergieva lavra at Zagorsk. Ushakov attempted to re-establish the art of the icon on its traditional foundations, whilst at the same time seeking to assimilate certain elements from western painting.

Vatican, Library of

Founded by Pope Nicholas V in the fifteenth century, the Vatican Library possesses, amongst other things, 4500 Greek manuscripts.

Vatopedi

The second great monastery on Mount Athos. The church (founded towards the end of the tenth century) is adorned with mosaics of the eleventh and twelfth centuries and with frescoes of the fourteenth. The chapel of St. Demetrius contains noteworthy icons from the thirteenth to fifteenth centuries. The monastic library. possesses 1536 manuscripts,

Victoria and Albert Museum, London

Rich in Byzantine objects, including an Epitaphios of 1407 and an exquisite mosaic icon of the Annunciation, fourteenth century.

Vienna Genesis

Several painters had a hand in the forty-eight miniatures of this 'Genesis' preserved in the National Library at Vienna; their sources seem to have been two-fold, Alexandrian and popular. In general their style is Hellenistic: it is only in isolated elements that an oriental influence is discernible. An Alexandrian naturalism impregnates most of the miniatures: landscape occupies an important place, the figures are treated in the antique style, the plasticity of the bodies and the third dimension are respected; on the other hand, some miniatures have an anecdotal and popular character which recalls the Coptic manner.

Villehardouin

French family, originally from Champagne, one branch of which won fame in the East in the thirteenth century as head of the principality of Achaea.

Vladimir

The city of Vladimir was the capital of Suzdal', a principality which reached its apogee under Prince Vsevolod (1176-1212). The church of St. Dmitri (1195) is ornamented with admirable Byzantine frescoes of the twelfth century. The Cathedral of the Dormition (1158) is ornamented with frescoes by Andrey Rublev and Daniil Chyorny (1408).

Vladimir, Our Lady of

Virgin of tenderness, the most famous of all the icons and the masterpiece of Byzantine classical art. Brought from Constantinople first to Kiev, then to Vladimir (1155) and finally in 1395 to Moscow, where it remained until the revolution in the Cathedral of the Dormition in the Kremlin. Now in the Tretiakov Gallery. Painted in distemper on a panel of limewood, the icon ($78 \times 54 \cdot 6$ cm.) has been frequently repainted and today bears the marks of these successive 'restorations'.

Volotovo

(U.S.S.R.) The church of the Dormition at Volotovo, close to Novgorod, contains frescoes (c. 1380) which surpass in boldness the ventures of Theophanes the Greek.

Weitzmann, Kurt

Eminent living Byzantinist. Chief publications: *Die byzantinische Buchmalerei des 9 und 10 Jahrhunderts* (Berlin 1935); *Illustrations in Roll and Codex* (Princeton, 1947); *Greek Mythology in Byzantine Art* (Princeton 1951).

Xenophon, Mount Athos

Convent founded at the end of the tenth century by the monk Xenophon. The chapel of St. George contains frescoes of the Cretan school. In the catholicon, frescoes by Antonios (1544), pupil of Theophanes of Crete. The paintings of the narthex (Cretan school) date from 1545. In the refectory, fresco of the *Last Judgment*.

Yaroslavl'

Town of Suzdal', north of Moscow. In the thirteenth century Yaroslavl' possessed a noteworthy school of icon painters. To this school, which followed Byzantine models very closely, should be attributed the splendid *Virgin Orans* and *Virgin*, now in the Tretiakov Gallery. Yaroslavl' again became a very active artistic centre in the seventeenth century (frescoes to the churches of the Prophet Elijah, 1650; St. John Chrystostom; St. John the Baptist).

Zeuxippos, Bath of

The baths of Zeuxippos at Constantinople were a veritable museum of antique art. Book II of the *Palatine Anthology* contains poems inspired by the statues in these baths.

Zica, Yugoslavia

The archiepiscopal church of St. Saviour, recently restored, was built about 1220. In the interior, the frescoes of the transept date from the thirteenth century, the rest from the time of the first restoration of the monastery, perhaps the beginning of the fourteenth century, and probably represent the work of Eutychios and Michael.

Ziza, Castle of

Palermo. A magnificent construction in the Arabo-Norman style, begun in 1154 by the Norman king, William I, and ornamented with Byzantine mosaics of oriental inspiration.

Zorzis

Painter of the Cretan school; c. 1547 decorated with frescoes the church of the Dionysiou convent on Mount Athos.

Printed in Italy.

Table of Illustrations

205

206

Bibliography

J. Beckwith: *The Art of Constantinople*, 1961.

G. P. Bognetti, G. Chierici, A. de Capitani d'Arzago: *Santa Maria di Castelseprio*, Milan 1948.

O. M. Dalton: *Byzantine Art and Archaeology*, Oxford 1911 (reissued 1961).

O. M. Dalton: *East Christian Art*, Oxford 1925.

C. Diehl: *Manuel d'Art byzantin*, 2 vols., Paris 1925-26.

J. Ebersolt: *La Miniature byzantine*, Paris 1926.

André Grabar: *La Peinture byzantine*, Geneva 1953; English translation *Byzantine Painting*, translated by Stuart Gilbert (*Great Centuries of Painting*).

W. de Gruneisen: *Sainte-Marie-Antique*, Rome 1911.

G. H. Hamilton: *The Art and Architecture of Russia*, London, 1954.

G. de Jerphanion: *Les Eglises rupestres de Cappadoce*, Paris 1925-6.

V. Lazarev: *History of Byzantine Painting* (in Russian), 2 vols., Moscow 1948.

V. Lazarev: *Old Russian Murals and Mosaics*, London, 1966.

Comte du Mesnil du Buisson: *Les Peintures de la Synagogue de Dura Europos*, Rome 1939.

G. Millet: *Recherches sur l'Iconographie de l'Evangile*, Paris 1916.

G. Millet: *Le Monastère de Daphni*, Paris 1899.

G. Millet; *Monuments byzantins de Mistra*, Paris 1910.

C. R. Morey: *Early Christian Art*, Princeton 1942.

P. Muratov: *La Peinture byzantine*, Paris 1928.

N. Okunev: *Monumental artis serbicae*, 4 vols., Prague 1928-32.

V. Petkovic: *La Peinture serbe du Moyen Age*, 2 vols. Belgrade 1930-1934.

K. Weitzmann: *Die bysantinische Buchmalerei des IX und X Jahrhunderts*, Berlin 1935.

T. Whittemore: *The mosaics of St. Sophia at Istanbul*, 4 vols. London 1933-1952.

J. Wilpert: *Römische Mosaiken und Malereien*, 4 vols., Freiburg in Breisgau 1916.

O. Wulff: *Altchristliche und byzantinische Kunst*, Berlin 1914.

A. Xyngopoulos: *The Mosaic Decoration of the Church of Holy Apostles at Salonika* (in Greek) Salonika, 1953.

Byzantine and Russian painting

This fifth volume in the series *History of
Painting* was printed and bound by
Officine Grafiche Arnoldo Mondadori
in Verona.

The text was
composed in Times 10 point type and the
first and third parts were printed on machine
coated paper and second part on blue
cartridge paper.

The cover and lay-out of the inside pages
were designed by Jean-Marie Clerc of
Editions Rencontre.